ENEMIES OF THE INNOCENT

Life, Truth, and Meaning in a Dark Age

N. A. HAUG

ENEMIES OF THE INNOCENT

Life, Truth, and Meaning in a Dark Age

N. A. HAUG

AcademicaPress
Washington~London

Library of Congress Cataloging-in-Publication Data

Names: Haug, Nils A. (author)
Title: Enemies of the innocent : life, truth, and meaning in a dark age |
Haug, Nils A.
Description: Washington : Academica Press, 2024. | Includes references.
Identifiers: LCCN 2023949403 | ISBN 9781680535419 (hardcover) |
9781680535433 (paperback) | 9781680535426 (e-book)

FOREWORD

Driven by neo-Marxist critical theories, identity activists promoting a distorted morality force their ideas of family, marriage, and sexuality upon society. In so doing, they aggressively confront established norms rooted in Judeo-Christian values which underpinning the Western culture. The result is a corruption of biblical principles imparting necessary rubrics for truth, morals and ethics, personal identity, meaning in life and its ordained purposes. These core components of a healthy society are under threat of replacement by progressive secular and neo-pagan agents claiming a social justice agenda, yet one of a fictious nature contrary to the public good of all citizens.

The Author's cutting-edge investigation into these existential issues is a much-needed exposure that requires in-depth reflection. He is clearly well versed in theology, philosophy, law, political theory and literature - disciplines necessary to address complex cultural concerns. Ongoing interpretive challenges to the enduring truths of scriptural authority and the Edenic Garden rebellion, where humankind attempted to usurp divine authority, are suitably addressed. Ramifications of this ancient insurgency are reflected in the destructive influences of Gnosticism, occultism, secular humanism and assorted New Age spiritual beliefs, all of which lead to the radical political and social hypotheses prevalent in the current era.

This study, then, examines how the social revolution has reshaped views of truth and reality, culminating in a desperate struggle for traditional values. All these factors illustrate the need for remedial action by concerned persons against gross distortions of the ordained order. An urgent social counter-revolution is therefore required to emphasize humankind's divinely created personal identity, the deep meaning and purpose of life itself, and the romantic reality of the Creator's love for all people. This book is a compelling read for all serious thinkers.

Dr. Henk Stoker, Professor of Apologetics & Ethics

September 2023.

DEDICATION

This book is dedicated to my children - Samuel, Ezra, and Keziah Ruth, all three being the joy, pride, and delight of my life and for whose future I have great hope.

And to my wife Ursula, with whom it is a great privilege to share life. A woman of noble character (Prov. 31), kindness, courage, faith and dignity without whose patience and deep love this work would not exist.

I dedicate this book also to the memory of my beloved parents, Arne Theodore and Ruth Johanne Blaalid Haug, for exemplifying strong family values, commitment, and unwavering love through years of trials. And I have to mention my kind and generous brother, Knut, my only sibling.

Above all, I dedicate this work to the Most-High God, Saviour of the World and the Lover of my Soul - Jesus of Nazareth, whose servant I am.

"Great and amazing are your deeds, O Lord God the Almighty!
Just and true are your ways, O King of the nations!

(Revelation 15:3)

ABBREVIATIONS

AFL	-	America First Legal
ANSIRH	-	Advancing New Standards in Reproductive Health
BBFC	-	British Board of Film Classification
BLM	-	Black Lives Matter
CGT	-	Critical Gender Theory
CRT	-	Critical Race Theory
CSJT	-	Critical Social Justice Theory
CT	-	Critical Theory
DEI	-	Diversity, Equity, and Inclusion
ECLA	-	Evangelical Lutheran Church in America
EU	-	European Union
JPS Tanakh	-	Jewish Publication Society Tanakh
MTD	-	Moralistic Therapeutic Deism
NAS	-	New American Standard Bible
NIV	-	New International Version Bible
NKJV	-	New King James Version
SBC	-	Southern Baptist Convention
SCOTUS	-	Supreme Court of the United States
UK	-	United Kingdom
US	-	United States
WSJ	-	Wall Street Journal

All quoted Biblical scriptures are from the English Standard Version ("ESV") unless otherwise indicated.

CONTENTS

CHAPTER ONE

SOCIAL TURMOIL

"We are on the edge of a totalitarian takeover of our culture, institutions, and lives. It is the greatest crisis of our constitutional system, individual liberty, and the rule of law that we have faced in 160 years"
(Newt Gingrich, 2023)

Western nations face serious social, moral, and political challenges arising from heretical assaults not only on the personal identity of individuals, but established biblical principles, truths, and values. Franklin Graham describes this as a "culture of confusion and lies which come from hell."[1]

The social conflagration is stimulated by radical identity[2] activists, progressive politicians and a woke media ecosystem. Consequently, traditional Judeo-Christian doctrines providing moral and ethical guidance are in peril. These principles have sustained the harmony, order, and common good of nations for many generations. The stakes could not be higher as this is no mere domestic squabble between the left and the right. Rather, the "New Left is at war with the West – with the moral, intellectual, and social foundations upon which our entire civilization rests."[3] Arkansas Governor Sarah Huckabee Sanders declared Americans "are under attack in a left-wing culture war that we didn't start and never

---

[1] Gryboski, M., Franklin Graham Warns Liberty Graduates, May 12, 2023.
[2] Activists consider identity a 'sacred self,' independent of all constraints.
[3] Roberts, K., Burkean Nationalism, May 24, 2023.

wanted to fight."[4] Yet, fight they must in order to preserve their culture, freedoms, values and truths.

Politics, Culture, and Religion

Conflicts initially start with politics. Politics, according to Marxist revolutionary Mao Tse Tung, can be described as "war without bloodshed" and the first casualty of coming war is truth itself, which socio-Marxist revolutionaries manipulate to justify their actions. The consequence, in Ron Paul's words, is that "truth is treason in an empire of lies."[5]As the concept of truth originates from natural law principles of Judeo-Christianity, a political conflict over truth inevitably leads to the core issue of religion. Richard Neuhaus explains, "we think it true to say that politics is, in largest part, an expression of culture, and at the heart of culture is religion."[6] A valid statement, to which can be added 'and the heart of religion is truth.' Therefore, a religious, theological, and spiritual contest underlies the cultural, political, moral and legal morass facing society. In particular, the engagement is residual Judeo-Christian truth pitted against secular humanist and neo-pagan ideologies in a struggle for the soul of humanity. Nobel Laureate T. S. Eliot clarified that this "conflict is between the theistic and the atheistic faith."[7] Great thinkers through the ages have faced this existential choice there being no middle-ground. One path leads to nihilism, the other to life and transcendence. All are compelled to embrace one or the other, the default position being atheism with its consequence of materialism.

---

[4] Miller, Z., Biden in State of Union, February 8, 2023.
[5] Paul, R., The Revolution: A Manifesto, 2008, p. x.
[6] Neuhaus, R., Putting First Things First, March 1990.
[7] T. S. Eliot, Selected Essays: Thoughts After Lambeth, 1932, p. 367.

The first ever political war began over legal issues during primordial times, at the beginning of creation, at the time of the first man and woman. The book of Genesis reveals details of this drama where a rupture took place of the Creator's eternal plan, a plan for his people to live in a peaceful, law-abiding, political theocracy under his loving oversight in Eden. The Edenic rebellion reflects Lord Acton's view that "politics is an attempt to realize ideals,"[8] meaning ideals of unconstrained personal freedoms like those so eagerly sought by Adam and Eve. However, freedom, identity, transcendence,[9] and morality are inextricably connected, and the demise of one of these pillars adversely affects all of them. Therefore, the First Couple, and subsequently all humanity, in seeking personal freedoms without borders, are compelled to create a new ideological worldview to replace lost meaning, purpose, and identity free of Divine's created order. The result is a humanist identity with new ideals of morality and purpose.

The damaging effect of a societal struggle over these issues can be described as follows, "We live in a time of ideological exhaustion. Our doctrines and ideals lie broken in pieces all around us, never again to fit into a whole."[10] This sequel is not surprising for hyper-individualism and independence lacking restraint, without accountability or definitive moral-ethical paradigms, leads to chaos. The biblical book of Judges (17:6) stresses this outcome, "In those days there was no king in Israel. Everyone did what was right in his own eyes."

---

[8] Himmelfarb, G., Lord Acton, 1952, p. 220.
[9] Transcendence of the self is understood as "reaching out beyond ourselves for something other than ourselves" (Kronen, S., Yes to Life, August 18, 2023).
[10] Gurri, M., How the Identity Cult Captured America, June 17, 2023.

A New Order

Social anarchists, seeking a new political and ethical order, comprise certain groups of feminist extremists, a determined abortion lobby, progressive politicians, racial and ethnic militants, LGBTQ+ campaigners, and various tribes of socio-anarchists. Their strategy is to recolonize society in the name of Identity Politics, while claiming a motive of social justice for all. However, the underlying idea behind this movement is not something new for it comes from treasonous transactions that took place in the Garden at Eden, as recounted in Chapter three of Genesis. And, just as heresies threatened the political order in Eden so, too, current ideological theories are "the greatest threat to the political continuation of our constitutional democracy,"[11] with its inherent personal freedoms, equality of all persons, and the rule of law.

A Clash of Ideologies

Society is thus confronted with a 'battle of ideas and ideals,' reflecting an internal clash of heretical idealists with biblical realists. The split of society into opposing camps of values stems from an attempt to enforce an authoritarian-populist idea of the common good of society under a façade of social justice. As a corollary, society faces a subjective morality designed to bypass established, definitive, biblical values. In this way, activists establish their moral and ethical objectives without hinderance. The prime target of this postmodern cynicism is destruction of an individual's uniqueness and self-worth as created by God. This is unsurprising for human beings are made in his image, the *imago Dei.*

---

[11] Lewis, H. & V., The Myth of Left and Right, 2023, p. 84

A Crisis of Western Civilization

Biblical values[12] are the central principles, morals, and ethics that support Western civilization and culture, for together they sustain the sacred *imago Dei* of humanity. Spencer Klavan lists the traditional issues under stress as: the crisis of reality; the crisis of the body; the crisis of meaning; the crisis of religion; and the crisis of the regime.[13] The proposed replacement is a form of pervasive non-religious, spiritual, secular ideology, via applied cultural neo-Marxist materialism[14] based on ancient Greek pagan Gnostic construals. The outcome is that the ethical and moral life of modern culture itself, developed over centuries of representative democracy, is subject to ideological refabrication. American political theorist Glenn Ellmer explains the "crisis of our country is also the crisis of Western civilization, of civilization itself,"[15] for America is the world's foremost cultural force.

Although the social disarray initially arose within an American setting, the destructive ideologies have spread to other Judeo-Christian grounded cultures. Examples are the various European and Scandinavian nations, the United Kingdom, Australia, New Zealand, Canada - all of which are established participants of the Western tradition. To some lesser extent, third world countries like Cuba and South Africa are also affected. It is widely acknowledged that what occurs in American society does not remain localised. The world witnessed this so-called 'Butterfly effect' in the financial crash of 2008-2009 which, due to systemic economic globalisation policies, eventually spread insidiously, in the mode of a

---

[12] The West's civilization is founded on biblical principles, Greek philosophy and Roman rule of law (Weigel, G., Pope, 2022).
[13] Klavan, S., How to Save the West – Ancient Wisdom for Five Modern Crises, Feb, 2023.
[14] 'Cultural Marxism' refers to "a collection of ideas rather than a collection of people" (Mahlburg, K., 2020).
[15] Ellmers, G., The Soul of Politics, 2021, p. xvii.

pathogen, throughout the world at large leading to a macro contagion. In this way, identity ideologies have growing influence in non-Western societies world-wide, as is obvious from the presence of abortion and same-sex marriage in several third world countries. It is true to say, then, that "no ideological revolution has ever been content to stay within the boundaries of one state."[16] This fact is particularly pertinent to the United Kingdom whose society has been negatively impacted by post-truth pagan identity concepts initially promoted by an elite cohort of American politicians, academics, and corporations. As in the US, a powerful UK cartel has "torn down the cultural guardrails used to hold people together – strong families, strong religion, a strong national identity, a strong grasp of history and achievements and a strong, shared set of values."[17]

A Search for Meaning

The egocentric 'sacred-self' identity theories involving race, sex, and gender issues, indicate a desperate search for purpose and meaning in life. Chief Rabbi Jonathan Sacks elucidates on this point, "The quest for meaning arises from the fact that God wanted us to be here for there are specific tasks he wants us to perform, this is the true reason of a search for meaning."[18] Once the original dignity, nobility, purpose, and emotional security of persons was lost through a rejection of divine qualities conferred upon Adam and Eve, questions concerning new personal identity became paramount. After insurrection in the sacred Garden and subsequent ejection from paradise, the predicament of humanity in relation to existence became a contentious matter. Lawlessness commenced with

---

[16] Lyons, N. S., The Upheaval, April 8, 2021.
[17] Goodwin, M., The Revolution of Liberal Economics and Radical Culture, May 28, 2023.
[18] Sacks, J., The Pursuit of Meaning, 2009.

the sin of Adam and Eve's first born, Cain, and such behaviour will continue until the coming finale of history. At such time, the ultimate restoration of the typological Garden scene, as revealed in the eschatological books of the two Testaments, will eventuate.

A Post-Truth Setting

Combined with the redefining of individual self-image and self-worth is the attempted elimination of the Fatherhood identity of the Creator. Various iterations of androgynous and often feminine identities of pagan, polytheistic, gods are substituted in replacement. To achieve an inversion of truth, a nihilistic and absurdist attempt to reconstruct and redefine central biblical doctrines commenced. The reason for the specific focus on the Fatherhood of God concept is to enable the dependant doctrine of the sacred *imago Dei* (the image of God) of humankind to likewise be moderated. In substitution, activists promote the narcissistic and esoteric *eritus sicut Deus* identity of Genesis 3:5 – the heretical desire 'to be like God.' The desired outcome is a fabricated, profane, *imago hominis* (image of man) or *homo deus* (man-god), an identity embraced by ideological humanist and neo-paganist advocates alike.

Furthermore, basic doctrines like original sin, the necessity of atonement, and God's plan of salvation can equally be denied upon elimination of the Fatherhood creed. This policy clashes with the West's cultural Judeo-Christian worldview, and has to be understood as a militant spiritual attack upon basic biblical principles. These trials culminate in the current period of social disorder, a perfect storm, in search of meaning through establishment of a fresh multifaceted belief system. Writer N. S. Lyons cautions that society experiences a neo-Marxian power struggle that has "turned itself into a mass movement scrambling every aspect of

traditional American political, cultural, religious, and even corporate life."
He elaborates that the traditional order is "being forcibly reconfigured by
an ideological revolution consuming the Western world."[19] All revolutions
commence with politics and, as Italian philosopher Niccolò
Machiavelli (1469-1527) famously stated, "politics have no relation to
morals." Established truths, identity, meaning, virtue, ethics, and morality
are casualties in the new political and social war on essential values.
Professor Russell Reno describes this scenario:

> *"The Rainbow Reich has become the leading engine of social
> transformation. It does more than advance LGBTQ causes. It wishes to
> transform the structure of society. In the past, we praised what was
> normal and censured what was perverse. Now we are encouraged to do
> the opposite."*[20]

A Multidisciplinary Approach

Richard Howe observed that to "effectively engage with the culture, you
will need a deeply integrated understanding of theology, philosophy, and
apologetics."[21] It is anticipated that this multidisciplinary treatise,
involving the above three criteria and more, will assist in explaining the
origins of the political, philosophical, legal, religious and spiritual
opposition to biblical doctrines underlining present society. This is
particularly so with respect to the heretical, self-deification, tenets of the
eritus sicut Deus ('to be as God') concept adopted so enthusiastically in a
post-biblical milieux, notably by radical identity activists.

The situation is exacerbated by the endemic rise of secular humanist
ideologies intersecting with postmodern New Age occultism, as expressed
through syncretic spiritualism and subjective moral ideas of neo-pagans,

---

[19] Lyons, N. S., The Upheaval, April 8, 2021.
[20] Reno, R. R., Sacrificing the Young, August 2023.
[21] Howe, R. G., Engaging a Post-Christian Culture, June 2021.

humanists, and compromised theists. To the detriment of the Judeo-Christian tradition, some believers capitulate to the politically correct 'woke' culture focused on fantasy claims of self-identity. Malevolent identity hypotheses are endorsed through statutory laws of the Legislature, enforced by juridical decisions of the highest courts of Justice and driven by the Executive branch of government. These combined political powers stimulate the social and cultural upheaval to an ever-increasing degree. Even so, this development is not new for, as King Solomon clarified, "What has been, will be again and what has been done will be done again; there is nothing new under the sun." Everything "under the sun" can be traced back to early biblical events for "it was here already long ago; it was here before our time,"[22] as this book explains.

About the Chapters

Each chapter supports the central contention that the identity crisis facing society has spiritual origin in the Edenic Garden. However, the literary interpretive method first needs to be determined in order to enable a clear reading of principal Genesis passages. This will be presented in Chapter 2, 'Interpreting Genesis.' The purpose of the remaining chapters is to justify the principal contention and to develop the main themes.

Essential Knowledge

Political theorist Yoram Hazony's concern is that there exists an "astonishing amount of ignorance" concerning the importance of political, cultural, theological, and philosophical principles crucially reinforcing the Western democratic order. He laments that "many well-intentional conservatives really do not know anymore why one would need to

---

[22] Ecclesiastes 1:9-10.

preserve and strengthen these things."[23] It was Alexander Pope (1688-1744) who said that "a little learning is a dangerous thing; Drink deep, or taste not the Pierian spring."[24] Therefore, the intent of this study is to "drink deep" - to explore issues crucial to society and to add knowledge which, as grieved by Hazony, is sadly lacking.

An Enduring Search

Since Edenic times, humanity's vital search for the purpose of life itself, meaning in life, and personal identity, has never ended. The words of that great apologist, C. S. Lewis, describe the search in this way, "Human history is the long and terrible story of man trying to find something other than God which will make him happy."[25] This cultural exploration recounts the essence of that "long and terrible story."

---

[23] Hazony, Y. Conservatism, 2022, p. 9.
[24] Pope, A., Essay on Criticism: Complete Poetical Works, Vol. 1, 1848, p. 404.
[25] C. S. Lewis, Mere Christianity, 1952, p. 49.

CHAPTER TWO

INTERPRETING GENESIS

"Literalist and midrashic modes of Biblical exegesis
were indeed features of early Christian preaching"
(R. N. Longenecker, 1999)

2.1. Introduction

Before crucial events in the Garden of Eden can be considered, it is necessary to decide on the interpretative approach to be adopted to the book of Genesis as a whole. A survey reveals more Americans believe in evolution theory (57%) than creation theory (38%). This means a majority do not believe the word of God as written. Strangely enough, the idea of descending from apes seems more appealing than the idea of a loving God creating individuals in his image with dignity, purpose, uniqueness, and an eternal future.

Inerrancy of Scripture

In this post-truth era, the Garden narratives of Genesis 3 have been widely rejected. These events are regarded as parables, legend, myth or fable. However, it is apparent they do not fall into categories of untruth, despite much controversy. In theologian Dwight Longenecker's view, atheists "miss the remarkable fact that the Judeo-Christian stories, from the beginning, are presented as history."[1] Just because the "stories" are

---

[1] Longenecker, D., Myth, 2022.

religious, does not make them untrue myths or other categories of fantasy literature. Longenecker's view is underscored by Chief Rabbi Jonathan Sacks, when he affirms the Genesis narrative "is truth as story."[2] While in Catholicism, the Second Vatican Council (1962–1965) declared "Christianity is not a pious myth or a collection of inspiring legends but a revelation of what God intends for humanity, which began when God spoke to the Jewish people through Abraham, Moses, and the Prophets."[3]

The Chicago Statement on inerrancy of the Bible categorically affirms the text of scripture is to be "interpreted by grammatico-historical exegesis."[4] In other words, scripture is narrative truth as recorded in the original languages. Pope Benedict XVI points out that the literal advent of Jesus is a "guarantee of the solid, realistic, truth of the Bible."[5] The recorded, literal, history, birth and life of Jesus makes it impossible to refute his authenticity.

Gnostic Influence on Biblical Views

Gnostic heretics at the time of the early church adopted a mythological interpretation of Genesis' pivotal texts, particularly chapters 1 – 3. They believed that if they could undermine the truth and historicity of those three chapters, then the whole theology of fundamental Judeo-Christian doctrine would be compromised. Elaine Pagels, in her study of these three crucial chapters of Genesis writes, "Gnostic Christians read the Adam and Eve story as myth with a meaning."[6] Once that perspective had been

---

[2] Sacks, J., Genesis: The Book of Beginnings: Covenant, Vol. 1), 2009, p. 6.
[3] Weigel, G., The World Church, December 14, 2022.
[4] Chicago Statement on Biblical Inerrancy, 1978, Article XVIII.
[5] Pope Benedict XVI, In the Beginning, 1990, p. 21.
[6] Pagels, E., Adam, Eve and the Serpent, 2000, p. 413.

embraced, it led to a vacuum wherein any fanciful, idealized, or allegorical embellishment could be warranted.

A similar strategy was evidenced in the Edenic Garden when Satan's agent, the serpent, persuaded Eve of his special *gnosis* - his omniscient, secret, knowledge of God's intentions, thereby inducing her and Adam into sin. This pre-Gnostic concept was willingly acceded to by the First Couple, providing them with the confidence necessary to rebel against God's restrictions. After eating the forbidden fruit, Adam and Eve believed they too possessed *gnosis*, convinced of their new status as sovereign gods. Satan's malevolent strategy continued through all subsequent ages, and it can thus be claimed the foremost heresy faced by the early Church was that of Gnosticism.

New Atheists

In the current era, 'New Atheists' like Richard Dawkins, displaying hostility towards the Creator, simply dismiss all religious narratives as superstition. On the other hand, great thinkers of the past like Augustine, Bishop of Hippo, affirm the authenticity of the Genesis saga by stating, "we believe the strict truth of history, confirmed by its circumstantial narrative of facts."[7] The literal and historical composition of Genesis was further confirmed by significant Patriarchs such as Clement, Tertullian, and Irenaeus.

Importance of Transcendence

The issue of transcendence (meaning of life beyond temporal matters) is a prime component of the current 'battle of ideas,' the social struggle to conserve traditional Judeo-Christian values and doctrine. The reliability

---

[7] St. Augustine, City of God, 1890, Book XIII, Ch. 21, p. 369.

and historicity of both Testaments, and the realism of the redemptive agenda of the Creator, relies upon the book of Genesis for its foundation as the inerrant word of God. This contest has vital implications as the emotional and psychological well-being of humankind is affected. Terry Mortenson correctly claims that "a person's view of the origin of man will profoundly affect his view of the purpose and meaning of life, his moral values and perspective of life after death."[8]

The philosophical hypotheses of Erich Fromm who believed "the concept of God was a historically conditioned expression of an inner experience," allow him to concede that certain ideas polymorph into cultural ideologies and this process "usurps the place of the underlying reality."[9] This deduction explains the irrational basis of identity ideologies empowering secular humanistic, anti-theistic, materialist and determinist schemes confronting the historicity and validity of biblical narratives. The actual issue is one of supernaturalism versus anti-supernaturalism - divine creationism contrasted with the physical process of naturalist materialism and determinism like evolution theory. This contest concerns the source of morality, ethics, and virtue governing human conduct.

The Primary Doctrines

The fundamental doctrines of Judeo-Christianity arise within the first eleven chapters of Genesis, emphasizing the importance of those chapters for the integrity of scripture. From early Genesis events come pivotal issues such as the Fatherhood concept of God; the sacred identity of persons; the corporate solidarity of imputed sin (where all humanity

---

[8] Mortenson, T., 2016, pp. 11-12.
[9] Fromm, E., You Shall Be as Gods: A Radical Interpretation of the Old Testament and Its Tradition, 1966, p. 17.

inherited Adam's sinful nature); and the promise of a Redeemer. Therefore, it is to be expected that "Genesis chapters 1 – 11 is the main focus of undermining biblical authority in our time."[10] The question of interpretive methods used in understanding Genesis is crucial in arriving at a solid doctrinal outcome.

Textualism

Later in this study, when considering the issue of Constitutional interpretation by the US Supreme Court, the concept of originalism - a form of textualism - becomes pertinent. In legal circles, the term 'Constitutional originalism' implies "the Constitution should be interpreted according to its original meaning," that is, "according to the intent of the Founders."[11] When exegesis of the Constitution is not undertaken in this objective manner but through an invasive eisegetical (subjective) approach, the original, literal, meaning is lost. Unsurprisingly, there is a close connection between a conviction of the inerrancy of scriptures and Constitutional originalism. A study by Columbia Law School found that originalism "has value not only as a legal proposition about Constitutional interpretation, but also as a political commodity and as a culturally expressive idiom."[12] Stated differently, "legal scholars have found belief that the Bible is literally true helps predict adherence to originalism."[13] Holding to a view of inerrancy of the scriptures has far-reaching implications, not only for validation of Judeo-Christian doctrine, but also for society as a whole especially in the areas of law, justice, and politics.

---

[10] Sarfati, J. D., The Genesis Account, 2015, p. 9.
[11] Steelman, A. L., Literalism and Originalism, 2022.
[12] Greene, J., Profiling Originalism, 2011.
[13] Steelman, A. L., Literalism and Originalism, 2022.

2.2. Scribes of the Two Testaments

In considering authenticity of the Genesis chronicle, it will be beneficial to look at how certain writers of the two Testaments understood the personages and events mentioned.

Moses and David

The First Testament scribe, Moses, audibly received the Genesis narrative direct from the Creator. Numbers 12:6-8 reads, "With him (Moses) I speak mouth to mouth, clearly, and not in riddles." God used plain, simple, language to communicate with Moses. Generally, First Testament scripture is straightforward history, relatively easy to understand, literal and historic. King David, too, emphasised a literal creation in Psalm 33:6, "By the word of the Lord the heavens were made, by the breath of his mouth all their host."

The Apostles

Second Testament writers validated narratives of the First Testament, making 200 direct references to the events or characters in Genesis. This includes 22 direct references to Genesis 3 alone. Jesus himself quoted directly from Genesis, implying that its words should be taken literally. The Gospel of Mark records his words, "But from the beginning of creation, 'God made them male and female'" (10:6). In the gospels of Matthew, Mark and Luke, Jesus referred his listeners seven times to the words of the First Testament by asking, "have you not read…" In like fashion, Jesus quoted scripture three times to Satan while refuting the temptations directed at him, each time countering with "It is written" (Matt. 4:1-10), using a grammatical-historical exegesis. Paul quoted directly from Corinthians, Galatians, and again in the Ephesians' letter.

So, to reject the inerrancy of the Genesis narrative is to reject the historicity of the Messiah and integrity of his words. The same argument applies to the Apostolic writers. To dispute the historical Jesus of Nazareth has been attempted over the centuries but always without success - as is evident in the discrediting of Docetic and Gnostic heretical views. Even secular historians like Pliny the Younger, Cornelius Tacitus, Suetonius and Thallus (100 C.E), affirm the existence of Jesus. The Roman Tacitus wrote, "In the reign of Tiberius, Jesus was executed by the procurator Pontius Pilate."[14] A second century text by Lucian of Samosata refers to the "man who was crucified because he introduced new mysteries into the world."[15]

The genealogies set out in 1 Chronicles 1, and in reverse order in Luke 3:23-36, commence with the line of Adam. If the historicity of Adam himself is dismissed so too must all the biblical personages recounted in various biblical genealogies, and the Messiah himself who descends from Adam through the female line. Plainly stated, if Adam is not understood as a literal, historical, person then no sin would have entered the human race and there would be no need for a Messiah-Redeemer and the plan of salvation becomes irrelevant.

Secondary Sources

Apart from extra-canonical sources and dismissing even the credible testimony of Jewish General Josephus,[16] archaeological verifications for the historical Jesus and biblical narratives keep emerging. An example is the Ossuary of the disciple James, Bishop of the early Jerusalem Church.

---

[14] Tacitus (55-120 C. E.), Annals: Books 13-16, Loeb Classics 322.

[15] Lucian (120-190 C. E.), The Passing of Peregrinus, Loeb Classics 302.

[16] Josephus Flavius (c. 37 -110 C.E.) in 90 C. E. wrote, "about this time lived Jesus, a wise man" (Testimonium Flavianum).

The Hebrew inscription on the Ossuary is specific in identification for it translates as, "James son of Joseph, brother of Jesus."[17] In the Israel National museum in Jerusalem lies the sarcophagus of King Herod the Great, a significant character of the Gospel narratives, with many other archaeological items and scientific discoveries presenting. In this mode, the much-disparaged account of the annihilation of the sodomite cites of Sodom and Gomorrah, finds validation in the 2021 'Scientific Reports Journal.' A large team of researchers in a fifteen-year multidisciplinary study, conducted by twenty-one co-authors in ten US States together with other countries, concluded in a voluminous report that:

> *"An asteroid entering the atmosphere resulted in a massive fireball that exploded about 2.5 miles above the ground. This devasted cities which had been settled since about 4,300 B. C. E. Air temperatures rose above 3,600 degrees Fahrenheit. The biblical account of destruction of Sodom and Gomorrah may have been the result of eyewitness accounts of the meteor strike."*[18]

Rabbinical Validation

Early Rabbinic sources, especially of the Palestinian school rather than the Alexandrian school with their allegorical penchant, likewise commit to the historicity of events recorded in Genesis. To this day, Orthodox Jewish scholars[19] firmly follow a literalist reading, the plain meaning, of scripture in the first instance. For instance, Rabbi Joshua Golding confirms, "the *Torah* of Moses is God-given, accurate, and a true record of historical events that happened to the Jewish people."[20]

---

[17] Tombetti, P., *Ossuary of James the Just*, 2019.
[18] Bunch, T. E., *et al*, *Airburst*, 2021.
[19] When UK Rabbi Louis Jacobs (1920-2006), "deviated from the traditional orthodox dogma regarding the literal revelation of the Torah," he was summarily "excommunicated from the orthodox establishment" (Nadler, A. L., 2011).
[20] Gordon, D., *Jerusalem or Athens*, October 31, 2022.

Chief Rabbi Jonathan Sacks also emphasized Genesis' literal-historical veracity when he wrote, Genesis is the "most significant element, the foundation, the principle, upon which the rest of the canon is based. Genesis is Judaism's foundational work, a philosophy and political treatise of the human condition under the sovereignty of God."[21] It is therefore legitimate to emphasize the literal and historical authenticity of the events, transactions, and individuals recounted in Genesis - the founding document of both Judaism and Christianity.

That being the case, the opening verse of the First Testament, "In the beginning, God created…" dogmatically asserts the Judeo-Christian God's primacy over all creation, both seen and unseen. Therefore, all competing ideologies and faith systems are rendered false including humanism, atheism, evolution, polytheism and pantheism, deism and dualism.

2.3. Early Jewish Interpretation

Accepting the historical-grammatical composition of the book of Genesis, it then becomes necessary to determine the interpretive methodologies to be used in understanding its prophetic narratives. Questioning how Rabbinical scribes from early Judaism of the Second Temple period, and thereafter, undertook exegesis of the book of Genesis is the main enquiry to be explored. The period of early Judaism closely covers the Second Temple period, and "dates from around the end of the third century B.C.E., until the end of the second century C.E."[22]

It is this formative period that will cast light on the interpretive approach used by early Jewish scribes. The contention is that Jewish

---

[21] Sacks, J., Genesis: The Book of Beginnings, Vol. 1, 2009, pp. 4-5.
[22] Charlesworth, J. H., The Old Testament Pseudepigrapha, 1985, p. 59.

exegesis strongly influenced early Christian thinkers and scribes, including the Apostolic writers. James Charlesworth, in discussing Christianity's Jewish heritage says it was "the heir of over a thousand years of traditions, both written...and oral."[23] In fact, Christianity in its early years was deemed a sect within Judaism itself for early Christianity, "did not envisage itself as a new religion but as a true manifestation of Judaism,"[24] says Scott McKnight. It is inconceivable, then, to detach Christianity from its foundational roots within an early Jewish interpretive framework.

The Problem of Allegory

Various schools of interpretation certainly existed within early Judaism but, by and large, two prominent schools prevailed. It has thus to be decided whether the interpretive background of the Apostolic writers was Hellenistic Judaism of the Alexandrian school, or Palestinian Judaism of Rabbinical Pharisees. This question is important for if the Jewish scribes used mainly Alexandrian Greek allegorical practices, then it would be very difficult, to say the least, to assert a historical-grammatical reading of Genesis. The struggle against Hellenistic influence on Judaism was due to Greek tendency to allegorize much of scripture. Their purpose was to arrive at a subjective, 'deeper meaning,' no doubt influenced by esoteric mysticism. Such interpretation could result in an understanding devoid of grounded, contextual, restraints.

---

[23] Charlesworth, *ibid.*, p. 61.
[24] McKnight, S. A., A Loyal Critic, 1993, p. 57.

The Palestinian Approach

However, mainstream Palestinian Rabbinical exegetes adopted a literalist view rather than the allegorical approach of commentators such as Philo of Alexandria (20 B.C.E – 50 C.E.). The guidance of ancient Rabbis in early Judaism, together with their exegetical successors, is a deciding factor of how to read Genesis, especially the Garden passages. Rabbi Paul, who wrote most of the Second Testament letters, revealed his Palestinian background in Acts 22:3, "I am a Jew, born in Tarsus in Cilicia, but brought up in this city, educated at the feet of Gamaliel according to the strict manner of the law of our fathers, being zealous for God as all of you are this day." Paul's mentor, Rabbi Gamaliel,[25] a member of the governing Sanhedrin religious council, was direct successor to the famed exegetical school of Rabbi Hillel. It was Hillel who formulated the dominant rules of interpretation, the *middot*. Hillel (110 B.C.E. - 10 C.E.) was not only the interpretive authority of his era, but significantly influenced subsequent ages. His exegetical tools continued as primary instruments of interpretive practice for "more than a thousand years in Judaism."[26]

Rabbinical Schools

The most influential Rabbinical schools at the time of the Second Temple were the Pharisees, Sadducees, and Essenes. From this setting came Hillel's rules of interpretation, later employed by the Second Testament scribes who were all Jewish. So, upon the arrival of Christianity, traditional exegetical methods continued as before in the two interconnected faiths. In concrete application, then, ancient Rabbinical

---

[25] Alfred Edersheim believes the Jewish patriarch Gamaliel II, "may have sat with Saul of Tarsus at the feet of his grandfather," the great Rabbi Gamaliel (1993, p. 15).
[26] Schechter, S., Gamaliel, 2021.

scribes were the theological and exegetical predecessors of Second Testament writers.

Peshat and Midrash

The renowned Rabbinic expert, Richard Longenecker, explains that Jewish exegesis "of the first century can generally be classified under four headings: *peshat*,[27] *midrash*,[28] *pesher*,[29] and allegorical."[30]

The Rabbis of Palestine maintained a strict literal (*peshat*) reading of the books of the Bible, except for writings like Song of Songs which can sustain a poetic or allegorical reading. The basis of Hillel's Rabbinical *middot* (rules) was use of the *peshat* (literal) sense as a reading in the first order. Only once the plain, literal, sense had been established then, in order to show a prophetically repeated pattern (a theme), could the cyclical, *midrashic*, technique be employed. First and foremost, then, Rabbis emphasized the *peshat* (literal) sense of the passage, establishing a rooted context for later elaboration.

A Holistic Approach to Prophecy

A *peshat* reading explains Garden events in a plain sense, and this method was endorsed by Jesus and Apostolic authors. Still, it is necessary to explore interpretive devices that can assist in understanding prophetic scriptures. The aim will be to not only arrive at a deeper understanding of Second Testament events, but to ascertain whether or not First Testament occurrences find any thematic correlation therewith, so many eons later. It is important to note, says Longenecker, that ancient Jewish exegesis is a

---

[27] *Peshat*: the literal, plain, straight-forward sense.
[28] *Midrash* means "study, exposition, explore" and used in 2 Chronicles 13:22 and 24:27.
[29] *Pesher*: an Aramaic term meaning 'solution' or 'interpretation' (Longenecker, R, Exegesis, 1999, p. 24).
[30] Longenecker, R., Exegesis, 1999, p. 14.

system which "thinks more holistically, functionally and practically than it does analytically."[31] Gerald Bruns agrees with this view when he writes Jewish *midrash* "is holistic rather than atomic or subject-centred." This approach is not simply for purposes of interpretation, but has a strong practical application for, as Bruns explains, "*midrash* is concerned with practice and action."[32]

The holistic method is well displayed in the *midrashic* interpretive strategy applicable to *haggadah* (prophetic passages). On this issue, Rabbi Jonathan Sacks writes "through *haggadah* passages we strive to understand the past."[33] Leon Kass goes even further, saying "the beginning of Genesis shows us not so much the past but what will always happen,"[34] thus emphasizing cyclical, holistic, characteristics of prophetic events. And, this is to be anticipated for the prophet of old, "is one who sees the end in the beginning. While others are at ease, he foresees the catastrophe. While others are mourning the catastrophe, he can already see the eventual consolation."[35] As always, Jewish exegesis relating to prophecy operates in a manner that provides guidance for both the present and future, derived from lessons of the past in a real-life application. In this way, eternal divine purpose, expressed cyclically in the midst of linear time itself, is highlighted.

In summary, Jewish exegesis of prophetic events is not simply a prediction and a single fulfilment as understood by Western exegetes, in other words analytic. Instead, it indicates a holistic and ongoing thematic

---

[31] Longenecker, R., *ibid.*, p. xxv.
[32] Bruns, G. L., Hermeneutics: Ancient and Modern, 1992, pp. 105-113.
[33] Sacks, J., Covenant and Conversation: Genesis, 2009, pp. 282-283.
[34] Kass, L. R., The Beginning of Wisdom: Reading Genesis, 2003, p. 10.
[35] Sacks, J., Counting Time, May 7, 2015.

pattern of prophetic events from an ancient inception, through various epochal reiterations, including a present era, with final recapitulation and resolution at the end of linear time.[36] The purpose is to demonstrate the dominant, the perfect and complete salvific and eschatological purposes of God, from the time of creation to the eternal order, being the ultimate destiny of humankind. The prophet Isaiah speaks to this in 46:1-10:

> *"I am God, and there is none like me,*
> *declaring the end from the beginning*
> *and from ancient times things not yet done,*
> *saying, My counsel shall stand, and I*
> *will accomplish all my purpose."*

Hillel's Rules of Interpretation (Middot)

Hillel's rules commence with *Qal wahomer* which means, "what applies in a less important case will certainly apply in a more general case,"[37] and commonly known as "from light to heavy."[38] This rule will be instructive when applied to Edenic events. For example, what was relevant at the beginning ("light") in Genesis, will be even more relevant ("heavier") in a later setting (the Second Testament context), and, finally, most relevant ("heavy") in the eschaton. The period of the Apocalypse, leading to the eternal order, is when the resolution of God's disrupted plan for humankind occurs in a restoration of the paradisical Edenic Garden setting. Many aspects of the Garden theme will be found repeated throughout scripture as a pattern, for patterns of past events are typological guides for interpreting future occurrences.

---

[36] Prasch, J. J., Final Words, 1999, p. 40.
[37] Bowker, J., The Targums, 1979, p. 315.
[38] Strack, H. L., Introduction to the Talmud and Midrash, 1992, p. 21.

Applied Derash[39]

The application of Hillel's *middot* is generally referred to as *derash,* meaning to seek out or to search. James Sanders explains that *derash* is used "to search scripture and tradition, to read them and seek light in new situations. This is precisely what prophets and psalmists practiced, as did their exegetical heirs who wrote early Jewish literature."[40] Professor David Halivni endorsed this view when he confirmed that "*derash* is the applied meaning," whereas "*peshat* is the plain meaning" of the narrative.[41] Ergo, it is quite sound to search (*darash*) for verification of a *haggadah* (prophetic) passage and to gather further illumination in subsequent scripture through the ancient hermeneutical tool of prophecy, that of *midrash,* applying the revelation to a fresh, cyclical, situation.

Yet, only once the plain reading (*peshat*) of the narrative has first been established, should other illumination be sought through use of *darash.* This restraint will ensure contextualization of the passage, and so avoid straying into conjecture. The ancient rule for first establishing the plain sense before seeking further meaning has been carried into the modernist era.[42]

Coherence of Prophecy

Concerning prophetic passages, Rabbinic exegetes believed "the pattern of the past is the pattern of the future."[43] This describes a *midrashic* hermeneutical application utilizing Hillel's rules, and is designed to divulge the future from historic thematic events. To sum this up,

---

[39] Alternate translations are '*derash,*' *derush*" or '*darash,*' used interchangeably.
[40] Sanders, J. A., Foreword, 1993, p. xii.
[41] Halivni, D., *Peshat and Derash*, 1991, p. xiii.
[42] Cohen, M. Z., The Rule of Peshat: Jewish Constructions of the Plain Sense of Scripture, 2020, pp. 6, 14.
[43] Russell, D. S., The Method and Message of Jewish Apocalyptic, 1964, p. 231.

interpretation through an applied *darash* (search) of pertinent prophetic narratives (*haggadah*) reveals a *midrashic* (ongoing) pattern, a cyclical *motif*, of events derived from disparate but thematically interrelated texts. An example is the creation saga described in Genesis 1-3, and the relevance thereof to a new situation with ultimate relevance at "the end of all things."[44] The new situation, for Second Testament scribes, would be certain events and revelations now requiring to be understood from a Christocentric point of view.

As a result, narratives in St. John's gospel would be examined in light of the creation events in Genesis 1-2 in order to elucidate related events. In turn, John's book of Revelation would be similarly examined and read together with Genesis 1-2 and John's Gospel. A *darash* of these three passages reveal that certain verses in John's Gospel are a *midrash*, a repeated intertextual verification, of the Genesis creation passages depicting typologically enduring *motifs*, with eschatological fulfilment as recorded in John's Apocalypse.

Especially noteworthy is the interconnected tripartite theme of creation - new creation - final creation, which arises in the Genesis chapter, later validated in John's Gospel and fulfilled in his Apocalypse. In so doing, the interdependence of all three texts with each other is validated for only when considered together, can the three texts add to what Apostle Paul refers to in Acts as the "whole counsel of God," and to what Halivni terms the "holistic coherence"[45] of scripture. Only in this way can the unity of otherwise seemingly unconnected narratives be shown to have a common, cyclical, and persistent thematic scriptural pattern, a mutual

---

[44] 1 Peter 4:7.
[45] Halivni, D., Peshat and Derash, 1991, p. xiii.

motif, from the commencement of time (Genesis), until the end of time (Apocalypse).

An Enduring Theme

There are many thematic parallels in the triptych of Genesis, John's Gospel, and the book of Revelation, but only three are considered here to demonstrate a *darash* of these separate texts describing events millennia apart:

- The theme of creation - fresh situation - final recreation, commenced with Genesis 1, "In the beginning, God created the heavens and the earth." This verse is linked to the Second Testament context, "All things were made through him, and without him was not anything made that was made" (John 1:3); and further connected to final recreation in the eternal order, "Then I saw a new heaven and a new earth, for the first heaven and the first earth had passed away, and the sea was no more" (Rev. 21). The creation theme commenced in Genesis is thus brought to completion.

- The theme of life-giving water: In Genesis 1, creation occurred when the Spirit of God hovered "over the face of the waters." Water, essential for life on earth. Likewise, in John 4, through the move of God's Spirit in the form of life-giving water, a new creation resulted for "whoever drinks of the water that I will give him will never be thirsty again. The water that I will give him will become in him a spring of water welling up to eternal life." The theme of life-giving water is fulfilled in the eternal order of John's Apocalypse, "Then the angel showed me the river of the water of life, bright as crystal, flowing from the throne of God and of the Lamb, through the middle of the street of the city" (Rev. 22:1-2);

- The theme of the presence of God with his people: The Genesis 3 account of God walking in the Garden at Eden, "they heard the sound of the Lord God walking in the garden in the cool of the day," is affirmed in John's Gospel, "the word became flesh and dwelt among us." Finally, in the "new heavens and the new earth," his presence will forever be with his people for there is located the "throne of God and of the Lamb" (Rev. 21:10). In the eternal order, his people will worship him and see his face (Rev. 22:3-4).

The Rabbinical interpretive pattern of repeated prophetic events (past, present and future), validates the tripartite theme of initial creation in Genesis, the new spiritual creations of the Second Testament, and the final eschatological creation of Revelation. In this way, it can be made clear that only in the eternal order, at the end of time, does the Creator's plan for full restoration of the interrupted Edenic utopia take place. Such event will be a holistic finale of earlier creation events, being the ultimate aim of prophetic scriptures.

Summation

The cyclical relevance of a thematic pattern is reminiscent of F. F. Bruce's "this is that"[46] technique, where he brings to attention Peter's speech in Acts, "But this is what was uttered through the prophet Joel," when referring to the outpouring of the Holy Spirit at Pentecost, which itself has eschatological relevance with a great harvest of souls. Here is further testimony of a First Testament prophetic *motif* (Joel 2:28), having pertinence in a fresh (Second Testament) situation (Acts 2:16), with ultimate implementation eschatologically (Rev. 7:9 ff.).

King Solomon underscored recurrence of divine prophecy when he said, "What has been is what will be, and what has been done is what will be done; and there is nothing new under the sun" (Ecc. 1:9). The scribe's task is to uncover the scriptural pattern of prophetic events.

2.4. Conclusion

Through ancient Jewish Rabbinical interpretive rules, the inerrancy, coherence, perfection, and historicity of the Creator's redemptive program for the pinnacle of his creation, humankind, is emphasized. In such

---

[46] Bruce, F. F., This is That, 1968, pp. 9, 51.

definitive manner is the literal and historical legitimacy of the Creation order demonstrated. In Chapter 3 following, the Edenic Garden events can rightfully be considered in their historic, literal, and prophetic context.

CHAPTER THREE
PART ONE

CONFLICT IN EDEN

"It all starts with Faith but ends in Politics"
(Charles Péguy, 1910)

3.1. Introduction

The vast, sacred, paradise of the Garden at Eden located between the Tigris and Euphrates rivers in Mesopotamia, now Iraq, was created by God primarily for communion with the first man and woman and the society that was to follow. In this utopian setting were located a variety of creatures, most notable of which was the serpent, representing the fallen Archangel Lucifer, known as Satan, the indefatigable enemy of the Creator. That Satan was present is confirmed in Ezekiel 28:13, "You were in Eden, the garden of God."

At some unknown stage previously, Lucifer had been ejected from heaven together with his angelic followers who became known as demons. Satan's rebellion was based on an arrogant desire to exalt himself as the highest Deity, to set up a kingdom structure under his own rule replacing the creator God. This incident is referred to in the book of Isaiah when he exclaims, "I will ascend above the heights of the clouds; I will make myself like the Most-High" (14:14). In the Cave of Treasures Targum, the Syrian writer Ephraim elaborates that when "Satan saw that Adam and Eve were happy and joyful in Paradise, that Rebel was smitten with jealousy, and he became filled with wrath. And he went and took up abode in the serpent."[1] The first encounter with this unique character, after his ejection from heaven, is when he appears as a serpent in the Garden sanctuary, confronting humans for the first time.

Responsibility for the Crime

Driven by hatred and jealousy, Satan instigated a plan to destroy the pinnacle of God's creation – a position he had enjoyed before his rebellion - and so disrupt the serene, loving, and beautiful relationship God enjoyed with his especially created man and woman. Although the rebellion was initiated by Satan, Adam and Eve were not totally innocent, being individually responsible for their own part in the drama. As the first-born individual, Adam was ultimately accountable for the couple's disaster. Knowing full well the commands of the Creator and the consequences of breaking them, Adam faced a choice of eternal life or death. In the words of Rabbi Aquiba, Adam "chose for himself the way of death."[2]

The methods employed by the deceitful serpent have persisted through the ages in an attempt to derail the Creator's program of redemption for his people. This evil strategy will continue relentlessly until Satan is defeated at the end of time when, at last, his diabolical agenda is exposed and he is permanently terminated. In chapter 20, the eschatological book of Revelation describes this event, "the devil who had deceived them was thrown into the lake of fire and sulphur where the beast and the false prophet were, and will be tormented day and night forever and ever."

---

[1] Ephraim, Cave, Fol. 3 b, Col. 1, The First 1,000 years.
[2] Bowker, J., Targums, 1979, p. 130.

3.2. Humanity and the Image of God

God imparted his sacred image, the *imago Dei*, to the apex of his creation, Adam and Eve. Genesis 1 records that "God created man in his own image, in the image of God he created him; male and female he created them." In a post-flood context, and after all the unrighteous had been destroyed, God emphasised the continued sacred *imago Dei* of humanity to Noah and his sons, "God made man in his own image."[3] The *imago Dei* of all persons was similarly confirmed in the Second Testament context by Apostle Paul.

Upon being endowed with God's sacred image, which includes his reflected glory, the First Couple enjoyed abiding fellowship with him in the secure Garden, a theocracy under his loving oversight. Genesis reveals the Creator intended to personally dwell amongst his people - exemplified by the Garden, then the sanctuary,[4] later the Temple, and then the arrival of the Messiah who walked and dwelt among his people (Jn. 1:10-11). But it will only be in the eternal order, after the end of time, when complete restoration of God again dwelling personally among his people occurs in a recreated Garden. In the interim, God lives within his people through "the Holy Spirit (who) dwells within us" (2 Tim. 1:14).

Attributes of God's Image

The divine image assigned to Adam and Eve, and equally to all people, includes elements of God's holiness, love, eternity, glory, divinity, cognitive ability, law, justice and mercy. These qualities were essential for God "predestined his people to be conformed to the image of his son." (Rom. 8:29). In order for that to transpire, he made them in his own image, breathing life through his Spirit and placing eternity in their hearts (Ecc.

---

[3] Genesis 9:6.
[4] Exodus 25:8, "Let them build Me a sanctuary that I may dwell among them."

3:11). In Targum Pseudo–Jonathan, Adam receiving the Creator's breath of life is explained as follows, "And the living breath was in the body of Adam for a spirit able to speak, for the enlightening of the eyes and for the hearing of the ears."[5] The literal reference is to the breath, the essence, of God and consequently man was to be a holy, transcendent, moral and rational creature.

The attribute of rationality is confirmed when Adam named the multitude of animals, and his able locution of poetic verse upon the arrival of Eve (Gen. 2:23). Adam possessed all necessary intellectual qualities, being created in the very nature of God, partaking of his spirit, and eternally connected to his creator. The capacity of intellect is crucial for, as the great medieval sage Rabbi Moses Maimonides (1135-1204), also known as Rambam, remarked that it is "through intellect that man distinguishes between the true and the false. This faculty Adam possessed perfectly and completely." Here, 'true and false,' "are employed in the science of morals,"[6] that is to say, the ability to determine morally right from morally wrong. Adam was left with no escape for his ethical culpability.

The 1646 Westminster Confession of Faith declares "in immateriality and immortality, the soul of man bears a resemblance to God."[7] Even after the fall from grace, "man is and remains a creature of God" for God nevertheless, "acknowledges our bodies and soul as His work."[8] Not to be overlooked is the holiness of God, for his people are called to be holy, the

---

[5] §1, Ch. 2, L. 9-10.
[6] Rabbi Moses Maimonides, The Guide for the Perplexed, 1956 (1190), p. 15.
[7] Shaw, R., Exposition, 1980, p. 64.
[8] Concorde, 1580, §1.

essence of divine attributes. The scriptures declare, "I am the Lord, who made you holy,"[9] and, "You shall be holy, for I am holy."[10]

The Natural Law

Connected to Adam and Eve's divine features is the natural, the eternal, moral law of the Creator. Holiness, for instance, cannot be unconnected to divine law, nor law unconnected to justice and mercy. At the time of the First Couple's creation the natural law was, as recorded in the Book of Concordia of 1580, "graven on their hearts because the Lord had created them after his own image." Similarly, "even our first parents before the Fall did not live without Law, who had the Law of God written also into their hearts, because they were created in the image of God."[11] Therefore, an unwritten legal code would have been imparted to Adam when he was made in God's image, as it has been to all human beings. Rabbi Paul points out in Romans 2 that even those ignorant of God, "show the requirements of law are written on their hearts." For sin to exist there must be laws which define sin, a concept implying potential contravention of God's laws. Adam sinned as did all his successors.

Ambrose of Milan (339-397 C.E.) directed that, "Law is twofold - natural and written. The natural law is in the heart, the written law on tables. All men are under the natural law." This was the law disclosed to Adam and Eve. Natural law jurisprudence has its origins in the Creator's eternal moral codes, and even secular philosophers like Aristotle affirm the existence of an eternal law, "Universal law is the law of Nature. For there really is, as everyone to some extent divines, a natural justice and

---

[9] Leviticus 22:32; NIV.
[10] 1 Peter 1:16; Leviticus 11:44.
[11] Concorde, 1580, §VI.

injustice that is binding on all men, even on those who have no association or covenant with each other."[12] Aristotle's approach, and works of subsequent theorists like Jean-Jacques Rousseau in his 1762 thesis 'The Social Contract,' eventually led to the "Natural law school of jurisprudence." This secular school attempted to fabricate a legal system based upon the principles of a natural law, "even if there is no God."[13] As Francis Shaeffer perceptively commented, there is a "serious problem in trying to construct a system of law upon nature *per se,* for nature is cruel as well as non-cruel."[14] A valid remark, for the ethical concept of *malum in se* – an act which is wrong or evil in itself – cannot originate from unpredictable nature for a rational determination is required as to the wrongfulness of an action (*actus reus*).

However, the divine natural law as imparted to Adam (and thus all humanity), amplified in the Mosaic codes and Messiah's precepts (the "law of Christ") is the only absolute and definitive source of ethical and moral action. All Western principles of justice have these principles as their foundation, leading to a vast collection of *malum prohibitum* – acts prohibited by law, ensuring the common good of society. C. S. Lewis explains the importance of divine natural law when he writes, "it is not one among a series of possible systems of value. It is the sole source of all value judgements. If it is rejected, all value is rejected."[15]

---

[12] Aristotle, Rhetoric, Bk. 1. Ch. 13 (1373 b).
[13] Rousseau, J-J., The Social Contract, 1762.
[14] Schaeffer, F., Live, 1976, p. 159.
[15] Lewis, C. S., The Abolition of Man, 1943, p. 21.

Law and Justice

Thomas Aquinas (1225-1274 C.E.) emphasised that the "participation of eternal law in the rational creature is called natural law."[16] Simply put, without suitable legal constraints and without law connected to justice, flagrant lawlessness ensues. An observable, divinely imposed, eternal standard of ethical behaviour, with penalties, is necessary for the proper functioning of all societies. As Frédéric Bastiat sees the situation, "it is not justice that has an existence of its own, it is injustice. The one results from the absence of the other."[17] The two are inextricably intertwined.

God's authority in setting the standard for justice and morality remains constant through all circumstances and all ages. This applies also to the post-moral setting, and remains incapable of being deconstructed despite attempts by philosophers and identity agents to do so. Moral laws of the Divine are eternal in form and immutable in application, whether in the past, present, or future. It is contrary to the divine nature and omniscient attributes of God not to know the future in fullness, and to not provide permanent and immutable guidance to cater therefor.[18] The Creator imparted his natural law to Adam and Eve in the Garden, and it continued in this unwritten form until fully explained through the codified laws of Moses.

Moral truths, reflected in imperishable natural law, are endorsed in the Second Testament context where, for instance, the Apostle John describes the Messiah as coming to earth, "Full of grace and truth."[19] Grace is only relevant, and necessary, in cases of breach of the God's divine constraints.

---

[16] Aquinas, S.T. I-II:90:1 ad 1.
[17] Bastiat, F., The Law, 2007 (1850), p. 19.
[18] Rhoda, A. R., Open Theism, 2006, p. 432.
[19] John 1:14.

In this interconnected way, law (truth), justice, and grace (mercy) remain co-existent in the economy of the Creator and need to be understood as transcendental matters, being forever relevant. Therefore, truth, justice, and mercy are the bedrock values of Western legal systems.

Law of Moses

Insofar as Messianic Jewish believers are concerned, meaning those Jews who accept Jesus as Messiah and Lord like the disciples, the Messiah fulfilled all requirements of the law rendering ceremonial dictates, like the sacrificial regimen, obsolete.[20] A further reason the "law of Christ" (Gal. 6:2) superseded the Mosaic code was that a change in the High Priesthood had occurred. The writer of the Hebrews' letter explains that when "there is a change in the priesthood, there is necessarily a change in the law as well" (7:12). Thus, a correction of the "weak and useless" law was necessary.[21] Accordingly, Messianic Jewish believers fall under a different law, but with moral laws remaining eternally pertinent. The gentiles, as believers in the Redeemer-Messiah, were never under the ceremonial and civil laws of Moses in any event, also fall under the law of Christ which is based on the moral and ethical principles of the unwritten natural law, explicated through the Mosaic moral code.

Law of Christ

As a result, in Messiah, neither Jews nor Gentiles are under the Mosaic written law which has been cancelled in many respects. That does not imply that there is no law regulating their actions. Far from it, for they fall under the immutable and perpetual "law of Christ,"[22] referred to in

---

[20] Fruchtenbaum, A., Israelology, 1996, p. 650 ff.
[21] Hebrews 7:18.
[22] Galatians 6:2; 1 Corinthians 9:21.

Romans 8:2 as "the law of the Spirit." The law of Christ reflects the eternal, natural, law for while nullifying ceremonial and civic directives of the Mosaic code, it includes all moral elements of the Ten Commandments. The law of Christ is to be complied with both internally and through external obedience. The moral law, as contained in law of Christ, is evident in the ethical teachings of the Messiah and the Apostolic writers, not to overlook valuable gleanings from prophets like David in the Psalms, and Isaiah. These eternal laws, with penalty, remain applicable to all of humanity.

Law and Grace

The matter of law is of utmost importance in understanding the Gospel, for the two concepts of law and grace underpin the great doctrines of both canons. It was only the finished work of the promised Redeemer who could repair the corroded nature of humankind by reinstating the *imago Dei,* as originally designed. At the same time, the Messiah satisfied the moral laws, holiness and justice requirements of the Father through a propitiation for, "without the shedding of blood there is no remission of sin."[23] In light of the aforegoing, Adam and Eve were without excuse. Of their own volition, having the necessary intention (*mens rea*), they resolved to rebel against the restrictions of their Creator while ignoring moral law imperatives directing their conduct. They thus became accountable for their *actus reus,* their unlawful actions. The same position applies to all of humankind, for all descend from Adam, carrying seeds of his original sin.

---

[23] Leviticus Ch. 1; Exodus 12; Genesis 3:21; Hebrews 9:22.

Right of Contrary Choice

God's gracious gift of free will to the First Couple included the power of contrary choice. Yet it was anticipated that this freedom would direct them towards compliance with the natural, moral, laws of the Creator. In this respect, God empowered them with a freedom that he himself did not possess for the Creator cannot choose to sin, cannot go against his holy nature. The prophet Habakkuk wrote in 1:13, "You who are of purer eyes than to see evil and cannot look at wrong." There existed no irresistible compulsion for Adam and Eve to comply with the normative precepts of the Creator. If there had been, they would not have had the power of contrary choice inherent in the very nature of their given freedom of will. Adam and Eve were able to choose not to sin, as part of this freedom. They were free to partake of the produce of the Garden, and even of the Tree of Knowledge yet subject to God's firm warning which should have been enough of a deterrent. Without the freedom of choice, they would be not be accountable for their transgression for they would lack the necessary *mens rea*, the intention driving their *actus reus,* their unlawful action. In the result, Adam and Eve created their own social, moral, and philosophical future, a fabricated ideal of life, liberty, and property driven by a naive idea of social justice and independence. The humanist social justice concept was subsequently perpetuated throughout history, culminating in the prejudicial actions of present identity ideologues claiming to act for the public good of society.

Restoration of Imago Dei

Through the representative Adam, all ensuing humankind transgressed and the restorative Messiah of Genesis 3:15 was awaited. Only through actions of a Redeemer-Messiah could humanity "be renewed in knowledge after the image of its creator."[24] Cambridge theologian, Douglas Hedley, phrases it this way, "Humanity always has the image but individual humans have lost the likeness."[25] And so, only in Messiah are individuals considered spiritually anew, their corrupted identity annulled, so that "if anyone is in Christ, he is a new creation. The old has passed away; behold, the new has come."[26]

Through redemptive work of the Messiah, full consciousness of the eternal natural law will be restored in his promise of a new covenant, "I will put my law within them, and I will write it on their hearts."[27] It is inconceivable that the law written on the "hearts" of the spiritually restored individual, would be different in any way to the moral laws assigned to the First Couple in the Garden. There is but one Creator who has but one set of universal, eternal, and immutable moral laws which are supernaturally imparted to all humanity, initially at the time of the Garden events and refreshed in the consciousness of the "new creations." Just as in terms of the new covenant where the law is to be refreshed in the heart of the individual, so would the law have been engraved into the hearts of Adam and Eve. Both instances reflect a divine, spiritual, transaction initiated by the Creator.

Guilty Conscience

After their transgression of God's law, the First Couple's guilty conscience led them to evade the Creator. The capacity of conscience was for enabling them, as free agents, to avoid transgression of divine constraints but this endowment was dismissed in preference for the ego-centric exercise of

---

[24] Colossians 3:10.
[25] Hedley D., Imago Dei, February 6, 2023.
[26] 2 Corinthians 5:17.
[27] Jeremiah 31:33.

free will. It was John Henry Newman who clarified that conscience is a "connecting principle between the creature and his Creator."[28] Newman is correct, conscience of moral truth is an inalienable trait of humankind's image of God, a factor which sinners through all ages anxiously endeavour to alleviate.

Law and Justice

Associated with the transmission of law to Adam and Eve, their conscience failing perhaps, was the element of justice. It is in the very nature of God that his law is coupled to both justice and mercy. John 1:17 clarifies, "For the law was given through Moses; grace and truth came through Jesus Christ." Even the Mosaic law contained strong elements of justice and mercy – hence the sacrificial system, the day of Atonement and the Passover. These principles, namely, the fair and equal application of the law coupled to justice and mercy, are pivotal to the harmony of human society.

Agape Love

Divine love can be described by the Greek word, *agape*. It is this category of love – supernatural, sacrificial, and unconditional love - that was given to the First Couple when the Creator breathed his attributes into them. As a sacred precept emanating from God, *agape* love is the interconnecting element in human relationships with the Creator; with his commandments (the *Torah*); and with one's neighbour. The esteemed Rabbe of the Chabad-Lubavitch movement, Rabbi Menachem Mendel Schneerson, explained the connection this way, "The three loves – love of G-d, love of Torah, and love of one's fellow are one. One cannot differentiate between

---

[28] Newman, J. H., Grammar of Assent, 1870, p. 113.

them, for they are of a single essence. And since they are of a single essence, each one embodies all three."[29] Consequently, the First Couple's relationship with their Creator reflected this sacred *agape* love, for it was *agape* love alone that enabled them to display their affection for God, his commands, and for one another.

Through the serpent's seditious deceit and their own power of contrary choice, the First Couple rejected the law and discarded the Divine's unconditional love, acting purely in their own self-interests. Ephrem the Syrian describes this situation, "God withheld from him a single tree, hedging it around with death, so that even if Adam were to fail to keep the law out of love for the Lawgiver, at least the fear of death that surrounded the tree would make him afraid of overstepping the law."[30] In rejecting the Divine's love, Adam and Eve severed their *agape*-founded relationship both vertically and horizontally, with the latter leading to future marital strife. A foundation of *agape* love is the essential ingredient of all human relationships with God and, by extension, of all compliant marital relationships.

The Golden Rule

The primary law imbued to the First Couple over and above all other laws, as important and interconnected as they are, is the law set out in Deuteronomy 6:4-5 and Matthew 22:37, "You shall love the Lord your God with all your heart, with all your soul, and all your might." The second most important law involves the consideration of others, one's neighbours.[31] This law is commonly but mistakenly referred to as the

---

[29] Tauber, Y., Love According to the Rabbe, January 17, 1951.
[30] Brock, S. P., Ephrem the Syrian, 1990, p. 5.
[31] Leviticus 19:18, Luke 6:31, Matthew 7:12.

'Golden Rule.'[32] It is disconcerting that the Judeo-Christian cultural tradition takes as its focus the second most important law over the first. The reason for this is that many believers can comfortably identify with the second rule but not the first, being the humanists that they are. While it is laudable for both believing and secular individuals to follow the Golden Rule, it is even more commendable, and mandatory, to prioritize the primary command of the Creator to which the second is subordinate. It can rightly be said that emphasizing primacy of the Golden rule amounts to what Pierre Manent calls, "the religion of humanity," the social gospel. He elaborates by saying, "many Christians today have been seduced by the humanitarian imitation of Christianity."[33]

Above all, the great obligation of the church, as the Bride of Christ, is to "love the Lord." Dedicated horizontal focus on humankind, rather than a vertical focus on God contravenes the overriding command. This mistake is exactly why the Messiah chastened the vibrant church at Ephesus saying, "you have left your first love" (Rev. 2:4). The Messiah also criticised religious leaders of his day, the Pharisees, for their focus on human tradition instead of practising an organic, *agape,* love for God, "This people honour me with their lips, but their heart is far from me; in vain do they worship me, teaching as doctrines the commandments of men."[34]

---

[32] The Golden Rule: "Do unto others as you would have them do unto you" (Gregg, S., Natural Law, 2021, p. 3).
[33] Manent, P., The Religion of Humanity: The Illusion of our Times," 2022.
[34] Mark 7:6-7.

3.3. The Matrimonial Arrangement

After creating Adam, God decided he should have a companion. This led to formation of the first woman, Eve, named by Adam and created from his rib. As with Adam, the woman was not derived from or related to other mammals which were made "according to their own kind" (Gen. 1:25). The unique *sui generis* (one of a kind) nature of the First Couple confirms humankind's creationist origins for no other creature was made in the image of God, nor had the divine breath of God instilled in them, nor had eternity in their hearts.[35] As Job exclaimed, "The Spirit of God has made me; the breath of the Almighty gives me life" (33:4).

The clear creationist origins of humankind demolish all materialist and determinist evolutionary claims to the contrary, such as Charles Darwin's view that "man bears in his bodily frame the indelible stamp of his lowly origins."[36] In fact, the opposite is true for humanity has holy origins and a sacred character, being created by God himself.

The First Marriage

Genesis 2:21 reveals the inauguration of the first intimate human relationship - a mutually beneficial, harmonious, monogamous, complementary, and permanent fellowship of "oneness in nature."[37] The two humans were a divine creation of opposite binary genders, male and female, so to enable them to propagate a race of other human beings. The directive was for them to form an archetypical nuclear family and, subsequently, a society. To achieve this aim, in the words of St. Augustine, the First Couple were to be of "two sexes manifestly different."[38] The

---

[35] Ecclesiastes 3:11.
[36] Darwin, C., 1871, The Descent of Man, Vol. 2, p. 405.
[37] Fairbairn, P., The Revelation of Law in Scripture, 1996, p. 38.
[38] Augustine, 1890, Book XIV, Ch. 22, p. 401.

heterosexual couple were created to love God, love one another permanently and to be intimate in a way that two members of the same gender cannot be. Upon declaring it is "not good that the man should be alone,"[39] God formed a person of the opposite gender, a female and not a person of the same or a third gender, to be the rightful companion for Adam.

In this way arose the disparaged concept of complementarianism, the roles of husband and wife in society. In the passage of Genesis 2:21-24, God distinctly set the pattern of stipulated biological dimorphic genders, male and female, so there can be no doubt as to a limit of only two genders. It was the female gender that was created to be in union with the man, to propagate the species for the Creator's redemptive purposes. Without the male-female gender difference there would be no Redeemer-Messiah issuing from the woman, as predicted in Genesis 3:15.

Sacred Marriage

Scripture reveals the institution of marriage (as such relationship later became known) is a creation ordinance, a template. It is a sacred pattern that reflects the relationship of God to his chosen people of Israel, and the promised Messiah to his Bride, the Church. Consequently, there is a transcendent, a sacred, quality to the concept of opposite genders in ordained matrimony. This is demonstrated by the eschatological marriage between the Bride (the Church), and the Bridegroom (the Messiah). The holiness of the marriage theme can better be examined prophetically through a short *darash* (a search) of biblical passages, from origins in

---

[39] Genesis 2:18.

Genesis into the new situation of a Second Testament context, and eschatologically, as follows:

- Genesis 2:18, "Then the Lord God said 'It is not good that the man should be alone; I will make him a helper fit for him.'" To be read with Genesis 2:24, "Therefore a man shall leave his father and his mother and hold fast to his wife, and they shall become one flesh;"
- 2 Corinthians 11:2, "For I feel a divine jealousy for you since I betrothed you to one husband, to present you as a pure virgin to Christ;"
- Revelation 19:7, "The marriage of the Lamb has come, and his Bride has made herself ready."

The concept of marriage is a preordained ordinance which cannot be replicated by a union of same-sex persons, irrespective of whether or not either attempts a gender metamorphosis to transition to an opposite gender identity. Biologically speaking, a person's birth gender cannot, in any event, be altered through surgery or chemical intervention for it is comprised of fixed chromosomes (DNA) that crucially determine gender.[40] Resultantly, any marriage outside God's created relationship, as exemplified by Adam and Eve, should be denounced[41] as a profanation, sinful, despite legal validation.

An Organic Relationship

The relationship between God and his people is an organic romance founded on *agape* love, and bound by a covenant.[42] There is nothing religious about it as shown by the interactions between the Creator and the First Couple in the Garden. Adam and Eve had no rituals[43] to perform in order to please their God, but only one prohibition - to not sin, to not eat

---

[40] Roselli, C. E., Neurobiology of Gender Identity and Sexual Orientation, 2018, p. 1.

[41] "The marriage bed kept pure for God will judge the adulterer and all the sexually immoral" (Hebrews 13:4).

[42] 1 John 4:7-10.

[43] It is faith not ritual that confers relationship (George, R. P., Rituals, 2022).

the forbidden fruit. Similarly, after establishing a covenant, there was nothing religious about the consummation of Abraham's relationship with God, apart from the invariable requirement of faith in attaining a righteous status.[44] Not to overlook Moses, a friend of God, who enjoyed great personal intimacy with the Creator, not undertaking ritualistic religious requirements to please him or to attain righteousness, apart from simple faith. The prophet Isaiah records God's promise to enter into personal relationship with his people without formalities, "Fear not, for I have redeemed you; I have called you by name, you are mine" (Isa. 43:1).

The Second Testament records that the Apostle John enjoyed a close personal bond with the Messiah, "One of his disciples, whom Jesus loved, was reclining at table at Jesus' side" (Jn. 13:23). The Greek rendition of "Jesus' side" translates as, "in the bosom of Jesus." The King James translation is similar, "Now there was leaning on Jesus' bosom one of his disciples, whom Jesus loved." Here is a picture of affectionate intimacy, quite unlike principles of organized religion. John Horvat underscores this essential relational element when he says, "we must recognize and respect the organic nature of man, full of vivacity, spontaneity, and unpredictability. This is the essence of a truly organic, living society."[45] By its very definition, an organic relationship with God refutes an organizational arrangement. Only an organic romance meets the Bible's greatest command to, "Love the Lord your God with all your heart..." (Deut. 6:4). This obligation can only be expressed organically for it relates to a personal romance, a deep matter of the heart.

---

[44] Genesis 15:5; James 2:23.
[45] Horvat, J., Return to Order, 2013, p. 150.

It is for this reason that Christianity (for want of a better word) is not a religion, and never should be, for it is a tender romance. After all, are believers not the Bride of a loving Bridegroom? There is little place for organizational applications to such concept. In the result, religion proper cannot offer a supernatural, *agape,* relationship with the Divine for, as Karl Barth says, religion "is the attempted replacement of divine work by one of human manufacture."[46]

A Personal Creator

For the people of God to love and authentically interact with him, it is incumbent upon God to supernaturally enable them to do so for, as Barth stressed, *agape* love cannot be of human origin. God validates the relationship by imparting his sacred love into the heart of his Bride. This transaction is mentioned in Romans 5:5, "God's love has been poured into our hearts through the Holy Spirit who has been given to us." It is only when read with Romans 5:5, that the passage of 1 John 4:19 ("We love because he first loved us") makes complete sense in application. The reason being that it is the gift of *agape* love by the Holy Spirit (Rom. 5:5), that enables his people to love him in return (1 Jn. 4:19), through the means of that same *agapē,* supernatural love, uncontaminated by a love of "human manufacture" such as *éros* or *philia.*

The verse of 1 John 4:8, "God is love," explains that God is the creator and perfector of true love. He requires his people to love him with sacred love, a love which cannot exist in a marriage not reflecting his ordained design. His holiness would not allow it and such relationship would not have his approval. True love, *agape*, is a divine attribute, essential to the

---

[46] Barth, K., Church Dogmatics, 1961, p. 52. An *agape* relationship with God is the heart of the gospel (Jn. 3:16).

love affair between God and his people. The tripartite relational template in the Garden typifies the Divine's close, personal fellowship with his people. This is clear from the intimate, covenantal, relationship of the Messiah with his Church which, like Adam and Eve, is urged not to sin.

Set Apart

The second most important rule is, "You shall love your neighbour as yourself."[47] Again, the word used for love is *agape*, sacrificial love. This is the depth of love required for loving God and for loving one's neighbour. It hardly bears mention that the closest 'neighbour' anyone could have is their marriage partner. Hebrew terminology for marriage means 'to make holy, to sanctify, to set apart.' The Jewish wedding ceremony reflects the concept of holiness in marriage for the parties are holy unto one another, set apart for each other. The term, 'to marry,' indicates the holiness of God and is seen in Genesis 2:3 when the sabbath was sanctified, set apart, made holy by him.

To emphasize this theme, an example is the High Priest[48] who, on *Yom Kippur,* was the sole person sanctified to enter the most sacred area of the Temple, the Holy of Holies. Although knowledge of the procedure of events on that day is available from a reading of the Bible, only the High Priest himself could subjectively know what it's like to actually enter into the most sacred place. Holy marriage in accordance with God's ordained ways reflects this situation because just as the High Priest alone is sanctified to enter the Most Holy Place, the Bridegroom alone is sanctified to 'enter' his Beloved, to consummate the marriage. This is typology for the marriage of the Bridegroom with the Church, his Bride. Same-sex

---

[47] Matthew 22:39; Leviticus 19:18.
[48] See Prasch, J. J., More Grain, 2002, pp. 10-11.

marriage, being outside of God's set precepts, is contrary to divine law, is profane and scripturally illegitimate irrespective of secular legality. Participants defile themselves, becoming spiritually unclean, for marriage is a transcendent, holy, and sacred concept with eternal ramifications.

An Evil Assault

Satan's malignant intent in the Garden was not only to cause a rebellion *per se,* but to destroy the intimate and harmonious tripartite relationship, the marriage, enjoyed by the parties. By so doing, he would destroy the proposed nuclear family and establishment of a society eventuating from a family unit. Subsequently, the personal identity[49] and emotional well-being of individuals, interpersonal relationships, sacrificial love, and harmonious societal order would also be corrupted.

The importance of family is a core tenet of Judaism for, as Rabbi Sacks explains, "The book of Genesis, the Torah's starting point, is not primarily about theology, doctrine, or dogma but about families: husbands and wives, parents and children, brothers and sisters. God himself defines his relationship with the Israelites in terms of family."[50] From this understanding comes the crucial doctrine of God as Father and his paternal relationship with humankind; a relationship the evil one attempted to annihilate in its infancy.

Love Rejected

The First Couple were endowed with all divine attributes required to lead holy lives yet they rejected the unfailing love of, and eternal fellowship with, their Creator. Instigated by the evil Satan, they claimed a subjective,

---

[49] Personal identity is deeply rooted on *imago Dei* –made in the image of God.
[50] Sacks, J., Covenant and Conversation: Genesis 1 - Family Feeling, 2009, para. 5783.

Gnostic-like,[51] secret knowledge of God's ulterior motives, coupled with their humanist desire for creative license and absolute independence. Their actions would enable them to formulate their own ideals of meaning, purpose, and identity outside of the Divine's parameters. And, ever since, the corrosive effects of the Fall from grace have been devastating for individuals in their emotional well-being, their marital relationships, and their society.

---

[51] Gnostic, meaning knowledge, wisdom, or insight - characteristic of early heretics claiming 'secret' revelation available only to elites (Moore, E., Gnosticism, 2022).

CHAPTER THREE
PART TWO

CONFLICT IN EDEN

*"The mind is its own place, and in itself
can make a Heaven of Hell, a Hell of Heaven"*
(John Milton, 1667, Paradise Lost)

3.4. Adam

Created in a state of innocence, Adam was the firstborn human being and endowed with the blessings, privileges, and responsibilities of his position. Upon the arrival of Eve, Adam was no longer alone but had a female companion for whose well-being he was responsible.

No Excuse

Adam's chief obligation was to keep the law, "So Adam had nothing to do there except for the law which was laid down for him. Nor was any work entrusted to him apart from preserving the commandment he had been given."[1] In this straightforward task, Adam failed dismally. Secondly, he failed in his matrimonial duties towards the well-being of his wife. It is for this reason, with Adam being the example, Rabbi Paul deemed it necessary to caution husbands in the Ephesian Church to "love (*agape*) your wives, as Christ loved (*agape*) the Church and gave himself up for her." (Eph. 5:25).

---

[1] Brock, S. P., Ephrem the Syrian, 1990, p. 4.

Rights of the First-Born

The law of Moses firmly established the concept of *prīmogenitus* – a father's acknowledgment of his first-born son's inheritance rights.[2] A loose analogy to Adam's position in his relationship with Eve and their ensuing progeny, would be that of the Roman law *paterfamilias*, "the one who has dominium over the house shall be called the *paterfamilias.*" So, as the firstborn, Adam can be deemed "the first in the hierarchy,"[3] a position carrying both rights and responsibilities. In a biblical context, God allocated a *paterfamilias* role to Abraham for the purposes of not only protecting his family but for guiding them in the ways of God, for that is the main purpose of the role. This is confirmed in Genesis, "I have chosen him (Abraham), that he may command his children and his household after him to keep the way of the Lord by doing righteousness and justice."[4] Here, God selected family as the conduit for eternal truth through all generations.

Marital Responsibility

As the firstborn human, Adam inherited everything necessary for a harmonious, righteous and privileged life in God's presence. He was appointed overseer of all creatures and of his environment. When Eve was formed, she was presented to him to be his helper and companion, for him to love and protect. Adam enjoyed, as did Eve, all the essential elements necessary for a secure emotional and spiritual existence. Even so, Adam had the responsibility of guardianship over Eve. Paul's letter to the Ephesian church clarifies this role, "Husbands, love your wives, as Christ

---

[2] Deuteronomy 21:17, "he shall acknowledge a firstborn by giving him a double portion.
[3] Zammit, A., What were the Powers of the Paterfamilias? 2011, p. 1.
[4] Genesis 18:19.

loved the Church and gave himself up for her."[5] That is to say, sacrificial love, *agape*, to act in the best interests of the wife and the relationship.

Affiliated with Adam's firstborn rights were certain responsibilities, and so the passage in Genesis 3:6[6] begs the question as to Adam's whereabouts at the very time Eve interacted with the Serpent. The Hebrew is somewhat imprecise, "with her" or as Genesis 25:11 reads, "near or beside." Whatever the case, Adam failed as protector of his wife. He permitted a development whereby they faced disaster and ejectment from the Garden. The directive of Genesis 2:15 was for Adam to "keep, watch and preserve" the Garden, and such mandate included preserving his wife from harm, which he failed to do. The possibility that Adam was somewhere nearby and not right next to Eve, does not absolve him of his responsibilities for he held the office of a *promakhos* - the first line of defense and the first into battle against possible assaults on his family. Lacking excuse, Adam failed to protect his wife and the result was a catastrophe not only for them, but for all subsequent humankind. The overall responsibility remained with Adam although, says Paul, he "was not deceived, but the woman was deceived." (1 Tim. 2:14).

Silence is Dangerous

When Adam should have spoken up, he failed to do so. Ambrose of Milan pointed out this obligation when he said, "In some causes silence is dangerous." When God chastened Adam, the first issue raised in condemnation was his failure to protect Eve. Adam instead listened to her repeat the lies of the serpent and then, without comment, ate the fruit

---

[5] Ephesians 5:25.
[6] Genesis 3:6, "she took of its fruit and ate, and she also gave some to her husband who was with her, and he ate."

offered. Adam had a clear choice to not participate in the evil act, but by accepting and eating the offered fruit, the evil spirit of the serpent entered him as it had done to Eve. In a Second Testament context, this situation was replicated when Judas Iscariot had the option to refuse bread offered to him by the Messiah, for the bread would identify the potentially seditious person in their midst. It was only when Judas took the bread, accepting culpability for his intended betrayal, that evil entered him (Jn. 13:26-27). Therefore, the physical bread, and the Edenic forbidden fruit, had severe spiritual implications. The second point is that Adam blamed God for giving him a wife who fed him the fruit. Adam refused to acknowledge his own shortcomings, namely, his pride, guilt, irresponsibility, and complicity in seeking independence and self-realization (Gen. 3:12). Thirdly, acting in a cowardly manner, Adam blamed his wife.

In present times, Adam's behaviour would be described as an instance of Freudian psychological projection, whereby he attributed his own behavioural shortcoming as defects in his wife's motives and actions.[7] Adam's protestations were without merit for he acted reprehensibly, whatever reasons he offered. Fourthly, Adam was especially without excuse for he was created in a state of innocence, with all divine impartations necessary to live a holy life. Fifthly, Adam had no direct discourse with the serpent to use as an excuse. The wise King Solomon explains this mystery, "God made man upright, but they have sought out many schemes." (Ecc. 7:29).

---

[7] The disorder is when "the interpreter projects onto others the thoughts and attitudes he wishes to deny in himself" (Smith, R., Deconstructionist, 2021).

Adam to Blame

Adam ignored God's direct order against eating the fruit. The fact that Adam (and Eve) saw fit to believe the creature instead of the Creator established the future basis for naturalist, pagan, creation worship which in itself impliedly rejects the Fatherhood of God doctrine, and so the *imago Dei* of humankind. Adam exemplified a catastrophic failure of headship, a failure to protect the more susceptible partner under his care. Not only was Adam's omission a complete lapse of his created headship role but, as he was the federal head of all ensuing human beings, his failure had a corrupting effect on future marriages and relationships. In contemporary society, Adam's deficit influenced the rise of feminist claims to lead roles in intimate relationships. When the man's headship role has been usurped or practically abandoned then enmity, discord, and disaster generally follow. For this reason, the serpent approached Eve first while she was alone, for he sensed a lack of protection rendering her vulnerable to his evil deception.

The serpent's strategy in approaching women first has continued ever since for, as Apostle Peter says, women are spiritually "the weaker vessel" (1 Pet. 3:7). A woman asserting headship is evident in the relationship of Abraham with Sarah. Abraham paid heed to his wife's advice not to wait upon God any longer for an heir, despite God's promise to provide one.[8] Sarah directed Abraham to procreate with the maid-servant Hagar, and so "Abram listened to the voice of Sarai."[9] The resultant offspring from this extra-marital action was "a wild donkey of a man, his hand against everyone and everyone's hand against him, who shall dwell over against

---

[8] Genesis 15:4.
[9] Genesis 16:2.

all his kinsmen."[10] Ever since, enmity has existed between descendants of Ishmael and those of the true heir of the promises, Isaac.[11] Furthermore, discord between Sarah and Hagar arose once Hagar knew she was pregnant with Abraham's offspring. It is recorded that Hagar, "when she saw that she had conceived, looked with contempt on her mistress."[12] The household was in disarray, and the friction resulted in Hagar and Ismael being cast out into the desert. This situation solely arose due to Abraham handing over patriarchal authority to his wife instead of exercising the role himself.[13] A further example is seen in 1 Kings where King Ahab allows his wife, Jezebel, to lead him and the nation of Israel, for which he was responsible, into idol worship and to acquiesce in the killing of the Prophets of the Lord.[14] The end result was a tragic death for both of them.

Complementarianism

Both Adam and Eve were guilty of inverting the principle of complementarianism, God's ordained roles for husbands and wives.[15] First, Adam capitulated to his wife's leading and, secondly, Eve usurped Adam's lead role in the relationship. The implications are seen throughout history in the prevalence of marital disputes between husbands and wives. This was predicted in the curse upon Eve in Genesis 3:16. In present times, statistics indicate 50% of marriages in Western societies end in failure. Marital discord, particularly the power struggle for leadership between

---

[10] Genesis 16:12.
[11] Genesis 25:18.
[12] Genesis 16:4.
[13] Genesis 16:6.
[14] 1 Kings 16:31-33; 1 Kings 18:4,13.
[15] Complementarianism is considered sexist (prejudiced) against women by feminists (Hernandez, A. D., 2021, p. 30).

men and women, is a major cause of social and relational turmoil in society.

Evil Ambition

Satan's ambition, and his vehemence towards God, is revealed in his malicious spiritual assault upon the first human beings. This is evident when his alter ego, the serpent, lied to Adam and Eve about why they were banned from eating fruit of the Tree of Knowledge. The serpent argued they were prohibited because God feared they would then be like himself, having full knowledge of all things and with creative powers. In effect, the serpent was projecting Satan's ambition of divinity onto Adam and Eve, enticing them with that same prideful desire while simultaneously blaming God for withholding that office from them, just as God had withheld it from Satan.[16]

The serpent's successful strategy was in proffering divine qualities obtainable through secret, privileged, spiritual knowledge (*gnosis*), in the exact manner of later heretics who became known as Gnostic Elites. The serpent claimed insight and understanding that purportedly only he, the avatar, possessed and not Adam or Eve or even the Creator himself. Here, he adopted a dualist structure of reality - a fabrication based on the forbidden Tree's advantages, resulting in a complex metaphysical theory of deification through superior knowledge. This theory was in direct contrast with the Tree of Life's attributes which were then to be understood as representing a corrupted and counterfeit reality.

---

[16] Genesis 3:5; Isaiah 13:13-15.

The Occult[17]

The serpent persuaded Adam and Eve to condescend to his superior *gnosis,* his wisdom, that eternity and transcendence through knowledge would be achieved by eating the fruit. Here, the serpent represents the original, archetypical Gnostic Elite, the first instigator of occultist principles. Accepting the serpent's secret revelation of truth would enable Adam and Eve to be 'like God' (*eritus sicut Deus*),[18] having supreme knowledge coupled with personal autonomy, leading to certain creative ideals. By choosing the Tree of Knowledge in their search for enlightenment and freedom, they could by-pass the Tree of Life with its divine restrictions, persuaded that it represented a compromised reality. So, in exercising free will, they acceded to temptation and ate the fruit, anticipating secret revelations. In successfully destroying the First Couple's privileged position, Satan revealed both his envy, ambition, and vehemence as they were the pinnacle of creation - a position which Satan himself previously enjoyed.[19] Humanity has ever since prioritized the Tree of Knowledge, forbidden *gnosis*, in their search for purpose, identity, and meaning while disparaging the Tree of Life as a false attraction. In this manner, the Tree of Life as the metaphor of all truth, is rejected in favour of heretical humanist hypotheses.

Tree of Gnosis

The Italian scholar, Ioan Couliano, in his impressive study, 'The Tree of Gnosis,' claims "Gnosticism – like any idea or system of ideas – originated

---

[17] Occult means supernatural, hidden, secret, dark knowledge. Other terms are arcane, esoteric, mystical, magical.
[18] Genesis 3:5.
[19] Ezekiel 12 -14.

nowhere else than in human minds."[20] While he is correct insofar as the emergence of formal Gnosticism in history is concerned, he is mistaken that the idea is of human origin. Rather, the concept has malevolent spiritual origins emanating from the fallen Angel, Lucifer, as articulated through the serpent. There are only two possible spiritual forces in existence: that of good and that of evil, one being of divine origin, the other of diabolical origin manifesting for the first time at Lucifer's exile from the spiritual realm. Humanism, in its secular expressions, originates from the dark realm.

The serpent's fabrication of a parallel reality was in a later age formulated by the Greek philosopher Plato, and his circle of scholars. Named 'Gnosticism,' the theory came to exemplify a Hellenist allegorical way of thinking in contradistinction to a grounded Jewish Rabbinical worldview. The latter was founded on the natural law as recorded in Masoretic codes – the sacred laws handed down to Moses on Mt. Sinai, located in the desert regions of Egypt and accessible to this day. Some 613 laws in all, they contained not only moral rules but civil and ceremonial regulations for the young Israelite nation. In due course, the codes gave rise to rubrics of interpretation by Rabbinic scholars, and have endured into broad modernity. The *Torah* (the Law), being the first five books of the Bible, "does not embrace dualistic concepts,"[21] quite unlike Greek proposals, being grounded rather in the precepts of scripture, not fictional humanist theories detached from reality.

In the result, Satan's nefarious dualistic methodology successfully disrupted the Creator's salvific and eschatological plan for humankind and

---

[20] Couliano, I., The Tree of Gnosis, 1990, pp. xiii, 59.
[21] Labron, T., Wittgenstein's Religious Point of View, 2006, p. 110.

their society. Nonetheless, the plan eventually becomes fully remedied at the end of time[22] through the predicted Messianic deliverer of Genesis 3:15.

3.5. Eve

In Rabbi Carlebach's opinion, Eve ate the fruit because she "knew that she is really like God, as to give birth to a baby is the most godlike thing in the world. Eve knew that inside she is something very special but didn't know how to do it."[23] The issue of Eve's claimed creative powers is mentioned by Rabbi Rashi when he says, "God ate of this Tree and then created the world, and therefore he orders you not to eat from it, so that you cannot create other worlds."[24]

Eve believed the serpent lies when he claimed God denied her fruit of the Tree to prevent her becoming like him, "you will be like God, knowing good and evil."[25] The serpent fraudulently misrepresented the Creator for he intended the First Couple to know that evil existed, but not to have personal experience of it; they were to know the existence of evil cognitively, not experientially by eating the fruit. The existence of evil was evident to Adam and Eve from presence of the Tree. Irrespective, Eve desired knowledge that she was not meant to know. Clement's 'Book of the Rolls' records as follows, "then she called Adam and he hastened to her, and she gave him of the fruit, telling him that if he ate it he would become a god."[26] Eve's desire, and that of her man, was to become

---

[22] Revelation 21 – 22.
[23] Carlebach, S., The Torah Commentary, 2012, p. 58.
[24] Rashi, Ber. R. 9:4.
[25] Existence of the Tree of knowledge creates an opportunity for profanation of a sacred place, hence the prohibition.
[26] Gibson, M. D., Apocrypha Arabica, 1901, 94b.

independent, free from oversight and accountability, and in this sense they desired a form of divinity, to become *homo deus* (a god-man), a sovereign-self.

Aspiring Divinity

By embracing the serpent's lies, Adam and Eve "aspired to divinity."[27] Eric Fromm suggests God was aware his only real rival could be man who, if he ate from both the Trees, would become like God himself, and so upset the outright power and control of God over his creation. It is for this reason the First Couple were ejected from the Garden. Fromm continues, "this absolute power of God over man is counterbalanced by the idea that man is God's potential rival." In this way, humanism emerged as the principal ideology, in fact a secular religion of sorts, replacing the pre-eminence of God in human affairs. In Fromm's words, man's "first act of disobedience is the beginning of human history, because it is the beginning of human freedom,"[28] meaning the beginning of secular humanism. In Matthew 16:23, the Messiah revealed that, despite professed benevolent intentions, humanism has infernal roots and that is why he rebuked Peter for his seemingly well-intentioned advice. He said to Peter, "you are not setting your mind on the things of God, but on the things of man."

Pride and Sin

Prior to Eve capitulating to malevolent deceit was a predetermined, but no doubt subconscious, weakening of her will to remain steadfast in her love for God. Augustine of Hippo clarifies this argument, "Our first parents fell into open disobedience because already they were secretly corrupted by an

---

[27] Wilson, A., The Human Fall, 1988, p. 53 [3]).
[28] Fromm, E., You Shall Be As Gods, 1966, Ch. 2, p. 23.

evil will." He adds, an "evil will" has origins in flagrant pride for, "pride is the beginning of sin." This would explain Eve's puzzling malleability.

The end result reflects Eve's "undue exaltation"[29] of self, which underpinned her failure to reciprocally love the Creator, focusing instead on her love of self. Eve became convinced she could establish her own truth, with independent identity, purpose, and meaning in her own right rather than as a mere companion to her husband. This agenda explains her solitary interaction with the serpent. Herein lie the roots of destructive radical feminism manifesting millennia later in the present postmodern environment. Feminism rejects the created complementarian order for men and women in favour of unrestrained personal freedoms, leading to the narcissistic, imperial-self, phenomenon.

The Curses

Due to her blatant rebellion, Eve was subject to certain curses by the Creator. For instance, "Your desire will be for your husband, but he shall rule over you."[30] Eve was now to be subject to her husband who would "rule over" her. The relationship between Adam and Eve was different before the Fall, as prior to Eve's transgression, they enjoyed a harmonious setting with spiritual and relational equality. Both enjoyed their intimate relationship, with Adam exercising a loving and sacrificial headship when necessary. In that sense, Eve was subordinate to her husband but was not to be ruled by her husband, as such action was unnecessary. But since the rebellion, Eve would be "ruled over," dominated, by her husband. The benevolent, selfless, and pleasant partnership was to become a recipe for disorder as Eve defensively and strongly reacted to what she considered

---

[29] Augustine, 1890, Book XIV, Ch. 13, p. 393.
[30] Genesis 3:16.

overbearing patriarchy. The forces of male patrimony, headship, and guidance now clash with Eve's desire for female liberation, leadership, and independence from all accountability. Ever since, radical feminists have tried to reverse the effects of the curse through reactionary tribal movements, motivated by their yearning to assert complete control over their own lives and bodies, irrespective of the cost.

Claiming intolerable chauvinist dominance, divorce becomes prevalent and a feature of subsequent societies. Divorce was not in the Creator's original plan for parties to the marriage had "become one flesh" (Gen. 2:24). Divorce becomes a contentious issue, "Because of your hardness of heart Moses allowed you to divorce your wives, but from the beginning it was not so."[31] "Hardness" of the man's heart was to become the new norm, so much so that Paul admonished the Ephesian Church, "Husbands, love your wives, as Christ loved the Church and gave himself up for her" (Eph. 5:25). And wives had become resistant to their complementary role but, according to Paul, should rather submit to their husbands and respect them (Eph. 5).

Eve's Transgression

Prior to her transgression, Eve exemplified the goodness of a woman made in the image of God, spiritually equal to her husband and blessed with capacity for procreation. She was to be the foundation of future society. Her position deteriorated dramatically after the Fall when curses for her misdeed destined her to a subordinate marital position, which was never the original status. She lost marital harmony, could expect pain in childbirth, and was relegated to a different relational role outside the

---

[31] Matthew 19:8.

Garden. Even so, the love and compassion of the Creator led him to provide suitable clothes for both Adam and Eve, thereby indicating the required procedure for atonement of sin, based on the hope of redemption prophesied in Genesis 3:15.

Eve's Emancipation

Eve was the archetype of women's struggle for emancipation. Her proclamation of autonomy, her self-determination, subjective morality and freedom were iterations of her narcissism and self-veneration. Eve's desire for creative license and autotheism[32] has enduring importance in present society through fervent feminist demands for sole existential authority over their unborn children, rationalised as women's health and civil rights. The feminist abortion lobby is founded upon such rationale, furthered by a subjective view of morality.

The issue of morality is explained by Friedrich Hayek who says no moral paradigms can originate within humankind. He writes that it is a "rationalist delusion that man, by exercising his intelligence, invented morals that gave him the power to achieve more than he could ever foresee."[33] Furthermore, Eve's idea of unfettered autonomy is well expressed through William Ernest Henley's poem, 'Invictus,' when he writes, "I am the master of my fate, I am the captain of my soul."[34]

Autonomous Gods

The First Couple came to the conclusion that their natural environment was dominated by an evil force purposely depriving them of freedom, creative license, and opportunity for a divinity of sorts. In their view, the

---

[32] Genesis 3:5.
[33] Hayek, F., Fatal Conceit, 1988, p. 137.
[34] Henley, W. E., A Book of Verse - Life and Death: Invictus, 1888, p. 56.

situation could not be typical of a loving Creator's blissful world, and so had to be rejected. The real, perfect setting could only be an alternative world awaiting discovery outside the Garden boundaries. It was up to them to discover this new reality, one free of imposed norms, through their newly acquired creative powers and superior knowledge derived from the forbidden fruit. This proposition accords with what later became known as Plato's dualism,[35] which describes a fundamental Gnostic construction leading to much heresy, such as Manichaeism in ancient times.

Along these lines, perhaps the First Couple longed for what Carl Jung described as that "secret life which holds sway in the unconscious."[36] But more than that, they sought life as autonomous 'gods,' a concept promised by the evil serpent. However, the concept was based on a flagrant distortion of truth, resulting in humanity ever since acting in a Gnostic-like manner to create their own destiny and reality. Like all Gnostics, Adam and Eve rejected objective truth, rationality and definitive moral rules, desiring instead to reshape truth to suit their personal agenda.

Secular Humanism

Adam and Eve embraced agent-centred humanism. The primary antagonist of theism, humanism is derived from the notion of secularism – understood to be independence from, and the non-necessity of, God and living as if he did not exist. In this context, Mary Eberstadt understands secularism as "ceding to nonreligious authorities territories once considered to be God's, and God's alone."[37] Secularism negates Judeo-

---

[35] Dualist theory is a heretical attempt to introduce the profane into a sacred space, an act which commenced in Eden and has continued throughout history.
[36] Jung, C. G., The Archetypes and the Collective Unconsciousness, 1959, p. 23.
[37] Eberstadt, M., Hope for Faith, December 15, 2022.

Christian doctrines but inevitably leads to a nihilist[38] end result as exemplified by the philosophical, anti-theistic, theories of extreme feminism, free of established truths.

Judith Butler

The attempt to create an authentic humanist worldview, and a personal identity from which to comprehend life's purpose, forms the agenda of identity activists such as Judith Butler, considered the "most famous theoretician of gender." While Butler acknowledges she has been "cast out of Eden and there is no final redemption," she also concedes she has "never found a place… a gendered place, where we can feel at home in our bodies or at one with ourselves." Her restlessness is further exposed when she confesses, "I am permanently troubled by identity categories," and yet she insists on an "anti-metaphysical truth of the human condition."[39] This was the type of philosophical dilemma Eve faced. The end result is deprivation of emotional well-being, purpose, meaning and identity.

Like Eve, radical feminists reject the fatherhood concept of God, ignoring his actual existence, and his moral and ethical tenets. By so doing, important doctrines like the image of God in humankind are also rejected. Consequently, individuals are forced into an eternal quest for alternative structures of meaning and values like love and justice, morals and ethics. Adam and Eve entered this quest reliant solely on their own subjective fabrications which terminated in a nihilistic endgame, with no secure future. T.S. Eliot warned about the outcome of such a quest when he wrote, "In my beginning is my end."[40]

---

[38] Nihilism in the post-truth era means "nothing means anything so one might as well do whatever" (Kronen, S., Yes to Life, August 18, 2023).
[39] Franks, A., Judith Butler's Trouble, May 2023.
[40] Eliot, T. S., Four Quartets: East Coker, 1959 (1944), p. 23.

3.6. The Fig Tree

The refrain from eating forbidden fruit was Adam and Eve's test of loyalty, obedience, and love. Their failure led to exile, as they had been warned. Experiencing disgrace for the first time through loss of innocence, and acutely aware of their exposed physical bearing through a lack of reflected divine glory, Adam and Eve realised their rebellion had caused not only a physical but a spiritual alienation. The inevitability of death entered their consciousness. They had become detached from their secure status that found its source in God alone. Moreover, they experienced estrangement from one another as a married couple, with Adam blaming his wife and she in turn blaming the serpent for the transgression. It was the Father's loving oversight, his constraints and provision, with their personal identity found in God alone, that had instilled in them a sense of well-being.

Instead of a stress-free existence as enjoyed before, they were now filled with dread. Meaninglessness, purposelessness, loneliness, confusion, *angst* and alienation followed and this "affected every aspect of their existence: God, work, family life, and society."[41] An environment of cosmic absurdity, life without purpose, confronted them as they lost their righteous standing with the Father and the reflection of his glorious presence. Their sudden awareness of personal nakedness illustrates that condition for, in an attempt to hide their exposure and recover a lost sense of righteousness, they covered themselves with Fig leaves (Gen. 3:7).

Reflected Divine Glory

A significant degree of reflected divine glory was ascribed to Adam and Eve in their innocent situation. Just as God would have been clothed in

---

[41] Vangemeren, W., The Progress of Redemption, 1995, p. 87.

glorious light, so too would the First Couple made in his image and living in his Holy presence. The Bible confirms those who surround God, whether angels or mortals, reflect his glory. The passage of Exodus 34:29 supports this, "When Moses came down from Mount Sinai, he did not know the skin of his face shone because he had been talking with God."

Nakedness and Mortality

Upon their sinful rebellion, mortality entered the First Couple's lives and they immediately lost their glorious divine clothing. So, with horror, they realised their nakedness, their lack of a holy covering. Being acutely aware of this precarious condition, they feared the Creator's presence. They no longer had glorified bodies, no longer "garments of salvation" (Isa. 61:10), but, instead, corrupted bodies suitable only for living outside God's presence, outside the Garden. Humiliated, they became aware of their physical and spiritual nakedness.

Self-Realization

Adam and Eve's effort to cover themselves with leaves is indicative of attempts at righteousness through a self-realization process, widely imitated through the ages. This was not successful, and never could be, for it transgresses the precepts of the Creator which dictate that atonement is only achieved through a blood sacrifice, "With the blood of the sin offering he shall make atonement for it."[42] The principle of expiation is exemplified by God providing animal skins (Gen. 3:21), to replace rejected Fig leaves. The fact that Fig leaves, or any natural objects, cannot satisfy God's legal requirements for atonement is recorded in Genesis 4:3-5, when Cain offers

---

[42] Exodus 30:10; Hebrews 9:22.

a sacrifice consisting of grain which is rejected as non-compliant with the obligation of a blood sacrifice.

The Tree and Nietzsche

When the First Couple chose to seek omniscience from the Tree of Knowledge, they expressly by-passed the Tree of Life with its ethical and salvific principles. In this way, they set an example for their ideological descendants into the postmodern era. The postmodern philosopher, Friedrich Nietzsche, is a prime example for he denied God's authority, proclaiming his death and irrelevance. He then proceeded to philosophically fabricate subjective structures to accommodate his search for alternate meaning and identity. Despite complex compositions, Nietzsche like other existentialists, could not rationally explain the purpose and meaning of a life free of the Divine. Confusion, alienation, *angst*, and absurdity of existence is consequent upon this outlook, leading to a fatalistic and nihilist end result.

Sexual Licentiousness

Prior to the fall from grace, Adam and Eve's gender difference was not an issue, nor was the fact that their nakedness was evident to each other and to God. Their physical awareness altered upon loss of divine glory, and their attention switched entirely to covering their lower regions. The covering of genital areas is perhaps a harbinger of humankind's subsequent pre-occupation with sexuality free of strictures. In Augustine's view, "all nations being propagated from that one stock, have a strong instinct to cover the shameful parts."[43] He goes on to say, "lust requires for its consummation darkness and secrecy; and this not only when

---

[43] Augustine, Book, XIV, Ch. 17, p. 398.

unlawful intercourse is desired but even such fornication as the earthly city has legalized".[44] Augustine reflects the culture of that time (410 C.E.), but in the existing milieux, the display of sexual organs and immorality is no longer disgraceful,[45] no longer private. The proud public display of immorality[46] reflects the pinnacle of secular emancipation and the gleeful rejection of traditional biblical values. In so acting, individuals believe they have become "the creator and absolute masters of their fate."[47]

Sexuality and Postmodern Society

Western society reflects a demise of conventional moral and ethical standards. The obsession with sexuality arose to prominence in the mid-sixties of the last century when promoted by Kinsley and Freud, exacerbated by the advent of the birth control pill, the sexual revolution of the hippy movement, and availability of unmitigated pornography.

Sexual imperialism has become vividly apparent in the Western world for sexual sin, as idolatry of the body, enforces its claim as chief manifestation of the fallen human condition. Describing these conditions, Malcolm Muggeridge writes "When mortal men try to live without God, they infallibly succumb to megalomania or erotomania." The veracity of this statement is found in the ego-centric theories of Nietzsche, and the sexual proposals of Michel Foucault.

Nonetheless, sexuality exercised within the boundaries of marriage is a concept created by God and not to be condemned. Sexual licentiousness

---

[44] Augustine Chapter 18, p. 398.
[45] W. J. Bennett's study, 'The Death of Outrage: Bill Clinton and the Assault on American Ideals,' pursuant to President Clinton's extra-marital affair with Monica Lewinski, is a case in point (Bennett, 1999, p. 3).
[46] There is no finer example than the annual June festival celebrating the 'Pride Month' of Alphabet tribalists.
[47] Glucksmann, A., The Original Birth of Freedom, Autumn 2010.

continues to pollute society to an even larger extent as the influence of cultural Judeo-Christianity, and the political philosophy of classic liberal democracy with social restraints for the common good, evaporates exponentially. Biblically, Paul warned against those, "who are depraved in mind and deprived of the truth,"[48] for "God gave them up in the lusts of their hearts to impurity, to the dishonouring of their bodies among themselves" (Rom. 1:24). All choices have consequences, as seen in the Sodom and Gomorrah scenario.

Restoration Awaited

Restoration of the full image of God in humankind only occurs through the power, love, and grace of the Redeemer-Messiah. His "new creations,"[49] are enabled through his supernatural power[50] to escape the snare of Satan whose attractions lead to moral failure. So those who "put on the new self, (will be) renewed in knowledge after the image of its creator,"[51] and be restored to an intimate relationship with the Divine.

In the case of the First Couple and many of their descendants, including their first-born son, they chose love of self instead of love for God. Despite claiming independence, Adam and Eve remained subject to the laws, justice, and providence of their Creator for his original decrees cannot be replaced by human agency. God's providence remains eternal and immutable for, "God is not man, that he should lie, or a son of man, that he should change his mind" (Num. 23:19). Lawless actions free of God's moral standards, free of his laws and justice, simply cannot exist without serious consequences.

---

[48] 1 Timothy 6:5.
[49] 2 Corinthians 5:17.
[50] 1 Thessalonians 1:5.
[51] Colossians 3:10.

CHAPTER THREE
PART THREE

CONFLICT IN EDEN

"Ideology offers human beings the illusion of identity, of dignity,
and of morality while making it easier to part with them"
(Václav Havel, 1985)

3.7. Aftermath

In 1766, Jonathan Edwards described the catastrophic consequences for humankind as a result of Adam's sin, "Adam's posterity needs to be looked upon and treated as though they were partakers with Adam in his act of sin."[1] The biblical doctrine of corporate solidarity, whereby the original sin of Adam and Eve is imputed to ensuing generations, finds credibility in the degraded nature of all human beings. Raging immorality is not only prevalent in present society but has been so from time of the Genesis rebellion.

Humanist Utopia

The Garden was a harmonious utopia, never to be repeated on earth until the end of time. Even so, the first humanist attempt was construction of the Tower of Babel by Nimrod. This Tower was to be part of a city whose individuals could "make a name for ourselves" (Gen. 11:4). Despite periods of relative peace in certain communities for limited periods, all

---

[1] Edwards, J., The Great Christian Doctrine of Original Sin, 1766, pp. 407- 408.

human endeavours for harmony and stability have, ever since the Fall, resulted in a dystopia as only in the eternal order will a sacred environment again be fully operative.

Abel and Cain

The relationship between two brothers, Abel and Cain, both born to Adam and Eve after their expulsion from the Garden, ended tragically with the murder of the younger Abel by the older brother, Cain. Cain's actions were reprehensible due to the fact that he was fully aware of the moral code assigned to him not only by the Creator but teaching from his parents, recounting details of their transgression. Cain executed a diabolical act in full view of his Creator, reminiscent of the criminal actions of his parents. Moreover, in bringing a grain offering he ignored the requirements of a blood sacrifice in making temporary atonement for sins. Faith in the promised Redeemer was also required, but Cain chose to follow neither of these commands for he, like his parents, followed his own way of life.

Genesis 15:6 records that Abraham believed God's promises and his faith was credited to him as righteousness. A righteous status allows a sinner to be adopted into God's holy family, and to be in his presence. The requirements have never changed for they remain repentance of sin, faith in God, and his promise of a Redeemer as mentioned in Genesis 3:15. This did not happen in the case of Cain, as his actions showed. His corroded nature manifest itself in a heinous crime within a single generation after his parent's exile. Claiming independence from God, Cain and his descendants were forced to search anew for transcendence, meaning, purpose, and identity in a search common to all humanity through all eons.

Enduring Strife

The theme of interpersonal friction was to become repeated throughout ensuing generations reflecting the moral and mortal struggle between those of the line of Adam – the line of man - against those of the line of the second Adam, God's Messiah. This age-old struggle continues unabated until God's redemptive design finds eschatological completion. The struggle is reflected in a societal divergence between God's principles and secular humanist ideologies, continuing unabated until final restoration of all things.

3.8. Fatherhood of God

The cardinal doctrine of Judeo-Christianity is the Fatherhood of God concept, that is, God is a personal Creator and Saviour from which all other dogma connected to human meaning is derived. These include the idea of personal identity arising from individuals being created in the image of God, while living under the auspices of a loving and interactive divine father. This very concept defeats pantheism (the denial of an independent Deity outside of nature); the universalism of progressive theists; the deist claims of other religions; and instead endorses the exclusivity of the Judeo-Christian God.[2] The First Testament has many occasions where God is referred to as the father of certain individuals and of Israel itself.

Abba Father

In the Second Testament context, the term of choice for God that Jesus used was 'Father,' in distinctive forms. This occurs 165 times in the Gospels alone. Despite the fact that the Fatherhood of God dogma is well

---

[2] Exodus 20:3: "You shall have no other gods before me." Second Testament: "I am the way, and the truth, and the life. No one comes to the Father except through me" (Jn. 1 4:6).

entrenched in both Testaments, the idea of God as personal father is under severe criticism in present society. God's capacity as a personal father is a metaphor for the paternal function that God plays in the affairs of humankind. God is a spirit, not a man, and cannot be constructed, depicted in images or imagined, and does not have gender as humans do. God also acts in a manner generally associated with the role of a mother, showing love, care, and concern for his children.

Roles such as those usual of a human father or mother does not make God a man or a woman as he is beyond classification in terms of gender roles. Adhering to the plain and literal sense of scripture, the Church has for many centuries addressed God as Father. In the priestly prayer of Luke 11:2, Jesus taught his followers to pray in a manner subsequently recited by many millions through the ages, "Father, hallowed be your name." The image of God as Father is entrenched in Judeo-Christian doctrine.

Fatherhood under Assault

The fatherhood of God concept is challenged not only by secular humanist thinkers and feminist ideologues, but within professed Christian institutions. The purpose of rejecting the image of God as Father is to enable identity activists to assert their egocentric sovereign-selves in the Father's place. Theologian Chad Pecknold says, "we are not saying that God is like a human father, but rather that human fathers are like God."[3] This view explains why radical feminists seek to abolish the fatherhood, the male, role in society.

Cancellation of the male figure is supposedly justified through accusations of systemic male dominance, overbearing patriarchy, and

---

[3] Pecknold, C. C., Why We Call God Our Father, 2021.

masculine toxicity. Here is confusion of maleness (masculinity) with the properties of fatherhood. The purpose is to rid society of the patriarchal concept by which activists mean maleness, and to substitute instead a feminist role and identity, exemplified by Eve's dominance over Adam. In this way, the Creator's fatherhood identity is purged. The true position however, is that God being a spirit, transcends human gender roles while exhibiting qualities of both a father and a mother, depending on the circumstance.

Mary Daly

Mary Daly is a pivotal figure in the so-called 'second wave' feminist movement. She commenced her influential study, 'Beyond God the Father: Toward a Philosophy of Woman's Liberation,' with the first Chapter titled, 'After the Death of God the Father,'[4] which speaks for itself.

In a Reintroduction to her original work some 13 years later, Daly promotes an image of God not as a Supreme Being but, rather, as a spiritual "*Be-ing*" - a verb not a noun, a phenomenological and nebulous structure, a work in progress, subject to variable, subjective, inclinations. Here, Daly echoes basic tenets of ancient Hellenist philosophy, specifically Plato's Gnostic[5] epistemology whereby a dichotomy exists between a true immutable 'Being' and an everchanging 'Becoming,' the latter being her concept of the Divine. In replacement, Daly proposes an authentic self-realizing "noun-goddess." Her use of the term "goddess" instead of God the Father, can "amount to a change as minimal as a transsexual operation

---

[4] Daly, M., Beyond God the Father, 1973, p. 13.
[5] Gnosticism can "overwhelm the historic Christian faith" (Walker, W., 1959, p. 51).

on the patriarchal god."[6] No wonder Ronen Shoval exclaimed, "There are some things so ridiculous that only an intellectual can believe them."[7]

A Feminine God

In a case of psychological cognitive dissonance, feminists propose an androgynous or neutered god, one more to their liking - a replacement god for the patriarchal Judeo-Christian Divine. Their ideal is a malleable god whose ambiguous sexuality can be imitated by those with transsexual, non-binary, gender proclivity. In so doing, Daly directly confronts the Judeo-Christian doctrine of created binary genders.

Even certain theistic feminists seek a female Deity. Rebecca Peters, without underlying theological support, simply composes a grammatical gender conversion of God to that of Goddess. Peters' work is titled, 'Embracing God as Goddess.'[8] Denying the patriarchy of God, as Daly and Peters propose, creates an oversight vacuum and this is their intention. Their idea allows for a feminine, gender-neutral or androgynous deity of choice. Events in the Edenic Garden when the First Couple rejected the paternal sovereignty of a Father God are repeated in feminist thought. The battle over the Divine's fatherhood status has a long history.

Friedrich Nietzsche

The search for individual purpose and meaning through a fresh identity, one free of the patriarchal Fatherhood of God and his created *imago Dei* of humankind, converges into a perilous struggle for the biblical foundations of Western civilization. The quest for meaning is a hallmark of the social and religious *Sturm und Drang* (a period of storm and stress)

---

[6] Daly, M., 1973, Re-Introduction, pp. xviii-xl.
[7] Shoval, R., The Daily Princetonian, April 25, 2023.
[8] Peters, R. T., Embracing God as Goddess, 2008, p. 157.

of the late 20th and early 21st century - the New Age, within the so-called Age of Aquarius. Adam and Eve's rejection of their sacred purpose and meaning, has resulted in human beings desperately trying to replace lost identity with a philosophically fabricated version.

The 19th century continental philosopher Friedrich Nietzsche, echoed the ideological ideas of Adam and Eve when he declared (albeit through the mouthpiece of his allegedly insane protagonist) that, "God is dead. God remains dead. And we have killed him."[9] Nietzsche took his claim of a sovereign-self and denial of the Fatherhood of the Creator even deeper with his comment that, "Man created God."[10] These remarks identify the essence of Nietzsche's philosophy where there are no absolute truths, no objective facts, only subjective interpretations. He rejects validated truths in favour of a personal outlook free of permanence, reality, and rationalism.

All Nietzsche's assertions stem from the following motive, "We deny God; in denying God we deny responsibility in God."[11] The denial of a supreme God leaves him morally unaccountable and free to create his own reality. He can then insert into his worldview a replacement Creator - one of his own composition which he calls the *Übermensch,* the superman, the overman, an amoral individual[12] - one who formulates an idealized morality to suit. Nietzsche's theories reflect irrational atheistic persuasions and probable signs of slow progressive schizophrenia. As a consequence of his obsession in denying the existence of God, Nietzsche became

---

[9] Nietzsche, Science, 2006, para. 125, p. 120
[10] Nietzsche, Science, 2006, Poem 38, p. 18.
[11] Nietzsche, Idols, 1998, p. 75 [Ch. 6; §8].
[12] Nietzsche, Zarathustra, 2010, p. 53.

clinically insane for the final few years of his life.[13] Psychoanalyst Carl Jung diagnosed this illness as a case of 'ego inflation.'[14] His arrogant claims to divinity, of substituting himself (in his *alter ego* of the *Übermensch*) as the sovereign-self - a type of Messiah, a *homo deus*, doubtless overcame his mental stability. In this context, Nietzsche ignored his own caution to the effect that, "when you stare for a long time into an abyss, the abyss stares back into you."[15] Emotionally and psychologically, he could not conquer the dark implications of personal destiny resulting from his nihilistic philosophy, one without hope. In considering various alternative philosophical avenues, Nietzsche should have taken cognizance of John Milton's advice, "The mind is its own place, and in itself can make a Heaven of Hell, a Hell of Heaven."[16] Nietzsche made his mind a place of hell which eventually drove him insane.

Nietzsche and Resentment

Nietzsche's philosophy is based on this question, "Is that what you want?"[17] This interrogatory reflects his secular, ego-centred, ethical outlook and inquiry into the meaning of life. His search reaches no concrete answers, has no sacred framework and no rational justification. It is clear that throughout his volume of work, Nietzsche has one main motive which is that of resentment, meaning hostility and cynicism towards his nemesis, the Most-High God. He outrightly rejects the sacred and definitive moral principles of the Divine, displaying a deep hostility

---

[13] Nietzsche, Science, 2006, p. xxv.
[14] Huskinson, L., Nietzsche, 2004, p. 2.
[15] Nietzsche, F. Beyond Good and Evil, 2002 (1886), #146, p. 69.
[16] Milton, J., Paradise Lost, 1667, Part I., 254-5.
[17] Nietzsche, The Gay Science, 2006, p. 248.

that "pervades the core of personality," being "beyond control of the ego." In all, Nietzsche harbours a "generalised field of suppressed wrath."[18]

Nietzsche reflects the same insidious humanist demonstrations of an autonomous, creative-self attitude first encountered in the Edenic Garden. Radical thinkers, like Nietzsche, cannot tolerate existence of eternal, definitive, absolutist natural law with its clear moral and ethical standards. They therefore focus on philosophically circumventing such restrictions, always without success. Yet, there is no escaping God's holiness and his standards of law, ethics, morals and justice, coupled with grace and mercy. This realisation is the cause of Nietzsche's resentment.

Argumentum ad Hominem

As for Nietzsche, hostility against the Divine was the underlying motive of Adam and Eve, and has continued ever since the Fall. While expressly denying God, Nietzsche impliedly acknowledges his existence. For antagonists of this class, God is dead yet alive enough, influential, and real enough to be vehemently rejected. The 1978 Noble Laureate Yiddish writer, Isaac Bashevis Singer, concludes these philosophers "might revile God but they cannot deny God."[19] This statement well describes the position of Nietzsche and his circle, hence their desperate preoccupation with the issue of God's existence. Even so, Nietzsche's arguments do not provide answers to deep issues of life, especially a life outside of God, and moreover do not offer clear moral and ethical guidelines. Fundamentally, Nietzsche's irrational and unconvincing arguments are directed at the character, motive, and fatherhood status of God himself.

---

[18] Masterson, P., Concept of Resentment, 1979, p 157.
[19] Singer, I. B., Old Truths and New Clichés, 2022, p. 70.

School of Suspicion

In the view of Paul Ricoeur, the writings of Nietzsche (with Karl Marx and Sigmund Freud) should be read with a 'hermeneutic of suspicion' for the trio "dominate the school of suspicion," their arguments nothing other than "truth as lying."[20] The same view applies to Mary Daly, notably in relation to her views of human sexuality and patriarchal authority.

The underlying motive of philosophers is to repudiate God's existence, especially his sacred Fatherhood status, his transcendent moral essentials, and his spiritual influence. Through a collection of sophisticated philosophical theories, they promote their own theories of knowledge and reality. This attempt is noticeable in the nihilistic arguments of Nietzsche, Freud and Jung, as well as the absurdist opinions of existentialist philosophers like Jean-Paul Sartre, Simone De Beauvoir, Albert Camus, and Frans Kafka. These philosophers claim priority of the self, particularly in the areas of ethical behaviour and meaning. In seeking to replace biblical tenets underlying Western culture, none of these great European thinkers offer a credible ethical alternative that can be applied to society as a whole.

In their philosophy, each creates their own meaning, their own morality, but one detached from reality, revealing a neo-Gnostic dualism. Their ideas and ideals have converged into powerful ideologies, underlying much of the contemporary social disturbance. These dualist ideologies are reflected in various humanist identity fabrications such as Critical Race theory and other identity hypotheses like a sex-gender[21] split

---

[20] Ricoeur, P., Freud, 2008, p. 32 ff.
[21] 'Sex' describes biological binary sex attributed at birth. In contrast, 'gender' refers to cultural expressions of masculinity and femininity or to a chosen gender identity different to biological sex. The context reveals the application.

and self-gender fabrications. Perhaps the nihilists among them should consider the moral dilemma posed by Fydor Dostoyevsky, "If God doesn't exist then man is the chief of the earth, of the universe. Only how is he going to be good without God? That's the question."[22] Secular philosophers vainly struggle with this vital paradox.

Relativist Morality

To replace the true God, philosophers assert a substitute god. In the case of Freud, Jung, Marx and Nietzsche,[23] it is the Greek icon, Dionysius, the characteristics of whom support their neo-Gnostic, dualistic, theories within an idealized reality. Their humanist position becomes coupled to a pagan god of their choosing, one more amenable to their desire for self-determination. In this way, they declare themselves free of absolutist Judeo-Christian values and boundaries. Their position gives rise to a form of subjective 'situational ethics,'[24] leading to a pliable morality determined only by their opinions. In explanation of the desire for unfettered rights of self-expression, Brazilian intellectual Plinio Corréa de Oliveira says these activists demand, "the right to think, feel and do everything their unrestrained passions demand."[25] All well and good except when they endeavour to enforce social, legal, and political compliance with their moral grandiosity upon those holding more moderate views.

3.9. Conclusion

In search of freedom, Adam and Eve discarded their faith and all definitive meaning and regulated morality, conveniently overlooking the natural law.

---

[22] Dostoyevsky, F., The Brothers Karamazov, 1963 (1880), p. 721.
[23] Ricoeur, P., Freud and Philosophy, 2008, p. 35.
[24] Fletcher, J., Situation Ethics, 1966, p. 26.
[25] Corréa de Oliveira, P., Revolution and Counter-Revolution, 1993 (1959), p. 52.

The shortcoming of this strategy was later emphasized by Alexis De Tocqueville when he wrote, "Liberty cannot be established without morality; nor morality without faith."[26] Adam and Eve's ideals collapsed into a void of subjective fabrications in vain seeking new meaning, identity, and morality.

Identity Ideology

Continuing from Edenic events, the rejection of God in contemporary times comes with rejection of definitive moral and ethical rules, and the limit of binary, heterosexual, genders as represented by Adam and Eve. The created institution of monogamous marriage between two members of opposite binary genders; and natural laws that permeate the core of the human *psyche,* also come under lethal assault.

Society's turmoil is reflected in the arena of Identity Politics,[27] that is, through dualist race, sex and gender construals – especially transgenderism. The theories behind gender dysphoria have morphed into an influential political ideology which has as its aim the deconstruction[28] of created binary gender. Fromm explains that "ideology serves to rationalize and to justify all irrationality and immorality that exist within a society."[29] And so, irrational and immoral ideas have become a practical ideology, leading to moral anarchism endorsed legally, and to a certain degree morally, in the public square.

As an expression of Identity Politics, LGBTQ+ ('Alphabet') dualist

---

[26] De Tocqueville, A., Democracy in America, 1835, Vol. 1, Intro.

[27] Identity Politics invoke the relationship between transgressor and victimhood (Mitchell, J., Identity, 2019).

[28] Originating from Heidegger's '*Destruktion*' and Nietzsche's 'demolition' (Wood, D., Bernasconi, R., 1988, pp. 1-3). The concept of deconstruction is used to refabricate original meaning through a subjective methodology.

[29] Fromm, E., Beyond the Chains of Delusion, 1962, p. 134.

identity ideology has arisen from margins of society into the conventional. A minority group of activists has excessive influence in the political arena, well out of proportion to the number of their followers, and exercise degrees of hegemonic power. Social validation of their narrative has led to legalised homonormative behaviour contrary to long-established, fundamental, values. This influence has resulted in restrictions of individual freedoms, such as freedom of religion and expression.

From dualist identity ideologies comes a "culture of death" like euthanasia of the infirm and disabled; legally-endorsed assisted suicide; the sanctioned eugenical strategy to eliminate both perfect and imperfect unwanted humans in their pre-born state, and the prevalent, pernicious, trade in their body parts; the genocide of various social, religious, and racial groups with the forced sterilization of millions in totalitarian contexts. These practices are contrary to Judeo-Christian principles and a humane society.

The democratic rights, obligations, and freedoms enshrined in Western Constitutions can no longer be assured. Instead, these values and rights must be considered fluid, subject to political whims of reactionary lobby groups and other influencers of society. This is especially so as leftists with their destructive anti-theistic ideologies, "control every significant cultural institution," and thus the culture itself.[30]

Free Speech

Ideological sex-gender influence in tertiary educational institutions can be attributed to "feminization of the American University." Heather MacDonald explains that the most "far-reaching effects are intolerance of

---

[30] Trueman, C., Dogma Drives Christian Life, 2021, pp. 1-2.

dissent from political orthodoxy, and the compulsion to conform to that orthodoxy." This, she adds, is "justified in the name of safety and inclusivity."[31] The inherent right to freedom of speech is accordingly compromised, and so the "long march through the institutions"[32] by ideological activists is nearing completion.

Ancient Origins

The current discordance of cultures can be traced back to Edenic events from where originate modern secularism, individualism, and the neo-occult. The internal confrontation of values within post-Christian civilization is typified in the microcosmic struggle between Identity Politics coupled with moral anarchism, all in contest with cultural biblical values within a democratic liberal[33] political dispensation. In the opinion of French intellectual, Andre Kespian, "radical individualism became the major philosophical impulse of political modernity when it was progressively stripped of its spiritual nature to become a political statement about the nature of man on earth."[34] Edenic events provide evidence of the ancient origins of this continuing process.

The Human Dilemma

Humankind finds itself captive to its reprobative condition. Jean-Jacques Rousseau in his 1762 work, 'The Social Contract,' crystalizes the human dilemma, "Man was born free yet he is everywhere in chains."[35] It is this predicament that iconic English poets like Keats, Shelley, Coleridge,

---

[31] MacDonald, H., In Loco Masculi, March 5, 2023.
[32] Rudi Dutschke (1940 – 1979); Zündorf, I., Bibliography, 2021.
[33] The main focus of liberal politics is "equal freedom of all citizens, meaning liberty of speech, press, and religion" (Burns, D. E., Liberal Practice versus Liberal Theory, 2019).
[34] Kespian, A., Rights Now, November 30, 2022.
[35] Rousseau, J-J., Social Contract, 1968, Book 1, p. 49.

Wordsworth, and Lord Byron of the romanticist period (1780 - 1850) were likewise struggling to resolve. Their emotive works display themes of "restlessness and brooding, the pursuit of ideal love, and the untamed spirit ever in search of freedom."[36]

Hope remains, nonetheless, in God's redemptive intent for, as in the story of 'the Prodigal Son,'[37] his "restless" and "untamed" children will ultimately be restored to him in righteousness. Upon such event, they will regain the fullness of their corroded *imago Dei* identity and the meaning of life, defeating *angst* and 'the fear of death to which they had long been held captive' (Heb. 2:15). In the interim, practical atheism and the occult advance hand in hand through post-truth culture, laws, and politics replacing the loving but rejected theocracy of the sublime Garden setting, with an ideological utopia destined for disaster.

Finale

In the end, secular humanist seekers after meaning are destined, like Cain, to be 'restless wanderers on the earth,'[38] each facing an unknown future in fear, alienation and *angst*. The great poet, John Milton (1608-1674), in his epic work, 'Paradise Lost,' romantically describes Adam and Eve's odyssey into the unknown:

> *"The World was all before them, where to choose*
> *Their place to rest, and Providence their guide*
> *They hand in hand with wandering steps and slow,*
> *Through Eden took their solitary way."*[39]

---

[36] 'Shelley' (poetryfoundation.org).
[37] Luke 15:11-17.
[38] Genesis 4:12.
[39] Milton, J. L., Paradise Lost, 1667, Book X, para. 1540.

CHAPTER FOUR

THE OCCULT EMERGES[1]

"Man was born free, yet he is everywhere in chains"
(Jean-Jacques Rousseau, 1762)

4.1. Introduction

In G. S. Faber's study on the seeds of paganism and idol worship, 'The Origin of Pagan Idolatry,' he concludes that "all nations in the infancy of the world must have been assembled together in a single region and in a single community." Therefore, all nations would have possessed a common worldview which was exported throughout the known world at the time. This worldview was founded on a paganist[2] faith system that developed in Mesopotamia on the plains of Chaldea (Babylonia), between the two rivers of Tigris and Euphrates and, "stamped a character upon the whole mass of mankind and which remains vividly impressed, even to modern times."[3] This was the location of the Garden of Eden from where Adam and Eve commenced their journey.

The First Civilization

Mesopotamia was seat of the "world's first true civilization," and as such was the "father of all cultures in the West."[4] The influence of the capitol,

---

[1] The 'Occult' can be described as the practice of supernatural pagan powers.
[2] 'Pagan,' named after Pan the Greek god of sex and violence. Depicted as a Satan-type figure resulting in magic, witchcraft and related evil practices
[3] Faber, G. S., Preface, 1816.
[4] Anderson, M. C., History of Mesopotamia, 2021.

Babylon, cannot be underestimated for, apart from its historical significance as the centre of world power, Babylon gave birth to a malevolent occultist challenge to God's kingdom purposes after the Flood. The same demonic influence affecting Adam and Eve, later empowered the early Babylonian ruler, Nimrod, and continued relentlessly through the epochs. In early pagan thought Babylon, and not the Edenic Garden, can rightfully be considered "the world's navel, whose buildings connect heaven and earth."[5] Assuming many disguises, Babylon represents the treasonous Archangel Lucifer - a spiritual, malevolent personality that awakened upon ejection from the heavenly realm, sometime prior to the Garden saga.[6] Revelation 18:23 identifies the archetypal Babylon as source of all occult practice recording that, "all nations were deceived by your sorcery." The supernatural combat between the Most-High God and Satan, with manifestations in the natural world, continue unceasingly until resolution at the end of time.

4.2. Nimrod

After the flood, Noah's extended family settled in Mesopotamia and this is where they abandoned God worship. By the third generation, Noah's descendants venerated various pagan gods. Nimrod was the primary instigator of pagan worship. Philo explains Nimrod was the first person of his era to desert the Creator and to take up arms against his friends. He writes, "Moses calls the seat of Nimrod's kingdom, Babylon, which means 'change' - a thing nearly akin to desertion."[7] Nimrod and Babylon are symbiotically linked, as is clear from Genesis 10.

---

[5] George, A. R., Bond of the Lands, 1997, p. 125.
[6] Isaiah 14; Ezekiel 28; Luke 10:18; 2 Peter 2:4; Jude 6; Revelation 12:4.
[7] Philo, On the Giants, 15:66.

The Antagonist

Targum Pseudo-Philo records that Ham's descendants elevated Nimrod to be their ruler, "Then came the sons of Cham and made Nembroth (Nimrod) a prince over themselves."[8] The Jewish historian, Josephus, says the Tower of Babyl event revealed Nimrod's desire to build an edifice higher than any future flood waters could reach and, in so doing, avenge the diluvian destruction of his forefathers. In a nutshell, Nimrod actively sought to "turn men from the fear of God to bring them into a constant dependence upon his power."[9] He sought to establish a hegemony, "a rival world power to God,"[10] with himself as the divine personage. Nimrod desired veneration of the self, leading to a façade of self-deification, a god-man (*homo deus*).

Ever since the Tower episode, humanity has lived in a Babylonian-type environment, trying to create a utopian city to replicate lost Eden. The overriding agenda of the Tower constructors was to create a substitute religion in a humanist setting, thereby establishing an idolatrous, self-glorifying, community. In an act of supernatural intervention, God frustrated Nimrod's endeavours for independence by introducing a mishmash of languages. A humanist engineered replicate of the sacred garden was not part of God's design. Even so, at this early stage of history, loosely estimated at around 5,000 – 3,000 B.C.E., idol worship arose on the plains of Shinar and escalated widely through the conquering exploits of Nimrod and his cohorts.

---

[8] Philo, Antiquities, Ch. 5:1.
[9] Josephus, Antiquities, 1.4.2 [113 f.].
[10] Quey, R., Babylon, 2016, pp. iv.

Arrival of the Occult

The 'Cave of Treasures' Targum reveals Nimrod was the first to engage in the occult, to worship nature and practise astrology, "Nimrod went up from the east, and began to practise the art of divining and very many men marvelled at him."[11] Genesis 10:10-11 records Nimrod was responsible for establishing Nineveh, a centre of bloodshed, "Woe to the bloody city, all full of lies and plunder" (Nah. 3:1). Led by Nimrod, the city of Nineveh was also a source of occult, "all because of the wanton lust of a prostitute, alluring, the mistress of sorceries, who enslaved nations by her prostitution and peoples by her witchcraft" (Nah. 3:4).

Nimrod was chief deity of the time, and this fact is confirmed in the passage of 2 Kings 19:37, "he (Sennacherib King of Assyria) was worshiping in the house of Nisroch (Nimrod) his god."[12] Although the account of Sennacherib was dated about 681 B.C.E., the deification of Nimrod is far more ancient for the First Testament, "claims to have knowledge of Nimrod's kingdom although two millennia lie between the days of the king of Marad and the biblical narrator."[13]

Ancestor Worship

Not only was Nimrod a mighty hunter contrary to the Lord, he became a heathen priest-king and was later worshipped as a divine manifestation of a Babylonian god. As Faber's studies reveal, "In the religious system of the old mythologists, demons were the same as hero-gods, and these hero-gods were acknowledged to be the souls of eminent benefactors to mankind who, after they had quitted this mortal sphere of existence, were

---

[11] Budge, E. A. W., The Book of the Cave of Treasures, 1927, Fol. 24b, col. 2.
[12] 2 Kings 19:37; Isa. 37.
[13] Kraeling, E., Nimrod, 1922, p. 218.

worshipped as deities by a too grateful posterity."[14] In this way, ancestor worship emerged on earth.

Idol Worship

Nimrod was a vehement opponent of Jehovah worship. Bowker explains, "Nimrod came to be regarded as the great antagonist of Abraham, and the conflict between them summarised the antithesis between polytheistic idolatry and the worship of the one true God of Israel."[15]

Nimrod, the hero-god, the king-priest, was the first to venerate natural objects like fire and the "starry hosts."[16] He engaged in astrological practices such as "dividing the heavens,"[17] and practised idol worship. As the primary persona of occult practice, Nimrod was deified by his followers, as were many subsequent notable personalities. Dedication to gods and goddesses of human origin has never ceased, some of whom have reappeared in New Age neo-paganism. The transition from individuals to deified hero-gods harkens back to when certain beings emerged from intercourse between the "sons of God" and the "daughters of man," in Genesis 6:1- 4. The product was a group of "mighty men who were of old, the men of renown," later becoming pagan myths, legends, and gods.

Paganism in Canaan

A question arises as to how the practice of idol worship appeared in Canaan, contrary to strict biblical prohibitions against such practice. Kraeling supplies the solution, "what is more natural than the news of the mighty king of Marad, the patron for every bandit and herdsman, should

---

[14] Faber, G. S., The Origin of Pagan Idolatry, 1816, Book 1, Ch. 1, p. 23.
[15] Bowker, J., Targums, 1969, p. 180.
[16] 2 Kings 17:16.
[17] Isaiah 47:13.

have passed into Arabia and through Arabia to southern Palestine?"[18] The
great pagan, Nimrod as the king of Marad, not only established Babylon
and major cities like Marad, but was responsible for the spread of idol
worship from Chaldea to far areas like Ashur in Assyria - also described
as the "land of Nimrod."[19] In ancient times both Babylon and Assyria,
geographically and historically, initially formed one country with a related
language. In both Testaments, Babylon is named as the original location
and source of idol worship and sexual immorality, instigated by Nimrod.
The Apostle John writes, "Fallen, fallen is Babylon the great, she who
made all nations drink the wine of the passion of her sexual immorality."[20]

Spread of Paganism

There existed a significant interconnection between pagan practice in
Chaldea, Assyria, and Persia and such practice soon made its way to
Greece, Rome, Egypt and the rest of the known world at the time. The
Hellenistic influence of philosophical intellectualism through Socrates and
Aristotle, but particularly via Gnostic dualist theories developed by
Plato,[21] Plotinus, and their followers, combined to advance secular
humanist and paganist constructions which thrive in current cultures.

Occult and Orthodoxy

The stark difference between believers in pantheistic, polytheistic, pagan
idolatry and the monotheists who worship the true God continues into
postmodern society. The spiritual contest between Judeo-Christian tenets
and paganism is the cause of much political, legal, and social turbulence.

---

[18] Kraeling, E., Nimrod, 1922, p. 218.
[19] Micah 4:4-6.
[20] Revelation 14:8; 18.
[21] The Greek, Plato, c. 428 – 348 B.C.E.

The occult involves worship of created entities or rationalized spiritual entities lacking grounded ethical attributes. These pagan icons are unattached to God's natural law resulting in their followers formulating subjective ethical and moral theories. To do so, they rely on contextual circumstances, emotivism, and subjective concoctions. This is the philosophical source of what later became known as 'situation ethics,' a personalised composition based solely on two principal factors, namely, that of a Platonic and Gnostic dichotomy, and a subjective opinion of ethical and moral conduct. Relativist, nuanced, ethics has evolved anew through the philosophy of Joseph Fletcher (1905 -1991), the promotor of situation ethics. Nonetheless, dualistic situationalism has ancient occultist roots from Edenic times and remains in contrast to the high ethical and moral order of rational and definitive Judeo-Christian principles, fundamental to the moral order of society.

Seed of Satan

Adam and Eve's rebellion was motivated by arrogantly desiring to be like God. This attitude was emulated by their post-flood descendants, Nimrod and his allies, who likewise rebelled against God. Even in present times, Nimrod's ideological successors claim independent secular identity, affirming their status as unaccountable sovereign-selves, while striving for a kingdom of man, combined with a neo-pagan spirituality arising from Edenic events. Nimrod is the earliest identifiable post-flood 'seed of Satan' (Gen. 3:15), having the same evil intentions as the diabolical serpent and his own treasonable forebearers, Adam and Eve. He exhibited great pride in establishing a new world order to replace the disrupted Edenic utopia, with himself as the Divine.

4.3.　Astrology

As a whole, the occult can be "viewed as a global phenomenon, at least in the modern period."[22] Astrology, a narrow expression of the occult, can be defined as, "the divination of the supposed influences of the stars and planets on human affairs and terrestrial events by their positions and aspects."[23] To search for understanding is the primary purpose of astrology, for once meaning through comprehension has been grasped then purpose and meaning can follow.

Astrology and Paganism

Astrology is a belief system involving worship of created, cosmic, natural objects such as "starry hosts." Astrology was a hallmark of pagan spirituality, and continues to be a feature of religious activity in many cultures. The original source of this form of nature worship, that is, divination of "starry hosts," was evident in early Babylon, as with the origin of all paganist beliefs, commencing from the time of Nimrod as cited in Genesis 11.

From Babylon, the practice of astrology spread to Persia, Greece, and India. As Nicholas Campion explains, "contemporary popular Astrology can be seen as a remarkable revival of the practical applications of an ancient, non-Western astronomy, that of Mesopotamia of 4,000 years ago, and one which predates all the other intellectual pillars of Western society from Greek philosophy to Judaism and Christianity, to modern scientific method." Not only is Nimrod's Babylon the original locale of pagan practice but also the spiritual source of astrology today, little different if at all from its ancient roots. Campion confirms, "it is possible to identify a

---

[22] Asprem, E., New Approaches to the Study of Esotericism, 2021, p. 3.
[23] 'Astrology,' Merriam-Webster.

fundamental continuity from the earliest Babylonian astrology to the present day."[24]

Prohibition Against Astrology

By the time of Moses, worship of the "starry hosts" was evident within the Israelite community. Moses cautioned the tribes, "And beware lest you raise your eyes to heaven, and when you see the sun and the moon and the stars, all the host of heaven, you be drawn away and bow down to them and serve them."[25] The warning against nature worship was written some 2,500 years after the Tower of Babyl episode, and so alludes to the early origins of this occultist practice. The passage of Isaiah 47:13 condemns worship of astrological heavenly bodies, which King Manasseh introduced into Judah, referring to "those who divide the heavens."

Popularity of Astrology

Astrology remains deeply influential in society. It ensures the continuation of paganism, of divination of the sacred (the essence of astrology), into modernity. Campion confirms that "Astrology in the 20th century West has a central place in popular culture."[26]

It is not only in popular culture that astrology has gained acolytes, but also among intellectuals for some of the great thinkers who significantly influenced the culture, were practitioners. For instance, the famed Psychoanalyst Carl Jung, a colleague of Sigmund Freud, was a practitioner of astrology, "Astrology was a lifelong interest for Jung" and he had a "great regard for it and other paranormal or occult practices." Additionally, astrology played a "fundamental role" in Jung's

---

[24] Campion, N., Astrology, 2000, p. 509.
[25] Deuteronomy 4:19; 17:2-3; 18:10-11.
[26] Campion, N., Astrology, 2000, p. 509.

development of analytic psychology and was an "important aid in his formulation of psyche and psychic process."[27] Jung and others of the renowned 'Eranos Circle' for intellectuals, considered astrology an adjunct of classic Gnosticism,[28] itself an occultist, dualist, belief system endemic in society since ancient days.

Freud and Jung

The interrelationship between astrology and the mystical leads to dualist philosophical structures such as reincarnation, pagan spirituality, Gnosticism, and other demonstrations of the occult. Jung claimed ancient Gnostics were the "virtual discoverers of 'depth psychology,'"[29] a central tenet of psychology known as "Jungian spiritual therapy."[30] Jung's own words, written in a letter to his colleague Freud, displays the firm grip of astrology on his psychological theories, "astrology seems indispensable for a proper understanding of mythology and I shall return laden with a rich booty for our knowledge of the human psyche."[31] Jung's statement confirms important thinkers of the 20th century, like himself and Freud, found pertinent material for their psychotherapy and phenomenological theories in astrology, pantheism, and Gnosticism. Their wide influence contributes towards continuing secular humanist and neo-pagan ideologies underlying present counter-culture instability.

Darwin's Evolution Theory

Freud's theory on the origin of humanity was based on evolutionary

---

[27] Buck, S., Hiding, 2018, p. 207.
[28] "Gnosticism of the Greek and Roman world" is "brilliant, spiritual, amoral, totally false" (Satinover, J. B., Jungian, 1994).
[29] "Jung identified 'depth psychology' as heir to the Gnostic tradition (Satinover, 1994).
[30] Hoeller, S., The Gnostic World View, 2021.
[31] McGuire, W., The Freud/Jung Letters, 1974, 254j, p. 421.

materialism for, as he confesses, "the theories of Darwin strongly attracted me."[32] The evolution theory promoted by Charles Darwin originates from his paternal Grandfather, Erasmus Darwin, who believed "all warm-blooded animals have arisen from one living filament" formed by "spontaneous vitality" in the "primeval ocean."[33] Rejecting the creationist account of humanity, the Darwin family, commencing with Erasmus through Robert the father of Charles, then Charles himself, fabricated a pantheistic alternative. The result was materialist determinism, a fiction with no rational, coherent, objective, scientific validation nor moral and ethical guidelines.

Evolution is a false belief system trying to combine ideology and science, but without the strict grounds of rationality, empiricism, and coherence. Evolutionism casually rejects the compelling facts, dogma, and data of creationism and has become fashionable among those denying God. The variety of contemporary identity ideologies of race, sex, and gender are derived from evolutionist theory which is an example of secular humanism, being a practical atheism.

Marvellous Phenomenon

Frederick Nietzsche was enamoured with that "marvellous phenomenon," the Greek god Dionysus through whom he discovered "the eternity of life… the very path to life…a holy life."[34] His work is founded on the concept of 'hidden knowledge,' esotericism, to be accessed through his protagonist, Zarathustra, the *Übermensch,* a figure reminiscent of Thomas Carlyle's archetypical 'Man of Letters.' The Gnostic idea of *gnosis* and

---

[32] Schweigerdt, B., The Gnostic Influence on Psychology, 1982, p. 225.
[33] Darwin, E., Laws of Organic Life, 1794, p. 478.
[34] Nietzsche, Twilight, 1998, pp. 79-80.

Nietzsche's 'hidden knowledge' are one and the same concept, that of obscure knowledge uncovered only by enlightened adepts. Here, Nietzsche follows Jung and Freud with their occultist interests. Such are the paganist beliefs of modernity's three foremost thinkers.

Light and Darkness

In Gnostic thought, an inferior 'Demiurge' god created the inconsequential temporal body but not the eternal spirit (the mind) which denotes the true self. To the contrary, the God of Judeo-Christianity created all components of the human being, material and immaterial, the spiritual and the natural. Isaiah 45:7 reads, "I form the light and create darkness. I, the Lord, do all these things." There is no duality in the true God, no aspect of human condition whether body or spirit, that is not designed to be harmonious, whole, and good. The various facets of creation are often distinct, to be contrasted with each another, yet united and complete and this includes the human form.

While Plato's dualism considers the human body corrupted, disposable, material created by the Demiurge, the true creator is one who created a dichotomy between the spirit (the mind) and the material body. It is the spirit which is all-important for through the spirit, knowledge, *gnosis*, is attained. The claims of Gnostics denying the importance of the body are accordingly defeated by the biblical passage of Isaiah 45:7 and others. Consequently, so is dualist justification for moral and sexual licentiousness conducted by an irrelevant body.

Dualist Gender Theory

Declaring the body to be of no consequence leads to fluid and malleable gender, one open to reconstruction. Gender can thus be fabricated into any desired form, whether male, female, transsexual, transgender, a hermaphroditic or androgenous combination. The reality of biological binary sex assigned at conception can be ignored for it is the spirit, the true inner-self, that is all-important and needs to be manifested. Unsurprisingly, this leads to mutilation of an individual's created gender. Immense emotional confusion in the minds of vulnerable persons results, often with critical outcomes including suicidal actions and tendencies. Contemporary gender dysphoria is the outcome of applied Gnostic concepts concerning the spirit and body split.

Reincarnation

In esotericism there exists an intersection between Gnosticism, astrology, and reincarnation. Astrologers explain their connection with reincarnation as follows, "The doctrine of reincarnation should have a special claim upon Astrologers, as Astrology comes especially under Saturn, and Saturn is the planet of Justice."[35] Hardly a rational, scientific, or pseudo-scientific conception but, instead, a misplaced faith system, not objectively verifiable, and contingent upon natural objects revealing a form of justice, but a justice unattached to comprehensible laws. Nonetheless, rebirth is pivotal to the application of astrology for, "the science of the stars stands or falls with karma and reincarnation."[36]

Astrology and Postmodernism

Commenting on astrology in the postmodern era, Samuel Kriss concludes that "Astrology is hip now; it is queer and diverse and empowering, maybe revolutionary, definitely unavoidable."[37] Ancient astrological concepts are adapted to accommodate fashionable terminology and ideologies. It is

---

[35] Hall, M. P., Astrology and Reincarnation, 1980, p. 9.
[36] Leo, A., Esoteric Astrology, 1913, p. vii.
[37] Kriss, S., How to Believe in Astrology, 2021.

estimated that although the "global astrology industry was valued at $12.8 billion in 2021," it is expected to increase to $22.8 billion in ten years.

Astrology is hugely popular with 70 million Americans checking their daily horoscopes, claiming "astrology is the language of the stars," so it "helps us to understand how to live in the world."[38] Carl Jung predicted the occult's flexible nature in accommodating new social and spiritual developments when he said, "Eternal truth needs a human language that alters with the spirit of the times."[39] Gnosticism, astrology, and other facets of the occult, remain prevalent in the post-truth age in various forms. In each form lies the prehistoric roots of secular humanism and paganism based on discontent with time-honoured theistic precepts concerning meaning, purpose, morality, mortality, ethics, and identity.

4.4. Age of Aquarius

Differing schools of thought exist among astrologers as to exactly when the astrological Age of Aquarius commenced, and even for how long each age persists. The wide consensus is that Aquarius commenced during the 20th century and will continue for some 2,160 years, being the average duration of each astrological age. Myron Magnet describes the Aquarian age as characterized by "a transgressive fling with sex, drugs and rock and roll, seeking liberation not just from morals but even from manners,"[40] while asserting primacy of the unconstrained-self.

---

[38] Page, S., Young People Flocking to Astrology, June 13, 2023.
[39] Jung, C., 2020, CW, 16, Para. 396.
[40] Magnet, M., About Those Self-Evident Truths, Winter 2020.

The New Age

Within the era of Aquarius developed the New Age,[41] a post-structuralist period in which the politically driven reset of Western society is underway. All tertiary academic disciplines, for instance, are subject to ideological deconstruction including political science, psychology, philosophy, theology and sociology. This social engineering reflects demise of the Judeo-Christian orientation upon which the traditional Western order is based. It is historically verifiable that "the Judeo-Christian worldview led to the formation of Western civilization."[42]

The political freedom of Western society has allowed identity ideology to develop. This is unsurprising as political issues are driven by the culture of society which in turn is a manifestation of the dominant religion. Richard Neuhaus describes this process as follows, "it is true to say that politics is an expression of culture, and at the heart of culture is religion."[43] The key opponent to reformulating society is cultural Judeo-Christianity with its values supporting the moral order of society.

Once culture has adjusted to a new normal, then a political drive for legal enforcement occurs. This is precisely what is taking place as significant intrusion by identity ideology comes into the culture, despite objection and resistance by conservatives, moderates, and classic liberal democratic political interests. Still, the advocates of secularisation have no interest in customary freedoms or constraints on morality. It is the creationist truth and otherwise exclusivity of Judeo-Christian dogma that offends in this post-Christian age of relativist moral and ethical

---

[41] 'New Age' beliefs reflect pagan spirituality outside mainstream religions.
[42] Simmons, R., Reflections on the Existence of God, 2019, p. xii.
[43] Neuhaus, R., Editorial, 1990.

monopolism. This factor marks it as a target for destruction, under the
fiction of a biased social justice theory.

Identity Politics

Political promotion and judicial enforcement of cultural ideologies are
commonplace. The term, Identity Politics, encapsulates these ideologies,
energised in public life through sundry action groups like the 'Alphabet'
(LGBT+) tribe. This group denies the realism of natural-born binary
gender, while promoting transsexualism and transgenderism
(autogynephilia) under the slogan, 'Born this way.' Activists promote
mainstream acceptance of homosexuality and same-sex marriage as
normative. Other minority groups include ethnic anarchists such as Black
Lives Matter ('BLM'). The latter, through a program of racial
readjustment, are driven by a Critical Race Theory resulting in the
resegregation of society into opposing ethnic classifications. This
prejudices other ethnic groups such as whites, Hispanics and Asians. At
the same time, BLM militants in combination with leftist, socialist,
cultural Marxists and other socio-anarchists, desire to refabricate the
capitalist economy for their own benefit.

Challenges to Orthodoxy

The main agenda of identity activists is destruction of Judeo-Christianity
in favour of secularism and occultist-driven pluralistic, spiritual paganism.
For example, reactionary feminists in striving for identity, assault the
Fatherhood concept of the Judeo-Christian Creator. By so doing, they
dismantle traditional marriage between created binary genders in favour
of same-sex marriage, polyamory, polygamy, and other permutations of
sexual relationships. To facilitate this motive, they denigrate the literal-
historical interpretation of biblical events and personae such as Adam and

Eve and the Garden at Eden. The Bible itself is dismissed myth or allegory. Furthermore, doctrines like the *imago Dei* of humanity; original sin; the necessity of the Cross; and the Resurrection of the Messiah of Israel, are particularly under pressure from both within and exterior to the Church. Secularism, coupled with neo-pagan ideologies, has resulted in widespread euthanasia of categories of persons, and associated instances of eugenics. Selective abortion constitutes as an extension of euthanasia and eugenics. These practices are applied to millions of both perfect, and suspected non-perfect, defenceless, unborn infants and the egregious trade in their remains.

The hallmark of the anarcho-social movement is that it is hate-driven, especially against those who hold contrary views. There is no attempt at human solidarity; no place for moderation; no true embrace of equality, tolerance, and diversity; no consensual common good; no substantive arguments but merely emotivist, irrational, idealistic, subjective and ideological identity constructs, all in the name of a narrow distributive justice.

Reprobate Clergy

Minority groups control the narrative, the politics, the media, the education, and to an ever-increasing extent, infiltrate and influence Christian Churches. For example, 943 clergy from the Swedish Lutheran Churches declared themselves a 'trans-inclusive institution.' Roman Catholicism itself is not safe from the influence of heretical ideologies. Some 100 Catholic priests in Germany endorsed same-sex unions by invoking God's blessing, contrary to an injunction from the 'Congregation for the Doctrine of the Faith' prohibiting such action. Bishop Müller revealed that these reprobate priests, "claim to have secret exegetical knowledge" that justifies them interpreting scripture in a blasphemous way."[44] This articulation of esoteric, secret, knowledge is a hallmark of neo-Gnostic mysticism, originating from the serpent's deception, continuing in postmodern religion.

Primacy of Gnosis

While it is understood Western culture is based on three main pillars, namely that of Judeo-Christian precepts, ancient Greek philosophy, and Roman law (the rule of law), there is another factor seminally influencing modern culture. That factor is "the importance of inner enlightenment or *gnosis* - a revelatory experience that entails an encounter with one's true self."[45] From the time of the ancient Garden, continuing through the ages into modernity,[46] the influence of esotericism through a wide variety of conduits such as philosophy, psychology and spirituality, remains a compelling source of meaning for those rejecting Judeo-Christianity. Therefore, many people "turn again to the basic principles of Gnosticism and hermeticism, often integrated with some kind of New Age thinking."[47] As can be expected, New Age spiritually has become the "fastest growing alternate belief system in the country."[48] A search for purpose, meaning, and identity apart from a Judeo-Christian cultural orientation is the basic motivation of secular, humanist, and neo-pagan ideologies.

The Psychic Scene

In describing the postmodern psychic scene, Robert Galbreath mentions "the idea of the Adept and Initiate in secret knowledge, the idea of a divine

---

[44] Müller, G. L., Blessing and Blasphemy, 2021.
[45] Van den Broek, R., Gnosis, 1998, p. vii.
[46] Modernity commencement with the industrial age.
[47] Van den Broek, R., Gnosis, 1998, p. viii.
[48] Geisler, N., Apologetics, 1990, p. 9.

man or woman, of the god-inspired, of the human with super powers, is in the air."[49] Although pertinent to a postmodern context, the description is fitting when applied to Eve's esoteric elitism, her determination to emulate the Divine's creative authority and the attempted realization of fresh meaning through a recreated self-identity outside her conferred *imago Dei.* This heretical expression is to be expected for, as Joseph Pearce points out, "forces of evil always return, like a fungus, to feed on the fallen fabric of the world."[50] The claim of Gnosticism's cyclical appearance throughout all ensuing eons becomes validated when examined through the lens of ancient Jewish interpretative techniques pertaining to prophecy. This exegetical method was discussed in Chapter 2.

4.5. Conclusion

The heretical desire to be like a god (*eritus sicut Deus*) lives through Gnostic-based astrology and other neo-pagan dualist demonstrations. Widely promoted by influential philosophers like Marx, Darwin, Freud, Nietzsche, Heidegger and Jung, supported by existentialist writers like Sartre, Camus, and Kafka; added to by atheists and evolutionists, secular humanism coupled with neo-paganist spirituality has become the fashionable, but morally contextual, new religion of Western society.

The focus on Freud and Jung's idea of a therapeutic-self as the sole determinant of meaning, purpose and identity reflects continuation of ancient *gnosis,* the basis for dualist identity theories. While activists claim "identity is the source of divinity," they seek divine identity not only in individualism but primarily "in shared group identities."[51] Sociologically,

---

[49] Galbreath, R., The Occult Today, 1971, p. 629.
[50] Pearce, J., 2016, Why We Should Revere Spain, March 27, 2023.
[51] Patterson, J. M., Wokeness and the New Religious Establishment, 2021.

they strive for personal connection, cohesion, structure, and emotional order. Hence their objective to reconfigure society into an idiosyncratic group identity, as exemplified by Alphabet sect acronyms. Yet, the crucial issue of a personal, transcendent, identity will remain elusive for only in the embrace of *imago Dei* is true meaning attained.

Originating in Edenic times, re-capitulations of secular humanist and mystical pagan syncretism - together amounting to the rise of the occult – will persist until eschatological conclusion. This claim is theologically verified through a *darash* of ancient Rabbinical Jewish exegesis of midrashic prophetic *haggadah* in following chapters. In the interim, welcome to the New Age of Aquarius.

CHAPTER FIVE

IDEALISM IN A POST-TRUTH ERA

"If God doesn't exist then man is the chief of the earth, of the universe.
Only how is he going to be good without God? That's the question"
(Fyodor Dostoyevsky, The Brothers Karamazov, 1880)

5.1. Introduction

Plato's theories can be summed up as "teaching based on Gnosis, the knowledge of transcendence arrived at by way of interior, intuitive means."[1] Adam and Eve sought their own "knowledge of transcendence" through secret revelations imparted by the serpent - the original Gnostic Elite - for the purposes of freedom from God and his restrictions.

The philosophy underlying Platonic Gnosticism has early roots, harkening back to events in Eden[2] when the First Couple rebelled to create a milieu free of God's parameters. Through irrational claims of self-divinity, autonomy, creative license and *gnosis*, they assumed a freedom in which to devise their own reality, a new personal identity and philosophy of life. Rejecting the creation order, they fabricated a secular order enabling them to assert the primacy of their individualism. Gene Veith elaborates, "New Age religions for all their pagan trappings, have in common the idea that the self is divine, that you are God, the creator of

---

[1] Hoeller, S. A., The Gnostic Worldview, 2021.
[2] Gnosticism's prime target are "stories of Genesis" (Borchert, G. L., Gnosticism, 1984).

your own universe."[3]   Similarly, Thomas White describes the situation thus, "the modern person is free to define his own meaning, free from the influence of religious authorities" with their "collective account of meaning. When it comes to defining or defending the meaning of life, it's every man for himself."[4] The Judeo-Christian position is explained by C. S. Lewis when he writes "it is a fatal superstition that men can create values."[5] Lewis is correct, values come from God's natural law and not from a humanism initiated by the First Couple and their ideological successors, including post-truth identity activists. Hence, true values cannot be invented for they already exist and have always existed, emanating from the precepts of the Creator. The heretical genre of Adam and Eve, embracing fresh humanist values, principles, and spirituality much later designated Gnosticism, persisted in multiple manifestations throughout the ages.

Fruits of the Forbidden Tree

The actions of Nimrod confirm the continuation of a Gnostic-like occultist elitism into the post-flood era for, like his ancestors, Nimrod acted in blatant contempt for God's divine boundaries. He established his own theories of life through humanist rationality and moral creativity. These actions are derived from fruits of the Tree of Knowledge of Good and Evil, enjoyed by his forebearers. In order to achieve his aims, Nimrod denied the concepts of righteousness and holiness as explained to Adam and Eve, relying instead on his own fabricated, "intuitive means." In the result, Nimrod became the instigator of pagan worship and self-veneration for all

---

[3] Veith, G. E., Postmodern Times 1994, p. 199.
[4] White, T. J., The Metaphysics of Democracy, 2018.
[5] Lewis, C. S., Christian Reflections, 1967, p. 73.

future generations of humankind. During his lifetime, he was deemed a demi-god and thereafter a god worthy of worship, setting the stage for a *homo deus* (god-man) into the New Age of Aquarius.

Gnostic Thought

Gnosticism is of ancient origin for it can be said, "the more these beginnings (of Gnosticism) are studied, the farther they seem to recede into the past."[6] Gnosticism's ties to ancient Babylonian religion was publicly explained in 1882 by Karl Kessler in Berlin emphasizing Gnosticism's link to Babylonian astrology. On examining ancient Gnostic texts discovered at Nag Hammadi, Pleše reveals that Gnosticism is not a benign creation but, rather, "a coherent doctrine of evil derived from a spiritual source, permeating all domains of a multi-layered reality."[7] This fact is evident in Gnostic-based Marcionite[8] doctrine which claims evil originates in the Demiurge, a false creator, so truth must therefore be found elsewhere. Marcion of Sinope (144 C.E.), rejected the Fatherhood concept of the Creator God and the *imago Dei* concept of humankind. Reality, true knowledge, consciousness, and meaning emanate from a higher spiritual source, the Monad, outside of creation and accessible only to Gnostic avatars. This theory justifies a dichotomy of the spirit (the incorporeal mind) contrasted with the inconsequential corrupted physical body. The hypothesis, like all ideological heresies, originates from transactions in the Edenic Garden and can be regarded as the "doctrine of evil" which has "permeated all domains"[9] of spiritual life. The search for emotional

---

[6] Catholic Encyclopaedia, 2021.
[7] Pleše, Z., Evil and its Sources in Gnostic Traditions, 2014, p. 101.
[8] Marcion (144 C.E.) rejected authority of both Testaments except for Paul's letters, claiming the Creator was a malevolent personage and only Paul a true disciple of God.
[9] Pleše, Z., Evil and its Sources in Gnostic Traditions, 2014, p. 101.

security, personal identity, purpose, knowledge and meaning in life through idealized versions of reality has continued ever since.

5.2. Gnosticism, Phenomenology,[10] and Psychology

Theologian Norman Geisler explains New Age spiritualism comprises the "occult, Gnosticism, and paganism." He says this spiritualism "stands within a long tradition for it is not new."[11] In his book, 'A Gnostic Study of Religions,' Robertson divulges that Gnosticism's relevance today is seen in the "philosophical and psychoanalytic affinities,"[12] influencing society. These two conduits for Gnostic thought are examined below.

The Gnostic New Age

The presence of Gnostic spirituality in the New age was highlighted in persuasive lectures delivered at Carl Jung's famed 'Eranos Circle' group, by intellectuals like Gershom Scholem, Mircea Eliade, and Henry Corbin. These three described themselves as phenomenologists of a "Gnostic mind,"[13] and can rightfully be considered "titanic figures in the history of 20th century religion studies," who "remain immensely influential."[14] It is believed that Edmund Husserl initially, and then Jung specifically, developed phenomenology to the extent that it became "one of the great intellectual movements of the twentieth century."[15] This is apparent from the fashionable therapeutic focus on an individual's 'inner-self,' widely promoted by Jung, Freud, and their circle.

---

[10] In phenomenology, "reality consists of objects and events understood in human consciousness, not objective reality.
[11] Geisler, N., Apologetics, 1990, p. 11.
[12] Robertson, D. G., A Gnostic Study of Religions, 2020, p. 75.
[13] Wasserstrom, S., Religion after Religion, 1999, p. 25, 30.
[14] Versluis, A., Review, 2001, p. 288.
[15] Brooke, R., Jung and Phenomenology, 2020, p. 968.

The philosophical outlook of these scholars was to the effect that roles of myth and mysticism should dominate in religion, and so absolutist moral laws and doctrines should be repudiated. As Corbin himself asserted, "The entire human drama is played out on the plain of *gnosis* and Gnostic consciousness. It is a drama of knowledge, not a drama of the flesh."[16] This view leads to a subjective experience of the sacred, lacking objective boundaries. Phenomenology as a science of the mind is simply a vehicle for rationalising Gnostic claims, hence Eliade's "fantastic reality" which led to the inference that "myth was real and history was not." In support, Corbin described phenomenology as "a revealing of the concealed, a revealing of secrets" and so his objective was to "discover the primordial image."[17] In his view, this aim could only be achieved through a subjective, neo-Gnostic, philosophical strategy to the exclusion of independent reality. Even so, the elemental image he anxiously sought was established in the primeval Garden of Eden – namely, the *imago Dei* of humankind – a concept he rejected due to its theistic origins.

Members of the Eranos circle exemplified the intellectual interplay between abstract ideas of Hellenist philosophy and the grounded principles of Jewish doctrine - the contrast between knowledge for its own sake and realist biblical precepts. Tim Labron clarifies this distinction when he writes, "the source of authority and meaning is found in concrete practices of Hebraic thought, while Greek thought seeks the transcendent realm of abstract objects."[18] Eranos members avoided definitive paths to meaning, preferring instead the unimpeded freedom of creating a new reality. Ancient Greek theory, not ancient Jewish realism, was their chosen vehicle

---

[16] Corbin, H., Religion, 1999, p. 30.
[17] Corbin, H., Religion, 1999, pp. 27-30.
[18] Labron, T., Wittgenstein's Religious Point of View, 2006, p. 100.

for speculating on concepts like the body – mind dichotomy, being the classic Gnostic notion of being and identity.

Jung and Gnosticism

Jung summed up the worldview of his three fellow philosophers as follows, "In spite of the great variety of these contributions in form and subject matter, they are all related to central and transcendent ideas – to the ideology and phenomenology of the way of salvation or redemption."[19] Gnostic adepts seek "salvation or redemption" through their own ideas, which is the purpose of Gnosticism. Jung believed *gnosis* was "valid knowledge"[20] and "psychologically empirical," implying he was "studying a reality." It is through their own version of reality they find redemption.

Scholars of Jung's persuasion merrily dismiss coherent, rational, objective truths and definitive ethical principles, instead enjoying a parallel reality. In a study of these scholars, Steven Wasserstrom explains "modern Gnostics arrived at their *gnosis* just as did their ancient counterparts,"[21] meaning, through subjective and esoteric ideas. It is without doubt that Jung was a modern Gnostic as these "occultist ideas are the predominate feature of Jungian thought."[22]

Eliade, Corbin, Scholem, and Plato

Wasserstrom further explains that the "theorists of esoterism at Eranos sought to perpetuate ancient secret teachings by publicly teaching those

---

[19] Wasserstrom, S., Religion After Religion, 1999, p. 28.
[20] Jung's Gnostic source was his "special spirit guide" called 'Philemon'- "an ancient magician with a white flowing beard, a kingfisher's wings and the horns of a bull" (Hart, D. B., Jung, 2013).
[21] Wasserstrom, S., Religion After Religion, 1999, p. 30.
[22] Satinover, J. B., Jung, 1995.

secrets today."[23] To this statement should be added, 'under the guise of philosophical phenomenology and psychotherapy.' These scholars sought knowledge through ancient theories emphasising the matter - spirit dichotomy, a hallmark of Gnostic initiates who found verification in Plato's dualism. Plato's key idea was his 'Theory of the Forms,' a dichotomist cosmology denying reality of the transient material world. As a replacement, Plato adopted an invisible world of eternal, intangible, objects discovered solely through reason. He believed this would lead him to some form of redemption.

The focus of early Gnostics was on the intangible world of ideas, the onus being upon them to discover the secret knowledge ('*gnosis*') of reality for this wisdom (*sophia*) led to transcendence. In consequence, the biological body being of no sacerdotal or eternal significance, was deemed plastic. From such theory, validation follows for moral license. In the current era, the rise of identity ideologies through a variety of identifications such as the blurring of sex-gender categories, originates from the dualist concept of the insignificance of the temporal body in favour of the eternal spirit, the mind.

In later Gnosticism, *sophia* became personified as a feminine entity, an element of the feminine quality of the Deity, and soon polymorphed into a female goddess in her own right. In the collective unconsciousness of Jung's analytic "depth" psychology, the personified *Sophia* was identified as the anthropomorphic *anima,* the unconscious feminine aspect of man. In a Nag Hammadi Gnostic text, 'On the Origin of the world,' the personified *Sophia* is described as the "ultimate destroyer of the

---

[23] Wasserstrom, S., Religion after Religion, 1999, p. 33.

universe."[24] The existence of feminine and androgenous manifestations of
deity have existed since prehistoric times and this practice continues in the
occultist New Age of post-Christian modernism.

The theories of Plato represented the pinnacle of intellectual secular
philosophy at that time in history, and became important not only in
Greece but in all surrounding city-states. Plato's theories, as further
developed by Aristotle and Plotinus (the founder of Neoplatonism),
continued to be effective through late antiquity and the middle ages,
becoming prolific in contemporary society through philosophies, faiths,
and religions. Plato's philosophical influence is so wide that Alfred North
Whitehouse concluded, "the safest general characterization of the
European philosophical tradition is that it consists of a series of footnotes
to Plato."[25]

5.3. Gnosticism and Religion

The occultist practice of attaining 'higher wisdom' (*sophia*) through a
mystical 'Elite,' is seen in popular support for eastern religions. Seekers
after mysterious 'truths' flock to Hindu Gurus, Sufi Sheiks, Kabbalism's
Mequbbāl, Islamic Ulemas, pagan Shamans and the like. Community
scrolls of the Palestinian Essene sect, for instance, indicate their 'Teacher
of Righteousness' possessed exclusive insight (*pesher*) into prophetic
passages. He alone was capable of revealing the mystery, the '*raz,*' of the
passage.

---

[24] Robinson, J. M., The Nag Hammadi Library, 1988, Codex II, Book V.
[25] Whitehead, A. N., Process and Reality, p. 39, 1979.

Facets of New Age Beliefs

The spiritual features of New Age beliefs include astrology, reincarnation, psychics, and a vague entity described as 'energy.' This 'energy' is apparently present in natural objects such as trees, mountains, rivers, rocks and other landscape features. This belief amounts to primitive animism, being nature worship, naturalism, in fact a pantheism which commenced with Nimrod and his sycophants. Syncretic pantheism is the most vigorous New Age faith system in the US, with approximately 60% of current Americans believing in at least one of these New Age features and some 30% believing in reincarnation and astrology. Amongst professed Christians, the situation is quite alarming for while 80% of Christians believe in a biblical God, 60% also believe in one or more New Age spiritual components. Among atheist or agnostic affiliates, the percentages are about the same as for professed Christians. Interestingly, women are more likely to hold New Age beliefs than men: 70% compared to 55%. This ratio would accord with the serpent's strategy in approaching Eve first. Politically, supporters of the US Democratic Party are "more likely than others to hold to at least one New Age belief."[26] This would explain their dedication to promoting dualist-founded sex-gender identity policies.

Gnosticism Never Dies

It is true therefore that Gnosticism, "is the heresy that never dies" and "is very much with us today."[27] This state of affairs is evident through many ideological fabrications, not least being Marxist[28] neo-Gnostic, bipartite ideologies arising from Critical Theories so adversely affecting society in

---

[26] Gecewicz, C., New Age Beliefs; Pew Research Centre, 2018.
[27] Del Noce, A., The Crisis of Modernity, 2014, p. 29.
[28] Political movements are "connected to Marxism which has changed the world" (Del Noce, A., 2014, pp. xix-xx).

areas of race, gender, and social justice. In a way, Gnosticism is like the Lernaean Hydra - a mythological, multi-faceted and lethal serpent, almost impossible to destroy.

5.4. Gnostic Roots of Identity Ideology

The philosophical roots of all identity ideologies spring from Gnostic dualism: the split between the physical and the metaphysical, with exaltation of the latter form. To exemplify, the heretical Gnostic text, 'The Gospel of Thomas,' describes a situation whereby a female, Mary, had capacity to not only become a physical male but an authentic spirit. The final paragraph reads, "Simon Peter said to them, 'Make Mary leave us for females don't deserve life.' Jesus said, 'Look, I will guide her to make her male so that she too may become a living spirit resembling you males. For every female who makes herself male will enter the domain of heaven.'"[29]

The physical human body, whether male or female, has a sacred dimension, a blessing and purpose from God, as is clear from Genesis. To deny the importance of the body, and for a person to mutilate their gender in an attempt to transmigrate to another gender, is to disregard the sacred nature of the body, to deny the Divine's created order and salvific dynamic for his people and their society. Refusal to accept one's birth gender, the assigned biological sex, also amounts to denial of a personal identity. The outcome is loss of emotional well-being, alienation, *angst*, and an uncertain purpose of life.

Joseph Fletcher (1905-1991)

Fletcher's promotion of 'Situation Ethics' is a repeat of Gnostic moral concepts for this post-structuralist age. Fletcher describes himself as a

---

[29] Pagels, E., 2004, Gospel of Thomas, c. 60 C. E., 114: 1-3.

'personalist,' claiming one's personality is "both the highest good and the chief medium of our knowledge of the good." His view reflects a Gnostic dualistic idea of the 'mind' versus the body, with emphasis on *gnosis* (secret knowledge). Fletcher goes on to say, "Why not call to order what is over against us and send it packing into the realm of objects? Physical nature, the body and its members are part of what is over us." He adds, "if we live by the rules and conditions set in physiology, we are not men, we are not *thou.*" Here, Fletcher argues that to be an authentic person, to be the essence '*thou,*' the value of the body is to be rejected. His proposal is designed to deny moral constraints for he says, "spiritual reality and moral integrity belong to man alone."[30] This theory advances subjective morality without objective or universal application, very much in the genre of existentialist theory. For Fletcher, gender is a materialist fabrication and the body should be relegated to the realm of temporal objects, being unimportant for attaining knowledge (*gnosis*) and transcendence.

The immense influence of Fletcher's proposals has resulted in the rise of autogynephilia (transgenderism), various sex-gender constructions and related examples of identity dysphoria. His theories are not new, coming from ancient Gnosticism, mainly the Plotinus version which says, "a person in a body can act solely on appetite or emotion."[31] Naturally, given the concept of original sin and the dearth of realistic ethical controls, the actions of a free agent will be directed towards immorality, the material body having no sacred dimension in their view. The body is understood as inferior, contemptible even, to be handled in any way the possessor desires, including the transitioning of gender through physical mutilation

---

[30] Fletcher, J., Morals and Medicine, 1954, p. xviii; p. 211.
[31] Gerson, I, Plotinus, 2018.

to achieve that aim. To search for meaning through a synthetic body in order to correct the Demiurge's creative shortcomings, and relying on the mind to create a new reality is futile, a fantasy, resulting in severe emotional damage.

Morality and Society

There are desperate and grim issues confronting the individuals of today. A Pew Research survey indicates a reversion to flexible ethics by the majority in Western society. The question posed to interviewees was, "Is it necessary to believe in God to be moral?" The recorded responses confirmed 65% of US adults and 58% High School students answered, 'no.' Over 73% of Canadian adults replied in the negative, as did 76% of Netherlanders; 74% of Spaniards; 75% of British; 90% of Swedes and 85% of Australians. The median negative percentile of 17 Western countries was 68.[32] While the substantial number of moderate, ethical, individuals in society is encouraging, the source of their moral principles requires explanation. If the source is other than definitive biblical precepts, then the only remaining possible origin, outside of other religions, lies within the variables of secular humanist and pagan thought such as pantheism (paganism), rationalism, pseudo-science, and situational ethics, none of which provide definitive guidelines.

The Sacred Body

From a biblical viewpoint, the body is inextricably connected to a person's identity of self. This is evident from Luke's passage (24:36-40) describing the Messiah's resurrected body. And so too will all his followers be resurrected in bodily form at the second advent. The sacerdotal importance

---

[32] Pew Research Center, Not Necessary to Believe in God to be Moral, April 20, 2023.

of the body is not to be disparaged for it has intrinsic importance, being a 'Temple of the Holy Spirit.' To accept any other proposition is to open all of creation to subjective rearrangements to suit whimsical ideas free of rational, empirical, or absolutist limits. Due to Fletcher's significant affect upon postmodern culture, he was voted 1974 'Humanist of the Year.' His nihilist theories justify mortal concepts like euthanasia, eugenics, abortion, infanticide and sterilisation.

Existentialism and Narrative

Influential post-war philosophers include Jean Paul Sartre, Simone de Beauvoir, Albert Camus, Frans Kafka, Martin Heidegger, Hans Jonas, and their circle. These continental intellectuals base their existentialist theories of meaning on neo-Gnostic metaphysical principles denying theistic, definitive, or historical truths and ethics.

The novelist-philosopher, Albert Camus, is more accessible to an audience for he describes complex issues through popular novels, essays, and plays grounded in a context of everyday life. Camus uses this method to explain his theories of the 'absurd,'[33] reminiscent of earlier existential novelists like 1920 Noble Prize winner Knut Hamsun ('Hunger,' 1890) and Franz Kafka ('The Trial,' 1925), which predate Camus' 'The Outsider' ('L'Étranger,' 1942). In a like way, the work of Miguel de Unamundo whose 'Tragic Sense of Life' published in 1912, is among the most significant existentialist novels of the early 20th century. De Unamundo rejects a life based on reason and reality in favour of an intense emotive individualism. These emotions, including *angst*, are evident in his

---

[33] Camus' theory of the 'absurd' is seen in 'The Myth of Sisyphus,' where he faces the irreconcilability of a "rational and reasonable" desire for meaning in an irrational cosmos (Camus, Myth, 1955 [1942], p. 34).

recount of the absurd-hero Don Quixote with his tragic-comic battle against windmills (reminiscent of Camus' Sisyphus and his struggle with the rock). These conflicts exemplify the passionate warrior striving to reconcile external cosmic irrationality with internal idealism, all within a confusing parallel reality of their own fabrication. Like most existentialists, De Unamundo prefers his own world of ideas for, as 1948 Nobel Laureate poet T. S. Eliot confides, "Humankind cannot bear very much reality."[34]

Truth itself is well revealed through narrative, explaining complex issues in a readable manner. This is illustrated by Bunyan's 'The Pilgrim's Progress' and the great plays of William Shakespeare delivering universal moral lessons while capturing the vast field of human experience. Not to overlook John Milton's 'Paradise Lost,' an example from which is the scene where Satan has been dispatched to hell and Milton writes, "The mind has its own place and of itself; can make a heaven of hell, a hell of heaven."[35] Here, Milton predicts the postmodern narcissistic emphasis on the sovereignty and creative license of the imperial-self, which inevitably leads to ego-centric bondage.

Albert Camus

A 1957 Noble Prize laureate, Camus is widely thought of as an existentialist but referred to himself, rather, as an absurdist – a concept which in fact can only be derived from existentialist theories depicting a search for authenticity. While Camus criticized the philosophy of existentialism in his play 'Caligula,' his essay 'Myth of Sisyphus' and others, his meta-narrative is that of absurdist existentialism. By this is

---

[34] Eliot, T. S. (1888-1965), Four Quartets, No. 1, Burnt Norton, 1943, p. 3.
[35] Milton, Paradise Lost, 1608-1674, Book One: 250, p. 40.

meant the search for individual meaning in an irrational cosmology, one where existence faces a universe without absolute truths. This conundrum is at the core of existentialism.

For Camus, lamenting the vacuum of meaning and purpose, but rejecting God as an external authority imparting meaning, life has a nihilistic endgame. Robert Royal describes Camus' position as a choice between "God and nothing."[36] He chose the latter. In contrast, English Poet John Donne (1572 - 1631) utters his amazement at life, "It is an astonishment to be alive and life calls on you to be astonished."[37] Unlike Camus, Donne rejoiced in life, enjoying its serendipitous beauty and opportunity for love and fulfilment found in the beneficent confines of Judeo-Christianity.

Nietzsche and Camus

Like the neo-paganism of three great thinkers of modernity: Hegel, Marx, and Nietzsche, described by Matthew Sharpe as "the evil geniuses of contemporary Europe," Camus was also "drawn to ancient paradigms." Camus was an enthusiastic pagan, complaining he could not "go to Delphi to be initiated."[38] Camus imitated Nietzsche's faith in the Greek art-deities of Apollo and Dionysus with their inherent contrast representing the primal context of human life, as articulated in ancient Hellenist tragedy. In a discourse on this split, Nietzsche in his work 'The Birth of Tragedy,' claims it can best be described as a contrast between 'dreams' (the Apollonian principle), and 'drunkenness' (the Dionysian principle). These antimonies co-exist in a sort of paradoxical and vigorous tension

---

[36] Royal, R., Camus Between God and Nothing, 2014.
[37] John Donne, Quotes, 1623.
[38] Sharpe, M., Camus, To Return to our Beginnings, 2015, pp. 5-6; 20; 31.

exemplifying life and the division of subjective and objective. In other words, a Dionysian (natural) universe of chaos as opposed to an Apollonian (civilization) ordered cosmos. In Nietzschean thought, the universe is chaotic (Dionysian), subject to the whims of happenstance, "the total character of the world…is for all eternity, chaos." In his nihilistic way, he goes on to say there are "no purposes, for the living are only a form of the dead."[39]

Dualist Theory

Nietzsche's philosophy is founded on Gnostic dualist heresy emphasizing primacy of the intangible spirit. Both Nietzsche and Camus endeavour to find explanation for existence itself, and individual moral guidance, within the roots of Greek tragedy - in the genre of playwrights Aeschylus and Sophocles. By so doing, they bypass all definitive moral truths. They distain external constraints or personal accountability in favour of a subjective moral assembly, one lacking verifiable and pragmatic archetypes. The English Romanticist poet, S.T. Coleridge, touches on this dilemma when he writes the imagination, "dissolves, diffuses, dissipates, in order to re-create or where this process is rendered impossible, yet still at all events it struggles to idealize and to unify."[40] Unable to unify complex and irreconcilable concepts, eminent thinkers like Nietzsche and Camus resort to romantically idealizing, and so creating, a reality of their own fancy but one lacking transcendence, an eschatology of hope and convincing moral equivalency. Transcendence is a crucial criterion in reaching a secure personal identity for it implies an afterlife, giving meaning to life. Professor Nemoianu emphasised this when he said of life,

---

[39] Nietzsche, F., Science, 2006, pp. 109-110.
[40] Coleridge, S. T., Biographia Literaria, 1817, Vol. 1, p. 296.

"religious transcendence was always part of the whole project."[41] His statement is valid for it is the existential element of transcendence that is vainly sought through subjective theories.

Camus and the Absurd

The hallmark of existentialism is the search for individual meaning, purpose and identity in an inexplicable universe. As Camus says, "the absurd is born of confrontation between the human need and the unreasonable silence of the world."[42] The "unreasonable silence," the alienation, that Camus refers to is unsurprising given he impulsively rejects theistic doctrines, ignoring its truths. His work, 'The Rebel,' describes Camus' rebellious mindset, that of resistance and resentment against restraint or absolutism, especially that of religion. Instead of seeking enduring truth, he hunts for meaning within the presumed absurdity of life irrespective of the conclusion that it is the absolutism of truth alone that conveys meaning. Purveyors of truth, as in the doctrines of Judeo-Christianity, are summarily dismissed in favour of his own idealized creation. Here, Camus embraces a bipartite concept - a rejection of the Tree of Life in favour of the desired Tree of Knowledge where human reason and wisdom, *Sophia*, are lauded as the supreme good.

Unable to form a coherent alternative reality without absolutes, existentialists like Camus are forced to explore critical issues such as nihilism,[43] and hence suicide. In his texts, 'The Rebel' and 'Myth of Sisyphus,' issues such as suicide and murder are made plausible due to

---

[41] Nemoianu, V., Teaching Christian Humanism, 1996.

[42] Camus, A., Myth of Sisyphus, 1955, p. 15.

[43] The "only adequate protection against nihilism is belief in God" (Markham, I., Plurality and Christian Ethics, 1994, p. 154). With rejection of God, comes rejection of truth and all that is left is nihilism – no eternal life, no meaning of life, no objective ethical-moral rules and values to guide thought and conduct.

absence of moral guidelines. For Camus, "without the aid of eternal values"[44] meaning is absurd, being without purpose. In an environment of cosmic uncertainty, nihilist actions become justified. Camus' nominalist theory is that there is no meaning to life, all is absurd. He ignores the paradox that the definitive moral and eternal precepts of Judeo-Christianity, which he summarily rejects, impart the purpose he so anxiously seeks.

Jean-Paul Sartre

Despite Camus' public profile, the most prominent 20th century continental existentialist is fellow Nobel laureate Jean-Paul Sartre, probably the most renowned philosopher of the 20th century. His theories captivated intellectual life after the war period. Sartre's 1964 Nobel Prize citation reads as follows, "For his work which, rich in ideas and filled with the spirit of freedom and the quest for truth, has exerted a far-reaching influence on our age."

Sartre, initially influenced by a range of philosophical predecessors such as Georg Hegel, Søren Kierkegaard, Martin Heidegger and others, went on to crystalise the concept of the absurd in his work, 'Being and Nothingness.' Here he explained, "Absurd. That which is meaningless. Thus, man's existence is absurd because his contingency finds no external justification." Quite ironic considering he rejected all definitive and absolutist values, all 'external justifications,' yet laments their absence. Sartre elaborates further that man's "projects are absurd because they are directed towards an unobtainable goal - the desire to become God or to be

---

[44] Camus, A., Myth, 1955, Preface.

simultaneously the free For-itself and the absolute In-itself."[45] Yet another acknowledgement of the futility of his quest.

Sartre, in 'Existentialism and Human Emotions,' incongruously claims "the fundamental project of human reality is to say that man is the being whose project is to be God. To be man means to reach toward being God. Or, if you prefer, man fundamentally is the desire to be God."[46] He therefore endorses the primeval heresy of *eritus sicut Deus* (to be like God), while arguing the impossibility of attaining divinity. This oxymoron results in existential 'nausea,' the 'absurd,' a cosmic meaningless. This deduction imitates Adam and Eve's realization that their declaration of independence, their freedom from absolute moral paradigms coupled to a lack of righteous status, was likewise untenable. Hence their experiment with fig leaves in a futile attempt at re-establishing their sacred position.

Destructive Existentialism

The terms existentialism, absurdism, and situational ethics are mere labels for a collection of philosophical ideas, integrating a belief system from ancient times. The structural hallmarks are secularism, humanism, antinomianism, moral pliability, value pluralism, division, and a form of spiritual paganism of a subjective fabrication. Existentialist philosophers, despite their significant literary contribution to society, merely regurgitate ancient heresies in popular new disguises.

It was Roger Scruton who deemed Sartre's contribution to modernity as an "undermining of structures of bourgeois society, the scoffing at manners and morals and ruining the institutions upon which he depends

---

[45] Sartre, J-P., Being and Nothingness, 1956, p. 629.
[46] Sartre, J-P., Existentialism and Human Emotions, 1957, p. 63.

for his exalted status."[47] He describes this approach as a "culture of repudiation,"[48] indicating Sartre's negative attitude towards life, ethics, morality, and culture. In Tony Judt's study of French intellectuals during the period 1944-1956, he recounts the fatalistic attitudes of existentialist philosophers like Foucault and Sartre. He writes, "Foucault waxed lyrical at the thought of the September massacres, while Sartre was nearing the apogee of his career as an apologist for political terrorism." Sartre admired Marxist thought and held condolatory views on "revolutionary violence."[49] The destructive force of existentialist theory will continue to permeate society for some time in areas of truth, ethics, morals, and the sanctity of human life.

Immanuel Kant

Compared to postmodern existentialists, Kant (1724-1804) developed his idea of the moral imperative to a finer extent by directing the individual should always, "act so that you might also wish the maxim of your action becomes a universal law."[50] Even so, like later existentialists, Kant denied moral legitimacy of objective or eternal moral absolutes. Instead, he relied on the innate faculty of reason and self-reflection by posing the deliberative question, "What ought I to do," in each particular situation.[51]

Kant is well known for his phrase, "morality inevitably leads to religion."[52] Yet the reverse order is true for the ethical principles of the Judeo-Christian faith define morality in society. Kant's view is therefore a secular, humanist, stance much emulated by existentialists and deists in

---

[47] Scruton R., T. S. Eliot as Conservative Mentor, November 1, 2003.
[48] Scruton, R. T., Conservatism: An Invitation to the Great Tradition, 2017.
[49] Judt, Tony, Past Imperfect: French Intellectuals 1944-1956, 1992, p. 126.
[50] Tim, A., Kant and Categorical Imperative, 2012.
[51] Johnson, R., Kant's Moral Philosophy, 2021.
[52] Insole, C. J., Kant and the Divine: From Contemplation to Moral Law, 2020, p. 262.

a later age. In general, humanists contend ethics emanate "through a continuing process of observation, evaluation, and revision."[53] The result is a cultural, subjective, and fragile understanding of ethical theory, one that lacks the absolutist parameters so greatly needed.

Existentialism and Ideology

It is a short journey for existentialist ideas to mutate into ideologies. This is what has occurred with the rise of identity construals advocating fluid morality and contextual truth. The inevitable outcome of reductionist thought, whereby the body is discarded as temporal matter, is found in the justification of mortal issues like euthanasia, eugenics, termination of unborn humans, and legally sanctioned assisted voluntary suicide. While activists claim to reflect aims and desires of a majority, they amount to a radical political faction with a powerful but narrow support base. Their identity theories lack universal scope or objectively verified truths, thus justifying classification as ideologies. Activists denigrate the inherent value and dignity of the human body with its authentic *imago Dei* identity, in the very mode of occultist, Gnostic, thought.

5.5. Conclusion

The objective of secular humanists is to purge the literal-historical nature of Bible narratives and to likewise abolish, in favour of their own ideological theories, the eternal moral laws of God. Rejection of natural law principles results in the default position of subjective morality for, as Pope Benedict XVI points out, "the natural law – traditional morality – is the sole source of all value judgements." In his view, the post-truth moral problem results from the fact that society has "separated itself from its

---

[53] Amsterdam Declaration of the World Humanist Congress, 2002.

primeval testimony,"[54] meaning, the natural law as amplified by the Mosaic codes and the law of Christ.

Carlyle's 'Man of Letters'

Having rejected his Calvinist background, the vehicle of Gnosticism is perhaps what 19th century philosopher Thomas Carlyle was seeking when he desired to couch, "the divine spirit of religion in a new Mythus."[55] In 1840, Carlyle proposed a 'Man of Letters' as suitable messianic replacement for the 'Hero-god,' previously considered the "predominant form of heroism."[56] Carlyle's theory became reality through intellectuals like Freud and Jung, and the philosophers Marx, Nietzsche, Camus and Sartre. Although these famed 'men of letters' promoted their metaphysical and mystical doctrines as replacement for biblical doctrine, they were not overtly concerned with the moral state of society. Sartre's much vaunted treatise on ethics failed to materialise for he, like the other existentialists, adopted a situational, nuanced, approach to morals and ethics.

Paul Johnson issued a warning to "beware of intellectuals" for, as he explained, "intellectuals habitually forget that people matter more than concepts and must come first. The worst of all despotisms is the heartless tyranny of ideas."[57] Modernity's 'men of letters' should perhaps have adopted, as examples, the ideals of classical philosophers and statesmen like the Roman patrician Cicero who emphasized rule of law, ethics, virtue, and morality in politics. This is not to overlook the crucial contribution to civilization by Greeks such as Aristotle, Plato, Socrates and their circle; and, of course, the values and dogma of great Jewish scribes.

---

[54] Pope Benedict XVI, Consumer Materialism and Christian Hope, January, 1988.
[55] Carlyle T., The Works of Thomas Carlyle, 1898, p. 154.
[56] Haynes, C., The State of the Disciple, 2005, p. 287.
[57] Johnson, P. B., Intellectuals, 1988, p. 342.

A focus on the wisdom, the principles of higher ideals, and nobility of character, emanating from the intellectual circles of Rome, Athens, and Jerusalem would contribute towards the common good of society instead of the narrow narcissistic and nihilistic theories of post-truth existentialists, causing much confusion and anxiety.

It is predictable that these noble 'men of letters,' these genius philosophers and intellectuals, would inevitably drive society into the 'murky waters' of neo-pagan humanism or whatever ideology, religion, or composition they desired, which is precisely what has occurred. So much for famed 'men of letters,' the intellectuals and leaders described by C. S. Lewis as "Men without Chests,"[58] and T. S. Eliot as "Hollow Men"[59] – those without virtue, without integrity of character, without courage or nobility, favouring their destructive theories over the common good of society.

Ralph Elliot's 'Little Man'

Ironically, it is Ralph Elliot's obscure "little man," the everyman, who is pivotal to the well-being of society. Elliot's 1978 essay explains the obligation of every individual to excel at whatever task they called to do, "even if it's only in the waiting room of Chehaw station." He adds, "in this country there will always be a little man hidden behind the stove"[60] at the station. In reality, the vast majority of individuals are 'little men behind the stove' but collectively they add cohesiveness, connection, stability and structure to society. The everyman's condition and status, in Elliot's touching words, "is an inseparable part of a larger truth in which the highly

---

[58] Lewis, C. S., The Abolition of Man, 1943, p. 11.
[59] Eliot, T. S., The Hollow Men, 1925.
[60] Elliot, R., The Little Man at Chehaw Station, 1978, pp. 25-26.

and the lowly, the known and the unrecognized, the comic and the tragic, are woven into the American skein." In this compelling view, it is Elliot's 'little man,' the forgotten man, who "on the lower frequencies" speaks for all.[61]

Finale

Malevolent spiritual assaults on the supernatural romance between the Bride and the Bridegroom will ultimately be unsuccessful for, as the determined words of the Redeemer-Messiah proclaim, "I will build my Church, and the gates of hell shall not prevail against it."[62] Until such time, foundations of the contemporary Western ethos remain faced with critical challenges from secular humanism and the occult. As William Buckley points out, "the duel between Christianity and atheism is the most important issue in the world,"[63] due to existential implications of the confrontation. The complexity of this duel and its effect on present society is further considered in chapters following.

---

[61] Elliot, R., Invisible Man, 1989 (1947), p. 581.
[62] Matthew 16:18.
[63] Buckley, W. F., God and Man at Yale, 1951, p. xvi.

CHAPTER SIX
PART ONE

THE CULTURAL REVOLUTION

"Modern history is the dialogue between two men:
one who believes in God, another who believes he is a god"
(Nicolás Gómez Dávila, 1913)

6.1. Introduction

With political and legal support, the cultural revolution marches on relentlessly in Western society. Based on heretical theories originating from Edenic events, and manifesting in the contemporary era through secular humanist and neo-Gnostic, neo-pagan, beliefs, society reels from this ideological onslaught. The reorientation of public life is spurred on by a deconstruction of long-established norms and values founded on Judeo-Christian principles. Applying contemporary terms to ancient heresies, anarcho-social zealots attempt an inversion of cultural biblical precepts in a repressive post-truth, milieux. Their aims are typical of revolutionaries for they seek to change the "history, culture, customs, religion, and political order of the past."[1]

Promoting equity (under the pretense of equality), love, tolerance, inclusion, and diversity,[2] activists seek justice - the supposed objective of

---

[1] Patterson, E., Moral vs Immoral Resistance, September 1, 2023.
[2] 'Diversity' results in divisiveness and disunity, fracturing society along ideological, ethnic, and religious lines.

social revolutionaries through the ages. This is evident from French, Russian, and Marxist revolutionary slogans. As in past European revolutions, the true objective is not justice but power and control, commencing with a revision of civil and religious authority.

Institutional Challenges

In the present situation, enshrined liberal democratic constitutional rights and obligations are under severe threat of replacement in favour of a fixated leftist and cultural Marxist strategy avowing justice for the common good of society. However, this is none other than the advance of practical atheism, the essence of secular humanism, which arose in the Edenic Garden. Robert Wilken wrote that the intent of atheism is "to dismantle the common Western culture, to turn everything into a sub-culture," and so "bring down the system." Hence, public Christianity is in danger of becoming a sub-culture in the very society rooted upon its tenets. This is to be expected for "secularism wants religious practice, especially Christian practice, banished to a private world of feelings and attitudes while at the same time, an earlier appearance of tolerance towards religion is now seen to have been a sham."[3] This is the dark agenda of all social revolutions.

Assault on Truth

Overall, established truths are under assault. The particular focus is on the person and deity status of the Judeo-Christian Messiah, the embodiment of absolutist truth and morality. As Karl Barth acknowledged, "the Word of God is itself the source and norm of all truth," which "cannot be

---

[3] Wilken, R. L., No Other Gods, 1993.

transcended."[4] It is this obstinate, metaphysical, enduring truth that is a 'stumbling block' to identitarianists aiming to circumvent established truths of the natural order, that is, those eternal laws founding society, as displayed in biblical tenets. In this context, reference can be made to the words and actions of Pontius Pilate when he rejected the exclusivity of truth found only in the Messiah who declared, "I have come into the world—to bear witness to the truth. Everyone who is of the truth listens to my voice." Instead, Pilate adopted a subjective attitude towards truth, preferring a humanist fabrication of truth as evident in his rhetorical question, "What is truth?"[5] Pilate's secular mindset was unable to grasp the transcendence of divine truth presented to him. Rabbi Paul explains this situation, "None of the rulers of this age understood this, for if they had, they would not have crucified the Lord of glory."[6]

Relative Truth

There are three pivotal biblical scenarios relating to the rejection of absolutist truth. In all cases, actors denied the plain truth in favour of a humanist version of truth. The first occurred in the Garden of Eden when Adam and Eve rejected God's absolutist truth, in favour of their subjective version; the second in Pilate's demonstration of pluralistic, variable, truth; and, thirdly, rejection of the Messiah as immanentization of truth by his society, in favour of a criminal.

Identity activists of the 21st century steadfastly hold to a plastic concept of truth in the heretical tradition set earlier. The standard response, therefore, to the question of objective truth mirrors that of Pilate's

---

[4] Barth, K., Church Dogmatics, 1961, p. 235.
[5] John 18:37-38; John 14:6.
[6] 1 Corinthians 2:8.

dismissive reply, "What is truth?" Once the question of truth becomes detached from all "burdens of reality," activists are then "free to think with their emotions and to reason with their feelings."[7] In this manner, idiosyncratic truths are justified.

Resentment

The early 20th century philosopher, Max Scheler, understood the social avoidance of Judeo-Christian ethics and morals was due to resentment - a deep hostility directed against the Creator with his unequivocal principles. In the modern social movement, says Alasdair MacIntyre, "resentment has become an important determinant, increasingly modifying established morality."[8] It was the hostility, the resentment, of the diabolical serpent against the person and status of the Most-High God, as Father of all creation, that motivated his attempted destruction of the Creator's relationship with the First Couple. Satan's successful strategy resulted in a unilateral declaration of independence contrary to the Creator's agenda. Exercising their right of choice, Adam and Eve were free to fabricate their own purpose in life, their own truth, and morality to suit.

The Secular Creed

The foundational creeds of identity ideologies are aimed at philosophically refuting Judeo-Christian dogma, specifically those relating to sacred identity, purpose and meaning. Their idea of social justice[9] is contrary to principles of natural justice and the idea of a common good[10] compact. Instead, their justice is based on a sectarian ideal contrary to community

---

[7] MacPherson, J., The Charms of Transgenderism, 2022.
[8] MacIntyre, A., After Virtue, 1981, pp. 2, 19.
[9] James Petts refers to biased social justice as "ethical deceit" (Petts, J., Reason, 2021).
[10] Vermeule defines this as "the flourishing of a well-ordered political community" (Common Good, 2020, p. 7).

standards of virtue, morals, equality, fairness, rationality, common-sense and decency. This polarization makes mutual consensus benefiting all of society, inconceivable.

Identity engineers first commenced their drive for mainstream acceptance by demanding recognition of same-sex marriage. This was followed by petitions for legitimization of biological men claiming to be women, known as transgenders, and their appropriation of rights hitherto enjoyed by women only. Thereafter came claims of systemic racism perpetuated against a victimized black minority ethnic group, who therefore deserved recompense and primacy in certain areas of public life. Developed from these events, activists formulated cliches, regarded as the 'Secular Creed,' which can be recounted and refuted as follows:

- 'Black lives matter' – which is quite correct, as is the fact that all lives matter equally;
- 'Love is love' - *eros* as the new, all-embracing, universal love language justifying same-sex relationships, while detached from sacred *agape* requirements. A deceptive imitation of biblical love;
- 'Born this way' – the fictional idea that same-sex persons are not responsible for their choices and their lifestyle should be accepted as normal from birth;
- 'Gay rights are civil rights' – this slogan indicates the new civil rights movement, ignoring the fact that all members of society have equal civil rights. At the same time, the slogan validates same-sex marriage under the umbrella of human and civil rights;
- 'Woman's rights are human rights' – the motive here is to emphasize the absolute authority of a woman's choice to terminate her pregnancy, should she so desire. It simultaneously denies recognition of the right to life of the unborn person;
- 'Abortion rights are woman's health care rights' – again, an intention to subjugate the unborn child's rights to life under the guise of a mother's health care primacy;

- 'Pro-choice: my body, my choice' – unless the woman's rights existentially infringe on the rights of others, particularly a fetal child, then such claim is justifiable;
- 'Transgender women are women' – the irrational claim that gender self-identification is a valid gender, even if contrary to biological sex allocated at birth.[11]

Woke Politics

The above slogans reflect the character of Identity Politics, colloquially referred to as 'woke politics,' to be understood as radical leftist, racist, secular humanist and pagan ideology. A public refutation of the slogans can result in a 'cancellation'[12] situation due to intolerance of truth and reality. The deceptive terms are indicative of social zealots' aims reformulating the human image, the *imago Dei,* into an anthropology of their own fabrication while controlling the public narrative. The slogans reveal a narcissistic focus on the 'therapeutic-self,' irrespective of reality, a communal good or balanced by the rights of others.

Lawyer Erika Bachiochi argues that the "enduing moral principles" which earlier feminist movements "employed to make a reasoned critique," no longer exist. Instead, the aims of contemporary, woke, feminists are "bereft of noble purpose and ultimately dangerous."[13] Identity actors, particularly feminists, become more extreme in their demands with each passing generation to the extent that objective reality is now a subjective construction, truth is relative, morality is optional, and so disarray in society increases exponentially.

---

[11] McLaughlin, R., The Secular Creed, 2021, p. 1.
[12] Professor Norris defines 'cancel culture' as "collective strategies by activists using social pressures to achieve cultural ostracism of targets accused of offensive words or deeds" (Cancel Culture: Myth or Reality, 2021).
[13] Bachiochi, E., The Rights of Women, 2021.

A Search for Meaning

In philosophical essence, therapeutic orientated ideologies constitute a search for personal identity, for meaning, through self-realisation in a secular environment lacking any guidelines. Activists denigrate the truth of humanity's divine origins while promoting their own fatuous hypotheses. To replace their rejected sacred status, ideologues seek a tribal,[14] shared, group identity. Still, the root issue says James Patterson, is that of transcendence for, "identity is the source of divinity but individuals are not divine on their own,"[15] but nonetheless consider themselves so within their clan identity.

A Crisis of Identity

Sociologist Peter Berger believes the emergence of multifaceted identity creeds indicate "modern man is afflicted with a permanent identity crisis." In his view, the crisis causes "a condition conducive to considerable nervousness." Berger holds the socio-psychological view that a solid comprehension of identity is what actually roots an individual to the reality of existence. His contentions appear correct for personal *angst* ("nervousness") arises from the "fluid and unreliable" characterisations of identity.[16] To the contrary, fixed eternal truths and moral values are contained only in Judeo-Christian tenets without which the individual is subject to life-long anxiousness and alienation.

The underlying *angst*, the "considerable nervousness" and "deep uncertainty about contemporary identity," indicates alienation from the

---

[14] For much of history, meaning, identity, and the concept of immortality was achieved through tribal, familial and clan membership (Weigel, G., Individual, 2022). However, the Messiah through his resurrection emphasised the unique identity, purpose, dignity (Gal. 3:28), and immortality of the individual person.

[15] Patterson, J., Wokeness and the New Religious Establishment, 2021.

[16] Berger, P., The Homeless Mind, 1974, p. 78, 92.

Fatherhood of God concept. This causes the "nervousness,' the "fear of death,"[17] to which all such persons are subject. Society's increasing estrangement from the Fatherhood of God identity, and thus the *imago Dei*, is reflected in a Pew Research survey of factors determining satisfaction with 'meaning in life' in 17 advanced economies. The survey indicates 'Spirituality, Faith, and Religion' are rated very low on the scale at only 2%, being 15th of 16 categories, just one category above 'Pets' at 1%.[18]

A Battle of Ideas

The 'battle of ideas' is a struggle between diametrically opposing positions. This ancient contest continues in many modernist guises such as philosophy, psychology, economics, sociology, secularism and manifestations of pagan spirituality. Together, these avenues lead to New Age identity creeds with multiple formulations. Cultural forces challenge religious doctrines and practice, and social values instituted upon their principles.

There are also challenges to established doctrines from within the Church itself. Sacrilegious Christians such as Christian Platonists, Christian socialists (cultural Marxists), Progressive Christians, Moralistic Therapeutic Deists and Open Theists, all promote a non-literal interpretation of the book of Genesis and allied canonical literature. Equally, Christian evolutionists and extremist Christian feminists seek to reconstruct society, churches, and synagogues to reflect new norms of inclusivity and diversity. The casual use of the 'Christian' label is simply

---

[17] A study on the 'fear of death' revealed an "overall hypothesis that anxiety or a lack of certainty about one's relationship with the Divine represents a threat to psychological well-being" (Henderson, W. M., Kent, B. V., Attachment to God, 2021).
[18] Silver, L., What Makes Life Meaningful, 2021.

a pretext to add credibility to these 'alien invasive' (to borrow a Botanical phrase) principles. The net result is that the 'world has infiltrated the Church' instead of the reverse.   Cultural Identity Politics can be regarded as the new dominant religion in the Anglo-American public sector, and that of many other countries. The new religion, says social commentator David Thunder, "has a set of dogmas to be unconditionally assented to; it treats dissenters as heretics who must be excluded in order to keep the faith of true believers strong; and, it has a sort of priestly class who enunciate its doctrines from the pulpits of Twitter, YouTube, Facebook, the Guardian, The New York Times, and CNN."[19]

Cultural Anarchists

To a significant extent, judicial authority has upheld identity rights arising, as they do, from a secularised and atheistic society. In practice, a vociferous anarcho-leftist minority,[20] seek cultural dominance for their narrow ideas. To clarify, the term 'anarchist' is not applied here in the sense of violent, armed, revolutionaries. Rather, it is to be understood as a philosophical abolition of conventional controls and the humane order, thereby enabling mainstream practice of non-traditional values and norms, irrespective of the majority's contrary views and rights. Still, revolutionaries they are, for while they constitute a minority of society, they "push a malevolent ideology, scaring everyone else into agreeing with them." As a result, says Ronald Dworkin, "danger lurks" for society.[21]

---

[19] Thunder, D., Is Wokeism a Religion? December 2, 2022.
[20] As Adrian Vermeule explains, the activists "while claiming to represent the real will of the people, or the best of our national ideals, form a tiny minority of the population, even a tiny minority of the intellectual class" (Vermeule, A., Imagination, 2021).
[21] Dworkin, R. W., Ideology and Terror, March 8, 2023.

6.2. Critical Theory

The key hypothesis of Critical Theory (also referred to as cultural Marxism or neo-Marxism) is that it provides, "a basis for social enquiry aimed at decreasing domination and increasing freedom in all their forms."[22] Critical Theory has a practical intent and is not simply an enquiry without concrete application. Its declared purpose is to transform traditional social systems to attain "freedom, justice, and happiness."[23] With such a broad field of application, it is unsurprising that Critical Theory is utilised as the underlying idea, the core ideal, empowering the interconnection of identity ideologies such as race, gender, and sexuality. Critical Theory, as an expression of cultural Marxism - itself a reinvention of classic Marxism - is a hypothesis that considers the human struggle for truth, meaning, and identity to be a power contest between social orders and identity groups.

In the Western context, the power discordance is between black and white race groups, women verses men, women against transgender identifiers, and homosexuals contesting with heterosexuals. Minority race groups claim racist oppression; feminists allege sexist and patriarchal oppression; and homosexual and assorted gender identifiers aver heterosexual oppression. Society, according to Critical Theorists, needs a complete make-over so as to reflect a true social justice. To achieve this, neo-Marxist actors highlight the division and inequality of society and endeavour to restructure the social fabric through a class struggle, one based on allegations of victimhood.

---

[22] Bohman, J., Critical Theory, 2021.
[23] Cooke, M., Critical Theory and Religion, 2001, p. 211.

A Crucial Conflict

Social zealots, like the Alphabet collective, seek new identity to replace the rejected *imago Dei*. They believe this can be accomplished through a tribal identity – an identity with its own peculiar, sacred, culture. The idea of tribalism, in dividing society into opposing ideological sects, finds support in Professors Hyrum and Verlan Lewis' 2023 study, 'The Myth of Left and Right.' Here, they propose a "social theory in which ideological camps are defined more by tribal attachments than by loyalty to any unchanging philosophical essence."[24] They claim that through tribalist commitment, a correlation of issues emerge to provide members with a sense of unity and common purpose. Still, whether through tribal attachment or partisan political alliance, the effect remains the same for these actors negate biblical claims to the effect that the purpose of life and personal identity come from the Fatherhood of God principle. From this doctrine comes the image of God personal identity. These are crucial, existential, issues going to the core of what constitutes a human being.

Façade of Social Justice

Critical Theory powered identity ideologies have been catapulted into mainstream thinking via the philosophies of Herbert Marcuse and others of the 'New Left,' who through their "activist scholarship, have made everything about race, gender and identity."[25] Helen Pluckrose elaborates that Critical Theory, under the façade of social justice, is "concerned with revealing hidden bias" in society and seeks to expose the purported power domination of a certain class of society in the vital areas of race, sex and

---

[24] Lewis, H., Lewis, V., The Myth of Left and Right, 2023, p. 6.
[25] Pluckrose, H., Cynical Theories: How Activist Scholarship made Everything About Race, Gender and Identity, 2020, pp. 1, 14.

gender. Emancipation, according to Critical Theorists, can only be achieved through a societal reorganisation in the areas of ethics and morality, as seen through ethnic and sex-gender ideals. Therefore, ideologues attempt to philosophically overcome the absolutist ethical and moral constrictions of monotheistic religions, markedly that of Judeo-Christianity whose moral precepts are foundational to the liberal democratic political dispensation.

The Frankfurt School

Critical Theory, originally derived from the construals of Marx, Hegel, and German Idealism, has as its focus the "cultural life of humanity."[26] This amounts to a revolutionary[27] motive imposing a "new order (where) socialism will triumph by first capturing the culture via infiltration of schools, universities, Churches and media, thereby transforming the consciousness of society."[28] In contemporary times, the instigators are scholars Horkheimer, Adorno, Marcuse, Fromm, Habermas and other members of the 'Frankfurt School' (the 'Institute for Social Research,' established in 1923). These intellectuals claim their theorems were intended for the "abolition of social injustice" and that "the future of humanity depends on the existence today of the critical attitude."[29] However, they have an anarchist purpose which Kevin Donnelly describes as the "overthrowing of Western capitalist societies."[30] To achieve this end, they reframe the established social, economic, and political order to suit their version of justice. The result is a form of social distinction

---

[26] Brincat, S., Critical Theory, 2016, p. 563.
[27] Revolution is overthrow of an existing order and establishment of a new (moral) order.
[28] Kiska, R., Long March Through History, 2019, p. 7.
[29] Horkheimer, M., Critical Theory, 1972, p. 242.
[30] Donnelly, K., Editor: Cancel Culture and the Left's Long March, 2021.

(privileged considerations) and elitist power – political, social and cultural power. Expectedly, society suffers severe upheaval through direct challenges to basic values, traditions, and freedoms. This is especially so on the college campus where activists prevent public speaking by those holding contrary views. This results in what Heather MacDonald refers to as "the hysterical campus."[31] In this way, the democratic principle of freedom of speech is undermined, leading to an illiberal environment and a form of social tyranny.

Marxist Strategy

In Marxist theory, "regimes are nourished by the belief that the world cannot be tolerated as it is and that it should be changed: the old should be replaced with the new."[32] This attitude justifies revolutionary intrusion into the social fabric of society. Through ideological re-fabrication, society would then enter a completely new era, giving life to the *homo novus*, a new person, or perhaps Harari's *homo deus* – a god-man. In so doing, the Messianic imperative of a "new creation" (2 Cor. 5:17) is bypassed in favour of an ideological assembly, being the aim of secular humanism. However, this is a *chimera*, an unrealisable dream, one which first emerged in the Edenic Garden and destined for failure. By attempting refabrication of an established society, neo-Marxist identity agents will likewise see their efforts destined for failure.

Karl Marx's distain for God is illuminated by his statement that the "criticism of religion is the premise of all criticism." An assault on religion is fundamental to reactionary strategy in establishing their atheist dogma in the culture, thereby affirming Marx's commitment to refabricate society

---

[31] MacDonald, H., The Diversity Delusion, 2018, p. 9.
[32] Legutko, R., The Demon in Democracy, 2018, pp. 5-6, 178.

for, as he stated, "philosophers have only interpreted the world in various ways, the point is to change it." To change society, in neo-Marxist terms, means transforming it into an egalitarian enterprise reflecting true distributive justice. In an ideal transformation, the 'innocent workers' (the victims of society) would be validated and the 'masters' (the employers and 'captains of industry') who oppress them, would be exposed and dealt with. Justice would then be achieved. But as with all social revolutions, neo-Marxian activists do not tolerate criticism or dissent for to identify as a victim is to hold the high moral ground, a sacred status. Financial repatriation is then demanded from oppressors, which are all those unable to identify as victims due to their race, ethnic, or gender set. Demands for financial recompense due to racial discrimination decades or even hundreds of years previously are deceptive ploys, designed for entitlement without merit or effort.

Power not Justice

A new civic religion, cultural wokeness is a concept created for an ideologically driven social transformation, in the name of justice and egalitarianism. This religion is superficially focused on social justice, but motivated by an underlying lust for power, for privilege. An ideological elite claims lofty esoteric knowledge, in the mode of Gnostic avatars, to justify their social agenda. Even so, their elitist paradigm cannot offer redemptive hope other than through tribal identity and claims of victimhood. They cannot offer a definable moral compass, or a rational basis for establishing normative truth. Biblical doctrine denies inequality of persons, for all are created equal, all descend from the same forefather in the Garden, and all have sacred identity as children of God.

CHAPTER SIX
PART TWO

THE CULTURAL REVOLUTION

"We are in the grip of an ideology that disowns our genius,
denounces our success, and distains merit.
If Western civilization dies, put it down as a suicide"
(Gerald Baker, 2023)

6.3. Critical Theory and Race

A minor academic discipline in the US educational system for the last three decades, Critical Race Theory ("CRT"), is a narrow aspect of socio-philosophical Critical Theory. CRT is connected to Critical Legal Theory for, as identity activists claim, US laws perpetuate marginalization of the Black minority and maintaining of such status.

The essence of CRT ideology is the proposition that the United States was established upon racist principles of a Eurocentric social dominance theory, resulting in black slavery. White-dominated society prospered through such racism, remains racist at its core, is systematically and inescapably racist. White social and economic privilege is solely to blame for the situation. These allegations are a nuanced version of original sin.

The application of CRT ideology has resulted in sundry repercussions such as social power divergence (economic, financial, and political power in favour of the Black minority) which will allegedly remedy racial disadvantage to some degree. These are fine intentions, but the realistic consequence will be an inversion of such goals in the form of reverse apartheid. This is precisely what transpired in the economy of post-apartheid South Africa – a situation described by Victor Davis Hanson as the "racial chauvinism of the new tribal South Africa."[1] The legislative bias against whites from official business contracts is a blatant form of revenge racialism, designed to punish whites for past apartheid policies. Even those whites born after majority rule in 1994, and having no knowledge of apartheid, are prejudiced against in the economic sphere. The result is near collapse of the economy which has led South Africa, one of the wealthiest countries in Africa, to the brink of a failed state. Marxian policies rule there as in neighbouring Zimbabwe, a failed state in every way.

Black Lives Matter

Bearing in mind Freud's theory of individuals harbouring a "repression of powerful instincts,"[2] the social neo-Marxists allege whites (as the oppressors) are unable or unwilling to forgo their privileged position. To good effect, these claims garnered prominence in social and political circles, validating CRT as a civil rights cause.

CRT principles empower anarcho-activist groups like the 'Black Lives Matter' ("BLM") movement founded by three radical feminists. The three, Patrisse Cullors, Alicia Garza and Opal Tometti, adopt a militant approach to the concept of social justice. Initially based on commendable objectives, BLM soon evolved into an anarcho-social crusade, which is unsurprising as Cullors describes herself as a "trained Marxist,"[3] as are the

---

[1] Hanson, V. D., 2023, The Baleful Cargo of Woke Diversity Worship, January 1, 2023.
[2] Freud, S., Civilization and its Discontents, 1961, p. 44.
[3] Steinbuch, Y., Black Lives Matter, 2020.

other two founders. In accordance with Marxian strategy, CRT promotors acting through the BLM action group demand a metamorphosis of society to remedy historic, repressed, racial prejudices.

Resentment

Black Lives Matter members are ideological successors to the Combahee River Collective group of radical black lesbian feminist socialists, active in the USA from 1974-1980. Mary Eberstadt explains that both these movements, "signify political identity has become a substitute for familial and communal bonds. Both are rooted in a fury at creation itself – anger at the disruption of the natural order which the creature now claims the right to re-order."[4] Eberstadt has identified the root of the matter which is resentment towards the Creator due to the perceived inferior role in society allocated to blacks generally, and females specifically.

A Racist Ideology

CRT is a fresh version of Marxist class schism whereby a minority troupe, acting upon a narrow ideology, attempts to overthrow the established order to achieve political advantage. In this way, activists endeavour to establish an idealized socialist society. But instead of traditional Marxian class distinction between oppressed workers ('slaves') and the employer oppressors ('masters'), the focus shifts to race and gender. The outcome remains the same, a socialist utopia in which the oppressed are liberated.

The ethnic requirement for membership in the BLM movement is valid only for those considered African-American, at the same time excluding all non-Blacks. CRT is directly prejudiced against non-Black groups who are intimidated, guilt driven, and shamed as systemic

---

[4] Eberstadt, M., Men are at War with God, January 2022.

oppressors due to atrocities perpetrated by unknown ancestors some 200 years previously.

Despite social equality achieved through earlier Civil Rights movements, BLM actors seek to establish race privilege as a dominant ideology in not only the US education system, but in all aspects of corporate life, in all public institutions including military and government agencies. This ultimate aim is a far cry from egalitarian principles redacted in foundational documents upon which the US was established. An editorial in the Washington Examiner of June 8, 2021 reads, "In this telling, all whites are inherently racist, stained by the racialist equivalent of original sin, and must become second-class citizens as a matter of policy in order to establish 'equity.'"

Equality and Equity

Around the year 350 B.C.E., Aristotle proclaimed that "everywhere, inequality is a cause of revolution." There is truth in his view for social and legal inequality has led to past uprisings like the French Revolution. However, enjoying social, political and legal equality (if not privilege) is insufficient for CRT activists for they seek dominance through equity (equal outcomes). The term 'equity,' has a significantly different meaning to that of 'equality' with which most Westerners are familiar. The idea of equality is a noble one, not so the principle of equity for in race ideology, equity is simply an example of neo-Marxist economic redistribution, with all the injustice that such term implies. Economic and financial equity leads to outcomes like State ownership of property rights; State control of the means of production; State coerced equal outcomes; and State reallocation of wealth and property according to the dictates of a disadvantaged minority.

In practice, equity refers to a socio-economic equality of outcome irrespective of opportunity, merit, investment, labour or effort. The Austrian economist Fredrich Hayek, a Nobel Prize laureate, explained that there is "all the difference in the world between treating people equally and attempting to make them equal," for the latter idea is a "form of servitude." Striving to make all persons equal when all are subject to the same rules governing economics for instance, is a socialist idea contrary to the capitalist, *laissez-faire,* economic principles of Western civilization. Hayek believes these "two traditions of thought, while bearing the same name, are divided by fundamentally opposed principles,"[5] with one resulting in freedom and the other in bondage. Outcomes in democratic capitalist societies are generally not equal, but they are pursued in freedom of choice and effort and this unequal result is what race agents wish to demolish. Charles Murray predicts that should the issue of equity versus equality not be resolved, "it will lead to thinking that the only legitimate evidence of a nonracist society is equal outcomes." Expecting to 'reap' what one has not 'sown' is unbiblical, as is clear from Luke 19:21-22. Personal responsibility for 'sins' of forebearers is likewise unscriptural.

Diversity, Tolerance, and Equality

CRT theory is represented through ideals of diversity, equity, and inclusion ("DEI"). In education, DEI is employed to achieve a slanted form of academic justice (a facet of social justice ideology). As Victor Davis Hanson writes, "Under the new reparatory and compensatory diversity, equity, and inclusion rules, those deemed non-white were to be hired and admitted to colleges in greater numbers than their

---

[5] Hayek, F., Individualism: True and False, 2017.

demographics." In theory, DEI is not about black versus white but, instead, social justice for historically disadvantaged ethnic groups. However, that is not the actual case for DEI is a form of black on white racism, seeking reparation and privilege for perceived past and ongoing prejudice. This is clearly a leftist neo-Marxist strategy focused on hostility and resentment against the white cohort – the 'oppressors.' The acronym DEI, then, really means "discrimination, exclusion and indoctrination,"[6] a vengeful, racist, policy.

Tertiary Education

Due to DEI policies, progressive universities like Princeton lowered their standards in the fields of the Classics, allegedly to facilitate emergence of a Black academic class.[7] Relatedly, in California, Professor Gordon Klein of the University of California, Los Angeles, was suspended for refusing a request that "Black students get easier final exams."[8] The irony seems to be lost on CRT-DEI activists that such actions constitute an insult towards black students. Lowering educational standards to accommodate black ethnicity amounts to "a surrender of dignity" says Glenn Loury, for it "reduces, not elevates,"[9] the student.

The lowering of academic standards to accommodate African-Americans is much like what transpired in certain Universities in post-apartheid South Africa. In particular, Medical faculties employ two differing standards of entrance requirements depending on the applicant's ethnicity, all under the guise of social justice and equality. With this

---

[6] Kumar, D., DeSantis Signs Three Bills, May 16, 2023.
[7] Stepman, J., Princeton Drops Standards in Name of Equity, 2021.
[8] Heine, D., Poll, June 7, 2021.
[9] Loury, G., 2023, Speech at Kings College Cambridge: Preservation of Western Civilization, UK., January 19, 2023.

motive, over 40 US medical training institutions, including Harvard, Columbia, Stanford, and Mount Sinai, lowered standards for entry by minority race applicants. However, misguided attempts to create educational equality to remedy past social injustice might very well backfire. As Professor John McWhorter points out, lowering standards is prejudicial to black students "for they are saying that Latin and Greek are too hard to require black students to learn."[10]

Secondary Education

The US education system also reflects a preferential strategy in the area of gender identity. For instance, the San Diego Unified school district "adopted principles of academic queer theory," inculcating such principles into their educational pedagogy. The end purpose, it is revealed, is to promote a wide ambit of "new sexual identities such as genderqueer, non-binary, pansexual and two-spirit."[11] The program is introduced at kindergarten level, continuing through to Year 12, and unmistakeably based upon neo-Gnostic theory promoting a body-spirit dualism. Apart from public schooling, choosing a private religious school is risky for "most of them are as woke as most secular schools,"[12] says Dennis Prager. Professor McWhorter supports this view when he claims schools "teach students an antiracism that sees life as nothing but abuse of power, and teaches that cringing, hostile, group identity against oppression is the essence of a 'self.'"[13]

---

[10] McWhorter, J., Problem with Dropping Standards in Name of Equity, June 7, 2021.
[11] Rufo, C., The Dismantlers, 2022.
[12] Prager, D., The Single Best Thing, June, 8, 2021.
[13] Schrader, A., Black Columbia Professor, 2021.

Home Schooling

Popular Broadcaster, Dennis Prager, recommends parents withdraw their children from the school education system. He warns parents children will be harmed "intellectually and morally" at schools which "teach them race-centred hatred of whites," hatred of America and its values. They are taught "gender is chosen," not biologically assigned at birth, and so are "prematurely sexualised."[14] This perturbing scenario is a fair indication of the West's public school system. Children are taught hostile ideologies, not biblical principles, nor tolerance, fairness, justice, diversity, and equality, as traditionally understood. Identity theories are atheistic ideologies devoid of the basic elements, the emotional attributes, of a moral human being such as compassion, virtue, altruism and decency. To the contrary, says Professor Chenyuan Snider, neo-Marxian theory is "filed with hate." On the other hand, the only faith with *agape* love as a core element is that of Judeo-Christianity. Expression of love is an essential attribute of the Divine and ideally should be reflected in society but, says Snider, "Christianity has always been the ultimate target in any society controlled by Marxists."[15]

Resistance to Critical Race Theory

Tyler O'Neil reports race-based education has "sparked a civil war in American education."[16] As parents and teachers resist the unconstitutional secular scheme of identity ideologues, many States pass legislation prohibiting CRT-DEI in public schools. Chris Rufo, the intrepid antagonist of CRT, calculates by so doing, "75 million Americans will be

---

[14] Prager, D., The Single Best Thing, June, 8 2021.
[15] Snider, C., The Church Must Respond to Marxism, October 17, 2021.
[16] O'Neil, T., CRT has Sparked a Civil War in American Education, June 10, 2021.

protected from state-sanctioned racism." He adds that "public schools can then no longer promote the principles of race essentialism, collective guilt, and racial superiority theory."[17]

The most effective method of countering CRT arises from a 'grass roots' level of concerned parents who pressurise their political representatives to enact laws protecting children from biased regulations. Parents across all ethnicities reject identity indoctrination, understanding its destructive social implications. Being aware of rising resistance, the far-left US president, Joe Biden, directed the Department of Justice to "scare parents, to punish them for speaking out for their children and to shut down First Amendment protected speech and assembly."[18] Nonetheless, concerned about vulnerable children, resistance by parents and educators escalates.

The Military

The malignant influence of identity policies prevails in the US Military, the world's dominant power. The implications for world stability and democracy are no minor matter for opposing external forces comprise the triptych of Marxist China, authoritarian Russia, and despotic Iran. Their leaders have hegemonic intentions, driven by illiberalist ideologies with which the classical democratic political framework has no political or ethical equivalency. Marxist China, especially, has world domination as its aim evidenced through a perturbing build-up of nuclear military power. China's militaristic predilection is contained within their nihilist political

---

[17] Rufo, C. F., The Battle Over Critical Race Theory, June 27, 2021.
[18] Hamilton, G., AFL, 2021.

ideology for, as General Carl von Clausewitz explained, "War is nothing but a continuation of politics."[19]

Power Vacuum

The clear reduction in US military prowess resulted in Republican Senator Tom Cotton publicly recounting "several hundred" reports from 'Whistle blowers' in the Military, complaining of enforced identity policies. Cotton said these policies have "set members of the military against one another," and led to resignations in all arms of the military. In the authoritative 2023 'Index of U.S. Military Strength,' the authors claim as "currently postured, the U.S. military is at growing risk of not being able to meet the demands of defending America's vital national interests."[20] Sombre words indeed. The new dominant military power would be communist China, aiming to enforce their Marxist ideology worldwide while subverting the Western political and cultural order with its essential democratic freedoms and human rights.

Internal Strife

Despite serious external threats to Western civilisation, it cannot be overlooked that internal civilian strife, where the social and moral fabric of society becomes compromised, coupled with military discord, has resulted in collapse of great civilizations. History is replete with examples, not least being the mighty Roman empire (410 C.E.). In 1971, US President Richard Nixon in comparing the USA with ancient Rome ominously commented, "as the great civilizations of the past became

---

[19] Carl Von Clausewitz, On War, Vol., III, 1832, p. 121.
[20] Executive Summary, 2023 Index of U.S. Military Strength, October 18, 2022.

wealthy, they lost their will to live, to improve, and they then became subject to the decadence that eventually destroys that civilization."[21]

Large Corporations

Enforcement of cultural Marxist principles continues to damage the West's democratic political order. As social commentator Bruce Abramson remarks, "Progressives move quickly to cement their transformation of the country's beliefs, attitudes, values, social structures, economic models and government organisations." His view is accurate for identity ideology has become a *cause célèbre,* not only in the public sector, but also the private sector. Corporations are keen to publicise their new social justice program, no doubt to increase their profits. For example:

- American Express Company, a multi-Billion Dollar financial conglomerate, trains employees to "deconstruct their own intersectional identities, mapping their race, sexual orientation, body type, religion, disability status, age, gender identity."[22] The purpose of "deconstruction" is to ascertain whether or not they have privileged status or are part of a marginalised category, so remedial action can be enforced. Predictably, it is the cohort of white heterosexual individuals who are accused of being privileged 'oppressors,' while ethnic and sexual minorities are classified 'oppressed' - a standard neo-Marxist dichotomy;
- Google demands staff attend antiracist re-education CRT programs, claiming "all Americans are raised to be racist" and "America is a system of white supremacy;"
- The two largest US Defence contractors, Lockheed Martin and Raytheon, instructed executives to "deconstruct their white male privilege."[23]

---

[21] Bendle, M., The Dire Lessons, 2021.
[22] Rufo, C., Lie of Credit, 2021.
[23] Rufo, C., Battle over CRT, 2021.

Corporates and Government

Corporate leaders regard themselves as a "morally conscious business elite." However, they have mutated into dictatorial lawmakers. Avowing an agenda of social justice, corporate oligarchs claim the moral 'high-ground.' The enormous wealth of capitalist elites who direct technology companies (the 'tech-giants') like Amazon, Facebook, Twitter, Google, Microsoft, Apple, Shopify and others, has catapulted them into powerful and unassailable positions. This enables them to influence political and social affairs outside of their normal corporate objective, which is simply to make a profit for the benefit of shareholders.

A wealthy oligarchy finds rapport with radical political theories of leftist Government Administrations. This symbiotic relationship compromises individual freedoms and rights inherent in a classic democratic liberal tradition. Mark Tooley refers to the ideological merger of leftist politicians and wealthy corporates as a form of "liberal imperialism." He describes this strategy as an "aggressive push to impose progressive values, joined to corporate power, contriving to spread the same order (of leftist imperialism) to the ends of the earth."[24]

The danger of such alliance, in the view of professor of Government Mark Mitchell, is that "big government and big business arise in tandem, feed off each other and perpetuate each other." The end result of which, he says, is "a concentration of political power."[25] This relationship is an unholy fusion between the two most powerful institutions in any nation. The aim is to create an authoritarian, secular, humanist ideological utopia for their own benefit.

---

[24] Tooley, M., Integralism, 2022.
[25] Mitchell, M. T., The Ironic Revenge of Karl Marx, 2022.

Summation

Identity agents aim for mass public conformity to their theories. To do this, they employ indoctrination, compromise of fundamental human rights like speech and dissent, and replacement of religion in favour of the secular State. The outcome is an elitist despotism. A principle of classical liberal democratic republicanism is that a majority of law-abiding citizens should not be forced to comply with extreme ideologies with which they disagree, and against which constitutional safeguards exist. Identity ideology is anti-democratic and therefore repressive in practice, imitating Marxist dogma which compels compliance with State sanctioned ideology. This ideology permeates and controls all aspects of society. In this way, activists politicise ideological expressions of sexuality, gender, and ethnicity throughout society in fields like education, sports, government, military, public institutions, and the business sector. No dissent is tolerated.[26] Subsequently, where laws are enacted with which the majority disagree, resistance soon follows causing societal disturbance. A Washington Times article opines that should "leaders of society continue to ignore vociferous objections of the majority populace, "they risk falling even further into disrepute and facing an even greater political backlash."[27]

---

[26] There is "no forgiveness of transgression in the world of Identity Politics for the arena is political, not religious" (Mitchell, J. Conservatives Struggle, 2019).
[27] Bayse, C., Backlash Against America's Governing Expert Class, October 11, 2021.

CHAPTER SIX
PART THREE

THE CULTURAL REVOLUTION

*"Supremely frightful would be the effect of any human endeavour
to mock the stupendous mechanism of the Creator of the world"*
(Mary Shelley, Frankenstein, 1818)

6.4. Radical Feminism

Contemporary feminism was birthed in the women's liberation movement of the last two centuries, much of which was admirable[1] and necessary for eradication of inequality between the two genders in society. Once a level of emancipation, that is, societal justice in equality of roles, had been achieved through efforts of so-named 'first wave,'[2] and successive feminists, the focus of traditional[3] feminism shifted to the primacy of the individual especially as concerns autonomy of the female body.

Sexual Revolution

The 20th century sexual revolution was a stimulating factor for hyper-individualism, the hallmark of contemporary feminism. Mary Harrington argues that the current emphasis on body autonomy is a radicalism that

---

[1] At its formative stage, feminism was understood as the "belief that men and women are politically and morally equal and should be treated as such" for they "possess the same natural rights" (McElroy, W., Feminism, 2008).
[2] First wave feminism arose in the 18th century through publication of Mary Wollstonecraft's two books in 1790 and 1792.
[3] Early feminism sought equality in all facets of society. Postmodern feminism, also referred to as radical or reactionary feminism, is the stimulator of Identity Politics.

does not seek, nor promote, the true features of feminism. These features include uniform societal roles and equal financial compensation for the same work. In contrast, postmodern feminism amounts to what Harrington terms "bio-libertarianism," understood as extreme gender leftism. In her opinion, the term describes a "worldview that for 50 years has claimed to act in women's interests but is increasingly at odds with those interests." Activists now believe, she adds, that "human freedom necessitates a radical unmooring from the givens of our bodies."[4] In other words, a view of sex-gender detached from the realism of biological dimorphic sex evident at birth. To justify proposed sex-gender dichotomy, post-truth radicals adopt a neo-Marxist, Critical Gender Theory, validating their personalized gender fabrications.

Feminist Standpoint Theory

Critical Gender theory, also referred to as 'Feminist Standpoint Theory,' seeks to eradicate distinction between female and male binary genders. According to this theory, natural-born binary sex classification needs to be abolished through creation of an egalitarian and somewhat androgenous situation wherein all claimed, self-identified genders irrespective of biological realities, have equal rights and privileges. The theory posits that gender discrepancy is a social construction, generated for the purpose of maintaining the patriarchal subjugation, the disadvantages and inferior status, of women. In the same way, racial distinctions were purposed to disadvantage Black race members. Social commentator, Mark Levin, remarks that these ideologies are not about just gender or race but rather about, "destroying existing society using race, using gender, using climate,

---

[4] Harrington, M., Feminism, 2021.

all developed by Marxists in Berlin some of whom became tenured professors" in the USA.[5]

Shulasmith Firestone

In her study, 'The Dialectic of Sex: The Case for Feminist Revolution,' the prominent 'second wave' feminist, Shulasmith Firestone, proposed that "just as the end-goal of socialist revolution was elimination of economic class distinction, so the end goal of feminist revolution must be not only the elimination of male privilege but of sex distinction. Genital differences between humans would no longer matter culturally, being reversion to an unobstructed pansexuality." The foremost strategy, she explained, is "freeing women from the tyranny of their reproductive biology by every means available." She said this scheme enables "the freedom of all women and children to do whatever they wish sexually."[6] Carl Trueman predicts that upon implementation of Firestone's ideology relating to "exaltation of the disembodied individual will," anything and "everything else follows."[7] A utopian, humanist, conviction predominates in the feminism of a post-truth era.

Feminist Humanism

Critical Gender Theory driving radical feminist humanism is articulated through prisms of gender self-identification; abortion; same-sex marriage; and eradication of biblical morals and norms, specifically the Fatherhood idea of God and the *imago Dei* of humankind. Through application of these nihilist theories, secular humanists aim to create a "tolerant world where

---

[5] Baker, T., Biden, 2021.
[6] Firestone, S., The Dialectic of Sex: Feminist Revolution, 1970, pp. 11, 209, 238.
[7] Trueman, C. R., Mary Harrington Takes on the Machine, April 28, 2023.

rational thinking and kindness prevail," so as to create a "better society."[8] However, there exists no more egregious understanding of 'kindness,' 'tolerance,' and 'rational thinking' than when humanists endorse termination of pre-born children. International humanists similarly claim to seek for everyone, "a life of dignity where universal human rights are protected and respected."[9] Here again exists a severe cognitive detachment, for does not an innocent, defenceless, unborn baby, have a right to life? This incomprehensible denial of reality has to be understood as a spiritual delusion. G. K. Chesterton explains this phenomenon, "The first effect of not believing in God is that you lose your common sense, and can't see things as they are."[10]

Motherhood

Widely accepted as the 'mother of feminism' in her time, the 'second wave' feminist Betty Friedan authored the controversial best-selling work, 'The Feminine Mystique,' in 1953. In her book, she disparaged domestic roles for women viewing them as victims of society. She criticised the conviction that women were destined to find fulfilment and personal identity only through marriage and children – both of which concepts are foundational to society.

To the contrary, President Theodore Roosevelt held a high view of wives and mothers, declaring in 1908 that "This is the one body that I put even ahead of the veterans of the civil war; because when all is said and done, it is the mother, and the mother only, who is a better citizen even than the soldier who fights for his country… the mother is the one supreme

---

[8] Humanists UK., Successful Campaigns, 2021.
[9] Humanists International (Copson, A., President), Annual Report 2020.
[10] Chesterton, G. K., The Oracle of the Dog, 1984, (1926), p. 96.

asset of national life."[11] And rightly so, for the mother is the primary carer of the child, strongly influencing the future citizen, the nuclear family, and so benefitting society. Emphasis on the importance of mothers has implications for social justice for, as Erika Bachiochi explains, "even before women had direct access to political power, through their churches and community groups, women persuaded a nation that ensuring stable economic conditions for the activities of nurture, care, and character-formation in the home was not a matter of charity but of justice."[12] Pro-family policies comprising matrimony, fatherhood and motherhood, are rejected by post-moral feminists in favour of total freedom from traditional social, domestic, and familial roles.

Fourth Wave Feminism

Friedan's work was followed by that of Gloria Steinem (1934) and then by Germaine Greer[13] (1939), both promoting sexual liberation as the avenue to personal freedom. However, fervent feminists of the third and fourth[14] 'wave' movement (with each 'wave' becoming more extreme), became motivated to advance feminist ideology from a narrow application into a mainstream destigmatisation. In her study, 'A Decolonial Feminism,' author Françoise Vergès aims to "first and foremost place women's rights at the centre of global politics." This method would "anchor decolonial feminism in the desire to smash sexism, racism,

---

[11] Roosevelt, T., First International Congress for Welfare of the Child, 1908; *cf.,* Presidential Address, 1910, Vol. VII, p. 1672.

[12] Bachiochi, E., The Justice Mothers are Due, May 12, 2023.

[13] Greer published two international best-sellers: 'The Female Eunuch' (1970), and 'The Whole Woman' (1999).

[14] 'Third' and 'Fourth wave' feminism "divides society into distinct classes defined by gender and race. Statist intervention is required to enforce equality (equity) of power and wealth throughout society" (McElroy, W., Feminism, 2008).

capitalism, and imperialism and to change everything." The primary motivation, therefore, is to "construct a post-racist, post-capitalist, post-imperialist, and post-hetero-patriarchal world."[15] In other words, to re-fabricate society in accordance with a narrow post-truth, post-moral, neo-Marxist, neo-pagan feminist[16] identity ideology, while curtailing social and domestic leadership of males.

Feminism and Evolution

Rejecting biblical principles, feminists follow the evolutionary theories of Charles Darwin's materialist determinism, particularly in the area of ethics and morality. In the feminist view of anthropology, once freed of any definitive order by denying existence of God, individuals are able to fabricate sexuality, gender, truth and morality in line with their ideological aspirations. Identity activists simply cannot accept the idea of God's existence for, as Rabbi Jonathan Sacks says, "Believing there is a God means that we are not the centre of our world. God is."[17]

In the Handbook of Humanism, Andrew Copson writes the "origin of morality owes nothing to outside interference and has its genesis solely in our character as social animals." He continues, "Individual humanists try to think about right and wrong and do without any single moral authority to which they can turn for absolute answers."[18] The irrational belief in a materialist origin of a non-materialist, metaphysical, concept of morality and meaning is lost on humanists. Adoption of situational ethical behaviour, very much a variable principle, and coupled with the nihilism

---

[15] Vergès., F., A Decolonial Feminism, 2021, pp. vii, ix.
[16] Margot Adler explains, "Feminists and pagans both come from the same source without realizing it, and head towards the same goal without realizing it, and the two are now beginning to interlace" (Drawing Down the Moon, 1986, p. 182).
[17] Sacks, J., The Greatness of Humility, Shoftim 5776, 5783, 2016.
[18] Humanists International (Copson, A., President), Annual Report 2020.

of secularism inexorably leads individuals to strive for purpose and identity in materialist identity ideologies, notably those of race, sexual practice and gender. Even so, they believe their neo-Gnostic secret knowledge of the dualist structure of their sex-gender identity ideology, imparts the eternal, spiritual, meaning they anxiously seek. In their view, they have transcended the limitations of binary heterosexual genders imposed by God, and are able to give full expression to their true identity, their true purpose, and true meaning in life. Feminists therefore believe they have overcome God's grand design for creation, with its prejudicial patriarchal precepts. To this end, the World Economic Forum ponders rewriting the Bible using Artificial Intelligence, presumably to issue a politically correct, ideological, version replacing canonical doctrine with a new humanist religion.[19]

Radical Humanism

There exists in feminism ideology a duality in the mode of Gnostic oscillation between the body and the spirit. As Pauline Johnson reveals in her study, Feminism as Radical Humanism, "a humanist feminist" believes in the "persistent truth of a timeless, eternal human essence."[20] In this approach, the material, physical, body can be reformulated into one of the identitarians' choice, should they so desire. The new body would reflect their true physical form, a true expression of their identity, which was incorrectly fabricated at birth. Furthermore, the immutable spiritual essence of their humanity remains eternal, satisfying their quest for transcendence. This essentialist theory amounts to a secular sanctification of the mind (spirit) over a reductive theory of the body (matter). Feminists

---

[19] Agius, J., The Church of WEF: AI to Re-write the Bible, June 26, 2023.
[20] Johnson, P., Feminism as Radical Humanism, 1994, p. vii.

regard creative control over sex-gender as a demonstration of their absolute freedom from the restrictive parameters of God's creation order, echoing the basis of Eve's emancipatory intent.

Public Approval

Activists vociferously claim an autonomous right to not only create their own destiny and physical body, but to demand public acquiescence with their eccentric versions of secular meaning and identity. Feminism, they declare, "needs to recognise itself as a major interpreter of the cultural ideals of modern humanism."[21] Needless to say, these terms have weighted meanings differing from conventional applications.

Personal Pronouns

To eradicate the firm boundaries of created heterosexual binary gender, activists demand public compliance with self-gender identifiers' preferred pronouns which describe their fabricated, synthetic, genders. Nowadays, students stipulate how they "identify in terms of gender, race, class, sexuality, religion" – while distaining empirical science and objective reality. The final indignity fostered upon vulnerable youth is proposed through the San Francisco School Board's 'Guidebook,' in which teachers permit children to adopt the "It" pronoun as a form of self-identity, should they wish to do so.[22] The Darwinian evolutionary cohort no doubt celebrate this direct link to the animal kingdom, and the complete erasure of *imago Dei*.

Hans Boersma understands the pronoun arrangement as a "linguistic rebellion against the creation and redemption of all mankind in Christ,"[23]

---

[21] Johnson, P., Feminism as Radical Humanism', 1994, p. 18.
[22] Rufo, C., Pronouns, 2022.
[23] Boersma, H., Saving Mankind, 2022.

and against a created order in respect of which the Divine declares, "I the Lord speak the truth; I declare what is right."[24] When identity actors use plural pronouns in self-description, such as "we" or "they/them," while referring to a single individual, an implication of divinity ensues. It was the Creator, as triune God, who described himself as "we" (Gen. 1:26). No created being has the right to appropriate a plural description, for it is a blasphemous act.

The feminist agenda of proclaiming primacy of concocted genders, sometimes in the plural, is a display of animosity towards constraints of the two created heterosexual genders. In God's economy, both genders have equal value for they bear the image of God, the *imago Dei*. But, while they have God's image, they do not have his divinity for that quality belongs exclusively to God himself.

Transgenderism

The aim of transgenderism is eradication of biological sex-gender distinctions between natural-born male and female. As Professor Reno points out, "transgenderism has tremendous metaphysical significance as a symbol of successful rebellion. Its open warfare on the body promises total victory." To justify their actions, gender self-identifiers embrace the neo-Gnostic bipartite theory of an ethereal spirit contrasted with the insignificant material body. Glenn Sunshine explains transgenderism as "an explicit neo-Gnostic rejection of the human body, treating it as largely irrelevant to our identities. Instead, who we really are is determined by some non-observable, non-empirical, secret knowledge known only to ourselves, but to which everyone else, and reality itself, must adapt."[25]

---

[24] Isaiah 45: 19.
[25] Sunshine G., Stonestreet, J., Ash Wednesday and Lent, February 3, 2022.

Stated otherwise, a concealed, authentic, persona resides within every person and constitutes the real self which awaits expression.

For feminists, deconstruction of the created *imago Dei* leads to a new idol, a non-binary person with autonomous creative license in the mode of a *homo deus* (god-man). Philosopher Ludwig Wittgenstein (1889-1951) cautioned against the tendency of creating fresh idols when he wrote, "all that philosophy can do is destroy idols... and that means not creating a new one."[26] In true revolutionary style, after tearing down established concepts like biological gender revealed at birth and the Fatherhood identity of God, visionaries fall into the trap of inventing a fictional idol - the narcissistic deified-self, which will itself eventually be deconstructed for something new.

Language, Truth, and Reality

Contemporary feminists ratify Nietzsche's statement in the 'Twilight of the Idols' when he says, "I am afraid we are not getting rid of God because we still believe in grammar." New sex-gender normality commences with new grammar, especially pronouns for everyday use. As Carl Trueman points out, feminist linguistic strategy highlights the desire for sovereignty and so they "assert that God and all that he created, from male and female, to notions of right and wrong, are simply linguistic constructs, mere con tricks that capture the imagination of the unthinking herd." This view is accurate for the furore over vocabulary is the conforming of reality to radical identity ideology in the minds of the populace. The redefining of language and grammar is indicative of the deconstructionist aims of postmodern thought. Gene Veith continues, "By its very nature, language

---

[26] Wittgenstein, L., Philosophical Investigations, 1958 (1953), §86-93.

shapes what we think. Since language is a cultural creation, meaning is ultimately a social construction," and therefore susceptible to deconstruction.[27] Subsequently, adds Veith, "all reality is virtual reality," which is an acceptable alternative to confronting positive truths and objective reality.

Professor George Weigel endorses this perspective when he explains the "postmodern world has lost its grip on the most fundamental truths, even those inscribed in our chromosomes."[28] In other words, all accepted knowledge coming via objective facts derived from disciplines like biology, history, archaeology, maths, and the sciences which combined give society and culture its context for truth and reality, is disparaged under the pretext of *gnosis* – superior subjective knowledge. The Polish-British novelist, Joseph Conrad in his book, 'Under Western Eyes,' describes a similar 20th century situation, "In Russia, all knowledge was tainted with falsehood for the government corrupted the teaching for its own purposes."[29] Meanwhile, Alan Bloom focuses on the root of the matter when he says, "the relativity of truth is not a theoretical insight but a moral postulate – the condition of a free society, as they see it."[30] Hence, there is no possibility of arriving at a centrist position for the two viewpoints are ideologically and morally exclusive: one founded on absolutist, definitive, positive principles, the other on relativist, sited, subjective ideas typical of existentialist situational ethics and Marxist propaganda.

---

[27] Randall Smith says, "Deconstructionism – unmasking the real author (and his words) by reducing him to his cultural, relativistic and psychological influences is all the rage in the academy." (Smith, R., Deconstruct Thyself, 2021).
[28] Weigel, G., The Sacred Earthiness, December 22, 2021.
[29] Conrad, J., Under Western Eyes, 1911, p. 100.
[30] Bloom, A. D., The Closing of the American Mind, 1988, p. 25.

The Fatherhood Identity

Pathological hostility towards the male gender and the Creator of life as a father figure, is the stimulating force behind not only extreme feminism but of all atheistic and secular humanist hypotheses. Once the father identity of God is deconstructed, neutered, androgenised, or feminised, and the connected *imago Dei* of humankind dispensed with, individuals are free to identify with any gender they chose and to ignore their biological sex. As a result, denying God's fatherhood role, as justified through neo-Gnostic dichotomist concepts of the Demiurge,[31] creates a vacuum in which gender agents claiming non-biological permutations of self-identity are possible. Yet these are speculative theories of ancient Greek origin, quite unlike Judaism's understanding of a personal, interactive, relational God. Tim Labron explains, "Hebraic thought sees the human characterization of God as a natural understanding of a relationship with their father for God resides among his people."[32] The Judeo-Christian ethos is represented by this belief.

A Sacred Identity

Philosophically and sociologically purging the Creator as a father figure, coupled with denial of the literal and historical nature of the Genesis narrative on fragile pretexts, indicates the feminist aim to likewise nullify the sacred genre of the individual. Mary Eberstadt suggests identitarians deeply "resent and envy their fellows born to an ordered paternity, those with secure attachments to family and faith and country"[33] – in other words, biblical principles. Understandably, those denying identity

---

[31] In Gnosticism, "non-recognition of reality is a matter of principle" (Voegelin, E., New Science of Politics, 1952, pp. 168-9).
[32] Labron, T., Wittgenstein's Religious Point of View, 2006, p. 114.
[33] Eberstadt, M., The Fury of Fatherless, 2020.

conferred by God will suffer *angst*, confusion, alienation, anger and insecurity. Blame for their predicament will, ironically, directed at God whose fatherhood status they reject.

To eliminate an individual's sacred identity, activists base their arguments on four main philosophical and theological components: one, belief in evolutionary materialist philosophy. Two, belief in the individual's creative rights as inaugurated by the first secular humanist, Eve. Three, rejection of God's identity as Father in favour of a feminine or androgenous spiritual figure. Four, rejecting the created body as work of a lesser god, thus defective and needing refabrication. In this way, activists justify recreating a binary, heterosexual, individual into an *imago hominis* (image of man) – an ideological person with sex-gender to suit. By so doing, they confirm Philip Rieff's view that "identity changes are the new idolatry," implying idolatry of the deified-self as expressed in sex-gender combinations free of realism. Walt Whitman reflected this attitude in his 1892 poem 'Song of Myself' when writing, "I celebrate myself, and sing myself; And what I assume, you shall assume; For every atom belonging to me as good belongs to you."[34]

The Demiurge

The original argument alleging an imperfect creation was proposed by the Edenic serpent when he, in true Gnostic style, disparaged the veracity of God's words. The serpent inferred the imperfect Garden scenario was the work of a lesser god, a Demiurge, irrationally denying the First Couple access to the Tree of Knowledge. By so doing the Demiurge prevented them from attaining omniscient and creative powers. The real Creator

---

[34] Whitman, W., Song of Myself, 1998 (1892), p. 1.

would have encouraged access to the Tree of Knowledge, leading them to transcendence and authenticity through superior wisdom. Transhumanist theory follows this concept.

Scientism and Transhumanism

To remedy an imperfect creation of the body, gender self-identifiers like transgenders and transsexuals, find relief in the concept of transhumanism – perhaps terms of post-humanism, anti-humanism, or even dehumanization are more suitable. Transhumanists aim to broaden "human potential by overcoming aging, cognitive shortcomings, involuntary suffering and confinement to planet earth." This concept is not new, having early beginnings such as that proposed by René Descartes in 1641 when he predicted advances in knowledge would result in freedom from "maladies of body and mind and perhaps even from the debility of age."[35]

Under the façade of a public good, philosophers, scientists and bioengineers strive to bypass the anthropological and theological confines of *imago Dei* and to re-create[36] humankind in their own fantasy, an *imago hominis,* in the very mode of post-structuralist sex-gender identity advocates. Scientism is supported by Stephen Hawking who stated, "there is a fundamental difference between religion which is based on authority, and science which is based on observation and reason. Science will win, because it works."[37]

Hawkins's dogmatic outlook is not quite the whole picture for scientific knowledge is not static, it constantly evolves as new discoveries

---

[35] Descartes, R., Discourse on Method, 2004(1641), pp. 48-49.
[36] "Medical, chemical and scientific technology result in the abolition of man and woman" (Longenecker, D. Abolition, 2022).
[37] Doane, J., Science Versus Religion, July 8, 2022.

present themselves. What seems to be scientific truth now, with benefits for humanity, might not be so in the light of subsequent empirical revelations. This will indubitably be the case with transhumanist theories. Transhumanism[38] reflects traces of Darwin's pseudo-scientific evolutionary theory which holds humanity to be product of a developmental process. Darwin wrote, "man has risen from a lowly condition to the highest standard as yet attained by him in knowledge, morals, and religion."[39] Perhaps Darwin's evolvement of the species was not progressing rapidly enough for the transhumanists

Homo Deus

In a sense, transhumanists seek to bring to reality Harari's futurist concept of *homo deus* (man-god), a species evolved from *homo sapiens* (wise-man), reflecting a divine status sought by the First Couple through the heresy of *eritus sicut Deus* (to be like God). Harari writes, "we will now aim to overcome old age and even death itself. And having raised humanity above the level of survival struggles, we aim to upgrade humans into gods and so turn *Homo sapiens* into *Homo deus*."[40] The lies of the nefarious serpent, appealing to human pride and their narcissistic desire for divinity of sorts, continue unabated in a contemporary setting.

Cyborg Feminism

Mary Harrison refers to a process of "Cyborg Feminism." She explains, the "final frontier for equality" is that of reproduction and the idea is to

---

[38] Transhumanism is "a political ideology based on the worship of technology, not the love of science. It is the enthronement of cleverness and the abandonment of wisdom" (Pearce, J., History, 2022).
[39] Darwin, C., The Descent of Man, 1871, p. 181.
[40] Harari, Y. N., Homo Deus: A Brief History of Tomorrow, 2016, p. 21.

"replace the sexes with an atomized, sexless, liberal person."[41] To do this, an artificial womb is required so as to eliminate God's creative process through technology. The outcome of scientific refabrication of human beings is well described by Frankenstein's author Mary Shelley as follows, "Supremely frightful would be the effect of any human endeavour to mock the stupendous mechanism of the Creator of the world."[42]

Transcendence

Christopher Dawson correctly believes the "development of scientific specialism has in no way reduced man's need for a historical faith, an interpretation of contemporary culture in terms of social processes and spiritual ends."[43] To the contrary, transhumanists insist "immortality is attainable in the physical world through applied technology," an anti-theistic stance. However, science in the form of technology, concerns the realm of empiricism and cannot convincingly enter into the realm of supernatural concepts. The corporeal cannot construct the incorporeal – the physical cannot create the metaphysical - and so a substantive moral and ethical paradigm becomes their nemesis. Their default position is a situational[44] ethic, free of universalism, transcendence, and objective validity. The situational ethic idea makes the unconstrained-self sole arbiter of virtue, identity, meaning, and social justice. In this context, reality and truth succumb to the fictional ideals of each individual.

---

[41] Harrington, M., Allen, E., Cyborg Feminism, December 8, 2022.
[42] Shelley, M. W., Frankenstein: The Modern Prometheus, 1985 (1818), p. 17.
[43] Dawson, C., Religion and the Rise of Western Culture, 1958, p. 13.
[44] Feminists refer to this as "standpoint theory" (Harding, S., Feminist, 2004, p. 3).

6.5. Fathers in Society

Dispensing with God as a father-male identity has concerning implications for fathers in society who suffer accusations of systemic male toxicity and patriarchal dominance. Disparaging the fatherhood principle leads to a negative feminist attitude towards the necessity of fathers in the common home. This gives rise to significant numbers of single parent homes run by the mother in the absence of an unwanted father. Fathers are then unable to represent a male role model to their children, to mentor their children and protect them, with adverse social consequences. Statistics indicate the primary cause of Black youth criminality, for instance, is the absence of a father in the home.

In her article on the social crisis surrounding absence of fathers in the nuclear family, Mary Eberstadt concludes the 2022 US civil riots, "exposed the three-fold crisis of filial attachment that has beset the Western world for more than half a century." In consequence, she says, "Deprived of father, Father, and *patria*, a critical mass of humanity has become socially dysfunctional on a scale not seen before."[45] Undeniably sombre words for civil unrest indicates a social crisis of paternity where, in an African-American home, for instance, 65 percent of children grow up without a present father. Using the year 2019 as an example, 34% of children in the USA came from a single-parent home and 25% grew up without any category of a father in the home.[46]

Sociologist David Popenoe concludes that "American fathers are today more removed from family life than ever before."[47] He explains the

---

[45] Eberstadt, M., The Fury of the Fatherless, December 2020.
[46] Green, S. K., The Feminisation of the Modern Man, 2021.
[47] Popenoe, D., Life Without Father, 1996, p. 1.

factor of fatherlessness, "predisposes children, especially boys, to academic failure,[48] criminal behaviour[49] and economic hardship, not to mention an intergenerational repeating of handicaps."[50]

Cultural Emasculation

A combination of feminist misandry towards males, resentment towards the father-male idea of God, the denigration of a father's role in the home, the high rate of divorce, and societal reluctance to engage in conventional marriage, coupled with freely available pornography, has effeminised and culturally emasculated men as a whole. Waldo Emerson summed up the situation when he wrote, "society everywhere is in conspiracy against the manhood of every one of its members."[51]

Researchers investigated claims of misogyny in contemporary society, looking for overt signs of toxic masculinity and affiliated expressions of male dominance. Instead of "detecting misogyny, they found something else…misandry, a bias against men, for there is overwhelming evidence of conscious, blatant, and widespread discrimination against boys and men in modern societies."[52]

The ominous words of Henry James in 1886 find context here, "The whole generation is womanized; the masculine tone is passing out of the world. It's a feminine, nervous, hysterical, chattering, canting age" which will "usher in the reign of mediocrity."[53] Understandably, the continued

---

[48] In fact, "66% of black degree recipients are women; they earn 70% of black Master's degrees and more than 60% of doctorates" (Hymovitz, K. S., Where Boys Aren't, 2022).
[49] 85% of youths in U.S. prisons stem from fatherless homes (Brewer, J., Fatherlessness and its Effects, February 15, 2022).
[50] Williams, W. E., Is Racism Responsible, 2021.
[51] Emerson, R. W., The Essay on Self-Reliance, 1908, p. 14.
[52] Tierney, J., The Misogyny Myth, Summer 2023.
[53] James, Henry, The Bostonians, 1886, p. 293.

assault on fathers leads them to avoid environments where they are not appreciated or wanted. The social effect on children and future generations is disturbing.[54]

School Shootings

The increase in US mass school shootings by teenage shooters can largely be attributed to lack of fathers in the home. In John Horvat's analysis, "almost in every shooter case, a true Christian father is missing from the home."[55] An article from the Heritage Foundation points out 75% of the "25 most cited school shooters since Columbine were reared in broken homes."[56] Similarly, psychologist Dr. Peter Langman, reveals most school shooters come from "incredibly broken homes of divorce, separation, infidelity, substance abuse, criminal behaviour, domestic violence and child abuse."[57] The diminution of male leadership roles is a reflection of the wider phenomenon of feminization of Western society itself. Hanna Rosin's essay, 'The End of Men,' captured statistics indicating women now comprise the "majority of the workforce." This role reversal has "vast cultural consequences"[58] for men have historically been leaders in society and the home.

Parental Alienation

The domestic situation is exacerbated through a prevalent form of emotional and psychological child abuse, legally designated in many jurisdictions as 'parental alienation.' Parental alienation occurs when a

---

[54] "Thousands of confused young men are a potential danger to their communities" (Horvat, J., Stop Mass Shootings, 2022).

[55] Horvat, J., *ibid.*, 2022.

[56] Kao, E., The Crisis of Fatherless Shooters, March 14, 2018.

[57] Langman, P., School Shooters: The Myth of the Stable Home, May 24, 2016.

[58] Rosin, H., The End of Men, The Atlantic, July/August, 2010.

custodian parent parts company with the other parent and then proceeds to disparage and denigrate the ostracised parent. These accusations are often unwarranted, but reach such a level of hostility that the children refuse to have any form of relationship with the rejected parent. Children's love for their expelled parent is practically deleted. Largely, the mother retains custody and so the alienating parent is invariably the mother resulting in fathers unable to have meaningful contact with their children. Parental alienation is difficult to prove in a Court of law and has severe effects upon the relationship of children and their fathers, both of whom are victims in the demise of their relationship.

Parental alienation is recognised as an "endemic world-wide health problem," having a serious effect upon the cohesiveness and psychological well-being of the nuclear family unit. Wilfred Von Boch-Galhou, an internationally respected researcher in the field, explains that "although some 1,300 professional articles and empirical studies exist from all over the world, there is still not enough awareness of Parental Alienation in professional practice."[59] Von Boch-Galhou is here referring to professionals in the fields of psychology, sociology, and psychiatry but the same sentiments equally apply to legal practitioners and the judiciary.

---

[59] Von Boch-Galhau, W., Parental Alienation, 2020.

CHAPTER SIX
PART FOUR

THE CULTURAL REVOLUTION

*"The real conflict is not between one set of moral prejudices and another,
but between the theistic and the atheistic faith; it is all for the best
that the division should be sharply drawn"*

(T. S. Eliot, Selected Essays: Thoughts After Lambeth, 1932)

6.6. Eliminating God

A new syncretistic religion of neo-Gnostic New Age neo-paganism and humanist secularism replaces Judeo-Christianity in the post-Christian society. A George Barna survey confirms "syncretism is the prevailing worldview of each generation in America today."[1] In this blend of spirituality emerge various feminine, gender-vague, and androgenous deities to replace the patriarchal Judeo-Christian Creator.[2]

A Syncretistic Worldview

Alphabet tribal members find comfort in a collection of assorted non-binary, transsexual deities, in a gender pluralist society. For instance, Naomi Goldenberg proposes an androgyne god in replacement of the "fallen patriarchal God" of Judeo-Christianity, dismissed as a tyrannical

---

[1] Barna, G., Cultural Research Center: Release #4, US Worldview, May 10, 2023, p. 4.
[2] Sallie McFague criticizes the traditional model for God as "triumphalist, sovereign, and patriarchal," which "contributes towards a sense of distance between God and the world." She suggests a more inclusive model of God, one as "mother (*agape*), lover (*eros*) and friend (*philia*) (Models of God., 1987, pp. 84-85ff.).

figure. Presumably, an androgyne figure is "beyond being a woman." A god of this genre was historically "used as a popular symbol of salvation in late Hellenism,"[3] for there is 'nothing new under the sun' as King Solomon said. Even Christians latch onto the feminist "Queen of Heaven" idea from Jeremiah 44:17-18, promoting a teaching described as 'Cakes for the Queen of Heaven.' This course has been well attended over the years by Congregationalist, Methodist, Episcopalian, Catholic, Unitarian and other religious groups.

Deathworks

Cultural revolutionaries aim to remove all traces of a conservative Judeo-Christian dispensation with its long-standing virtues, truths, and freedoms founded on the Fatherhood concept of a supreme God. As L. P. Hartley frames the situation, "the past is a foreign country, they do things differently there."[4] This 'difference' is what activists wish to repel, and so pave the way for a complete refurbishment of societal values and of truth itself.

Phillip Rieff's "Deathworks" theory, a nihilistic composition, well describes the attempted abolition of traditional doctrine connected to the Creator's Fatherhood identity. This fundamental principle is the source of humanity's personal identity. Therefore, both the Fatherhood of God concept, and that of *imago Dei,* are deemed "sacred symbols" of a by-gone age which require removal from present culture. As Rieff explains, "sacred symbols" are "coordinators of moral demand systems," the constrictions of which are unacceptable in a setting of flexible morality. He says the

---

[3] Goldenberg, N., Changing of the Gods, 1978, pp. 78-9.
[4] Hartley, L. P., The Go-Between, 1958 (1953), p. 1.

current cultural clash is "directed against all sacred orders in any of their historical or theoretical manifestations."[5]

The honouring, through statue and memorial, of notable individuals due to their laudable achievements, virtue and integrity of character, is passé in the present secular climate lacking positive values. On this point, G. K. Chesterton writes "The mission of a great spire or statue should be to strike the spirit with a sudden sense of pride as with a thunderbolt. It should lift us with it into the empty and ennobling air."[6] Nobility, dignity, courage and commitment are qualities reflected in those who historian Mark Malvasi describes as "great men of the West." These virtues are no longer deemed worthy of honour and reference to them is to be abolished, 'cancelled.'

The same sentiments apply to works of famous writers such as Roald Dahl, Agatha Christie, Shakespeare, and, incredibly, the humourist P. G. Wodehouse. In 2023, Penguin Books took it upon themselves to edit works of Wodehouse by removing "prose deemed unacceptable to present day readers."[7] Here, critics censor what they deem unacceptable, ostensibly for the common good of society but contrary to the authors' narrative and culture of the times. Again, an instance of situational ethics.

The de-platforming of individuals promoting views different from woke religion is reminiscent of the 15th century Spanish Inquisition removing from society those with divergent ideas of truth. The end result, says Malvasi, is that "critics may succeed in expunging from the great traditions and history of the West, those aspects to which they take umbrage but they have yet to explain what they recommend as a

---

[5] Rieff, P., My Life Among the Deathworks, 2006, pp. 7-8, 43.
[6] Chesterton, G. K., The Defendant, 1901.
[7] Zymeri, J., Penguin Edits P. G. Wodehouse Novels, April 17, 2023.

substitute."[8] This is the case with the sacred principles of Judeo-Christianity unpinning the rich Western tradition, especially the Fatherhood of God concept which provides the source of natural law, ethics, morals, transcendence, virtue, and the divine identity of humanity for which there is no possible replacement.

The establishment of seminal cultural, religious, and civilizational landmarks, emblems, images, and symbols has biblical precedence for, as King Solomon instructed nearly 3,000 years ago, "Do not move the ancient landmarks that your fathers have set."[9] In modern times, Alexander Solzhenitsyn explains the deleterious effect of Deathworks, the loss of sacred symbols, on established culture and the need to resist such attempts when he writes:

> *"To fight against untruth and falsehood, to fight against myths, or to fight against an ideology which is hostile to mankind, to fight for our memory of what things were like – that is the task of the artist. A people which no longer remembers has lost its history and its soul."* [10]

While leftist agents demolish the traditional symbols of society, they revere their own versions. For instance, the LGBTQ Rainbow Flag is considered a 'sacred symbol' as is the 'Pride Parade' itself.

Hate speech

Demonstrations of unrestrained sexual freedom, in all its aberrant forms, publicly highlight a major victory for identitarians intent upon refabricating values of society. Condemnation of this public display is considered 'hate speech.' In July 2023, a black Councillor in the UK, one King Lawal, was suspended from the Conservative Party, fired from his

---

[8] Malvasi, M., Cancel Culture and the Great Men of the West, May 31, 2022.
[9] Proverbs 22:28.
[10] Solzhenitsyn, A., Warning to the Western World, March 1, 1976.

employment and as Governor of a local school and, moreover, refused access to local library facilities for the purpose of meeting constituents as before. His offence was tweeting a message that read, "Pride is a not a virtue but a sin." In explanation, the Conservative Party local leader incongruously said they are committed to "creating a fair and inclusive environment for everyone."[11]

Moral Autonomy

Loss of the biblical tradition results in reversion to post-flood paganist culture for, "where there is nothing sacred, there is nothing,"[12] says Rieff. His words are similar in concept to those of Pope Francis who elaborated, "If there is no transcendent truth in obedience to which man achieves his full identity, then there is no sure principle for guaranteeing just relations between people." The reason being "the transcendent dignity of the human person" is derived from the "visible image of the invisible God,"[13] meaning *imago Dei*. Refusing recognition of the sacred status of human life,[14] identity activists view themselves as morally autonomous, without objective or absolutist thresholds to moderate their actions.

And so, reactionary feminists, among others, reveal their unrealistic worldview based on a personal sex-gender ideal, freeing them from a patriarchal concept. In their view, "individual sexual preferences, marriage, and prudence, all things historically valued by liberal democracy, have no place in the feminism of the 21st century."[15] The

---

[11] Dalrymple, T., Before the Fall, July 21, 2023.
[12] Rieff, P., Deathworks, 2006, pp. 7-8, 43.
[13] Pope Francis, Fratelli Tutti, 2020, para. 273.
[14] The personal identity of individuals is sacred. Humans are made in the image of God and have divine status, only "a little lower than the heavenly beings," but still "crowned" with "glory and honour" (Ps. 8:5 ff.).
[15] Schultz, M., Is Sex Political, 2022.

piercing view of novelist Joseph Conrad (1857-1924), finds relevance in this era when he writes, "Visionaries work everlasting evil on earth. Their utopias inspire in the mass of mediocre minds a disgust of reality and a contempt for the secular logic of human development."[16]

Tribal Villages

Migration towards a tribal entity – a figurative family - by fatherless persons implies a desperate quest for personal identity, for meaningful familial relations, and social connection. In a September 2020 manifesto on their website, BLM followers vow to "disrupt the Western-prescribed nuclear family requirement by supporting each other as extended families, and 'villages' that collectively care for one another, especially our children, to the degree that mothers, parents, and children are comfortable." However, detachment from an integrated society is contrary to the common good, peace, and harmony of society as a whole, and of the tribe itself.

6.7. Sex and Gender

The struggle for feminist emancipation and personal identity through sexuality is stimulated by a combination of Freudian sex theories, the pseudo-scientific Kinsley Reports[17] of 1948 and 1953, the advent of the liberating birth control pill, the sexual reformation in the decade of 1960, and the legalisation of pornography commencing with the 1973 Supreme Court decision in Miller versus California.

Demonstrating a Marxist class-struggle philosophy, oppressed women in society rebel against patriarchal dominated society, the oppressors, to

---

[16] Conrad, J., Under Western Eyes, 1911, p. 92.
[17] Alfred C. Kinsley founded the 'Institute for Sex Research' at Indiana University.

assert not only their individual sexual identity,[18] but a dreamy authenticity, equality, and freedom. Over the last few decades, the issue of sexuality has become more prominent in mainstream society, and is now firmly established as the primary focus of feminist liberation.

The Therapeutic Self

Psychologists Freud[19] and Jung strongly influenced sexuality and identity, being key prisms of their psychoanalysis. Psychoanalysis, an intense therapeutic method, has been widely popular since inception, having its aim as the 'salvation of the suffering self.' A program of regressive introspection was introduced to reach previously unrevealed and suppressed "sources of psychic suffering," leading to an assumption of sexual repression. Freud postulated that both males and females are "bisexual in nature," and their sexual drive was the "engine of personality."[20] In this manner, Freud approved "atypical sexual expressions," now embraced in society legally, socially, and politically.[21] Adopting Freud's therapeutic theories, the activists' attitude to sex is "the more fantastic a sexual identity, the more it expresses individuality." Freud's theories are not unexpected given his devotion to the androgenous Greek god, Dionysus, whose dualist character is represented in his title, *Dimporphos* - a god of two-forms.

---

[18] Carl Trueman says identitarians "take pride in their sexual identity, even consider sexual desire to be an identity." He adds this, "is a deep perversion of what it means to be human" (Pride Month, 2022).

[19] Jung claimed that "Freud's god was *eros*" (Satinover, J., Jungian, 1994), that is, physical, sexual love and desire.

[20] Paul, D. E., Under the Rainbow Banner, June 2020.

[21] The focus on sexuality is a result of "three evolving stages: first, the self was psychologized; then psychology was sexualized; then, sex was politicized" (Trueman, C., Triumph of the Modern Self, 2020).

In line with his gender-vague theories of deity, Freud claimed his concept of psychoanalyses would "eliminate father-gods through scientific reasoning." But, as Naomi Goldenberg submits, "feminism may prove to be more effective."[22] Dedicated feminists, not least Judith Butler (a progenitor of gender theory) and her circle of third and fourth wave feminists, centre their sex-gender hypotheses on Freudian sexual theories, coupled with the dualist philosophy of cultural Marxist Critical Gender Theory. The popularisation of psychotherapy has brought attention to the 'therapeutic self' – a narcissistic focus on an inner psychological condition. In Carl Trueman's view, this focus has "created a world driven by subjective emotions," leading to the "collapse of traditional, external, anchors of identity – those of religion, nation and family."[23]

Turning Inwards

The narcissistic obsession with neo-Gnostic ideas of self leads to a fresh application, a recapitulation, of Eve's *eritus sicut Deus* (to be like God) heresy. Denigrating God's created *imago Dei* of humankind implies denial of an individual's ordained, sacred, makeup. As a result, narcissists "turn inwards" for identity at a time when, "they desperately need external validation to maintain their precarious sense of themselves."[24] In dismissing objective validation, they reject authentic life found only in the precepts and love of the Divine.

Mini-Gods

Feminists consider traditional sexual ethics hateful, outdated, insulting, restrictive, a demonstration of toxic masculinity, phallocentric and

---

[22] Goldenberg, N. R., Changing of the Gods, 1979.
[23] Trueman, C., Dogma Drives the Christian Life, August, 2021.
[24] Smith, B., The Narcissism of Hyper-Politicism, 2022.

misogynistic – all resulting from the patriarchal influence of the Judeo-Christian God. They remain convinced that biblical principles perpetuate societal power of domineering male clusters. The freedom from sexual bondage enables women to abolish customary sexual norms, and identity, in favour of self-created gender-sexuality, assuming this will bring meaning to their lives. Noelle Mering therefore believes Western culture has become a "society of mini-gods each in pursuit of its own power," for being able to "speak into existence your identity in defiance of any bodily reality…must feel godlike."[25] A sentiment Eve would endorse. The result is that, apart from race, the sex-gender split remains the most pressing public policy issue of a post-truth society.

A Question of Freedom

With right to sexual freedom comes denial of conventional sexual ethics. Here exists a misunderstanding of the concept of freedom, for the right to personal freedom is inextricably constrained by obligation - the obligation to not infringe upon coexistent rights of others. In other words, freedom should be exercised for the common good, the good order, the harmony of others, of society itself.

Isaiah Berlin discussed this concept in his essay, 'Two Concepts of Liberty,' delivered at the University of Oxford in 1958. In short, Berlin distinguished between two forms of freedom: the liberty to do as one liked (negative liberty) and the freedom to do as one ought (positive liberty).[26] The common benefit of society requires personal constraints and the embrace of positive liberty. This will impinge on certain personal freedoms but is an altruistic act in the interests of a free and harmonious

---

[25] Mering, N., Our Rainbow Religion, 2021.
[26] Berlin, I., Two Concepts of Liberty, 1958.

society. Still, ideologues disparage positive freedoms in favour of negative liberty unconducive towards the harmonious order of society, all while averring a motive of social justice under deceptive CRT and DEI acronyms.

Alphabet Recognition

Despite dictatorial behaviour by activists, there is some public support for sex-gender identifiers, meaning those affiliated with the LGBTQ+ acronym. Revealed in a Gallup poll, a "record-high 70% of people in the US support same-sex marriage."[27] With wide public acceptance of sexual immorality, zealots[28] seek to enforce a cultural reorientation[29] of sexuality through promotion of every permutation of sexual appetite. And so, each activist demands their own alphabetical recognisance to affirm a claimed identity. Striving to obtain alphabet recognition for their narrow instance of gender dysphoria emphasises the terminal nature of identity loss for, as Judith Butler perceives identity, "I think that gaining recognition for one's status as a sexual minority is a difficult task…but I would consider it necessary for survival."[30] Tribal, social, and imitation familial membership is achieved by inclusion in the LGBTQ+ adage.

Political Endorsement

Political and legal support is required in order to establish mainstream acceptability for gender identitarians. With legislative endorsement,

---

[27] McCarthy, J., Gallup, 2021.

[28] There are many activist groups, e.g., the GSA Network (Genders & Sexualities Alliances) comprising "student-run organizations that unite LGBT+ and allies to build community and organize issues impacting them" (GSA Network, 2022).

[29] A 2021 Gallup survey indicated "5.6% of American adults identity as LGBT – compared to 4.5% in 2017. Furthermore, nearly 17% of Gen Z adults (born between 1997 – 2002) claim to be LGBT (Gallup, LGBT, 2021).

[30] Butler, J., Gender Trouble, 2007, p. xxvii-viii.

society is forced to condone aberrant sexual and behavioural predilections. Butler admits that a "variable construction of identity is a methodological and normative prerequisite, if not a political goal."

Viewpoints that diverge from Butler's sex-gender theories are dismissed as "anti-feminist, homophobic, and transphobic," while alleging "anti-gender ideology is one of the dominant strains of fascism in our times."[31] Butler's claim is rather ironic for it is the identity cohort themselves who are fascist in repelling criticism of their position. In this manner, coupled with legal and political validation, a form of authoritarian popularism emerges.

Lost Identity

These are but sad examples of lost identity in a confusing[32] world, and suggest desperate attempts to find meaning, purpose, and authenticity through sectarian Alphabet tribes. To gain an atomized individual identity, gender ideologues present ever expanding variations of sexuality. Social norms are challenged to the limit, activists proudly demonstrate their perceived emancipation, their unique sexual identity, and their enigmatic concept of authenticity. Unaware of impending severe psychological damage, they reject their birth physicality, an essential component of the created order.

In by-passing all traditional concepts of identity, extremists are left with a nihilistic worldview leading to personal *angst*, hopelessness,

---

[31] Rusk, A., Prominent Feminist, 2021.

[32] In March 2022, U.K. Shadow Minister for Women and Equalities, Anneliese Dodds, was asked on BBC as to "what is a woman?" She answered, "It does depend what the context is surely." Madelaine Kearns commented, "unfortunately this incoherence carries real-life consequences. In legislation, policies, and rulebooks throughout the Western world, the objective definition of sex is being replaced with the elusive fiction of gender identity" (Kearns, M., What is a Woman, 2022).

confusion, suicidal tendencies, and precarious dependence upon on a narrow identity centred around the Rainbow ('Pride') flag - a clan concept.[33] Yet, security of being is mainly based on individual identity but those of co-mingled or self-chosen gender tend to oscillate between the "psychological and social,"[34] between the therapeutic-self and tribal membership. This circumstance leads to what Trueman labels, "a socially constructed sub-category of humanity," the result of which is a "crisis of anthropology."[35]

Jean Baudrillard, referring to his work 'Rituals of Transparency,' says slogans of postmodernism indicate a crisis of identity and meaning, "I exist, yet I have no name, no meaning, and I have nothing to say." He adds that the "absolute urgency" of the Alphabet tribe is to "verify their existence."[36] Hence, the gathering of vociferous zealots under a Rainbow flag tribal identity in search of sociological factors like connection, cohesion, participation and infrastructure, emotional support, personal identity and, philosophically speaking, ontological security and meaning in life.

A Parallel Reality

Without an acknowledgement and understanding of the divinely ordained character of humanity, the "centre cannot hold" – as per the ominous words of W. B. Yeats in his poem, 'The Second Coming.' Western society, with its Judeo-Christian foundations, is subject to added polarization for the Alphabet assembly believe they alone harbour the true identity of

---

[33] Anthony Mills believes, "the politics of identity is driven by the desire for recognition on the part of those minority groups whose identities have been shaped by a history of marginalization by the majority" (Mills, M. A. Common Good, 2020).

[34] Relojo-Howell, D., Being a Snowflake is Bad for your Mental Health, August 9, 2021.

[35] Trueman, C. R., Christmas Amid Chaos, December 22, 2022.

[36] Baudrillard, J., Ecstasy of Communication: The Rituals of Transparency, 1987, p. 30.

human beings.[37] Estranged from pragmatic moral codes, sectarians remain convinced of the validity of their ideology as seen through a hyper-individualistic, neo-Gnostic, elitism. They are therefore detached from authenticity, subscribing instead to a parallel reality as indicated by Plato in his simile of the cave. Events in the cave revealed, "truth would be literally nothing but the shadows of the images," as stated by protagonists Socrates and Glaucon. The shadows are manipulated by those in authority behind the scenes, as is the situation with activists in society today.

The Pride Flag

Upon legal endorsement of same-sex marriage through the 2015 Supreme Court case of Obergefell versus Hodges, together with the controversial 2020 decision in Bostock versus Clayton County prohibiting discrimination on the basis of sexual identity in any public sphere, the Alphabet family adopted the Pride flag as symbolic of the new civic religion of the USA. By so doing, they indicated primary allegiance to a parochial ideology superseding loyalty to the US national flag, the 'Stars and Stripes.' Biden's administration subsequently ordered US Embassies throughout the world to fly the Pride flag alongside the US national flag, affirming the national importance of Pride ideology.

On the 1st June 2022, and as ordered, the US Embassy at the Vatican displayed the Pride flag "in celebration of the LGBTQIA+ community," right in the heartland of conservative Catholicism. The Pride flag, in such environment, constituted a direct challenge to, and attempted subversion of, the Vatican flag representing conservative Judeo-Christian values. Even so, the situation has deeper implications, for just as the Pride flag

---

[37] James Forgas says these tribal groups "consider their own ideology to be morally absolute" (Populism, p. 7, 2021).

annually celebrates the Alphabet community for the whole month of June, the Vatican also celebrates the month of June as one dedicated to the 'Most Sacred Heart of Jesus.' This is a "devotion which goes to the very heart of Christianity,"[38] says theologian Chad Pecknold. The direct cultural and religious confrontation was made obvious for all to see.

Relegation of the US national flag alongside a sectarian 'Pride' flag in equal hierarchical importance, advertises the priority of the US Administration's ideological strategy over national interest and unity. This rather treasonous act is an insult to the patriotic majority of Americans. The Pride flag proudly "proclaims to the world our new genital dogmas and pelvic creed," scorns Mering.

National unity is a hallmark of American exceptionalism despite diverse characteristics of a multicultural society. While Philip Rieff laments the destruction of traditional sacred symbols,[39] the Alphabet clan created their own "sacred symbol" as replacement, namely the Pride Flag, presenting a façade of national unity when displayed alongside the national flag.

International Recognition

The US administration's demand for international acquiescence to its identity ideology continues unabated. The US called a meeting of the United Nations Security Council – the most crucial UN council – with the proposition, "Integrating the Human Rights of LGBT+ Persons into the Council's Mandate for Maintaining International Peace and Security."

---

[38] Pecknold, C., The Two Cities in June, 2022.

[39] The Alphabet group's misappropriation of the rainbow as an emblem can be considered "Deathworks," that is, the profanation of a sacred symbol. The reason being that the rainbow is considered in the Judeo-Christian tradition to be "a sign of God's love and faithfulness" (Trueman, C., Welcome to Pride Month, 2022).

Reno claims the administration wishes to "strengthen the Rainbow Reich and ensure that it attains global hegemony." He continues, "the US leads an international ideological crusade to conquer the world."[40] All this foolishness while contenders like China, Russia and Iran, with alliances, seek global military dominance. On the other hand, the US tempers its own military prowess through enforced identity requirements resulting in declining numbers of military personnel. The US has created a military power vacuum, enabling the rise of pretenders. In so doing, the US fails to act as a global *katechon* – a biblical concept concerning restraint of evil - and so the international order becomes increasingly unstable.

Unity not Diversity

In Professor Helen Krieble's view, "America's strength and especially its endurance do not spring from its diversity but comes, instead, from its unity."[41] It is this unity that is under treat of schism through allegiance to competing ideologies for the Pride flag represents not societal unity but diversity – a diversity arising from two diametrically opposing concepts. The ideology of Identity Politics supported by a minority of the populace, is the first; the second is founded on Judeo-Christian principles providing justice, ethics, and morality in society. Carl Trueman writes the ubiquitous public display of the Pride Flag, especially during the Pride month of June, "should be particularly egregious to Christians for it is the primary instrument by which the LGBTQ+ movement asserts its ownership of the culture."[42] This is not new, for public immorality comes from an early age (2000 B.C.E.). The first 'Pride day' was mentioned in Genesis 19:4-5, "the

---

[40] Reno, R. R., America's Imperial Ideology, May 2023.
[41] Krieble, H. E., The Things We Believe In, December 10, 2022.
[42] Trueman, C., Welcome to Pride Month, 2022.

men of the city, the men of Sodom, both young and old, all the people to the last man, surrounded the house and called to Lot, "Where are the men who came to you tonight? Bring them out to us, that we may have sex with them." As King Solomon confirms, "there is nothing new under the sun" (Ecc. 1:9).

CHAPTER SIX
PART FIVE

THE CULTURAL REVOLUTION

"The culture dominant in the West today teaches that the creation of life
is ours to control; more precisely, that it is for women to control"
(Mary Eberstadt, 2022)

6.8. Feminism and Abortion

Feminist rights to abortion are expressed through slogans like 'women's rights are human rights,' 'my body, my choice,' and 'abortion rights are women's rights.' In a just and equitable society, principally one established on biblical norms, the right to life is paramount with innocent human life protected in law. These elementary ethical values are repeated in every significant Judeo-Christian Creed and Confession of Faith through the ages. They are also included in a Preamble to the American 'Declaration of Independence' of 1776 which reads, "We hold these truths to be self-evident, that all men are created equal, that they are endowed by their Creator with certain unalienable Rights, that among these are Life, Liberty and the pursuit of happiness." The principles were later integrated into the US Constitution and Bill of Rights which influenced other Western nations. The founding documents of the USA reflect these biblical principles, with early pioneers being Protestant Puritans, initially of the 1620 Mayflower arrival.

The Issue of Personhood

The biblical position is that unborn children are considered persons, as these passages indicate:

- All human beings are created in the image of God (*imago Dei*) and have equal value (Gen. 1:26);
- The developing fetus in Hagar's womb was understood to be a child (Gen. 16:11);
- God revealed to the prophet Jeremiah (1:5) that, "Before I formed you in the womb, I knew you and before you were born, I consecrated you; I appointed you a prophet to the nations;"
- In Psalm 139:15-16, King David acknowledges, "Your eyes saw my unframed substance;"
- The prophet Isaiah writes, "The Lord called me from the womb, from the body of my mother he named my name" (49:1-5);
- The unborn child to be John the Baptist, "leaped for joy" in the womb upon his mother, Elizabeth, receiving Mary's greeting (Luke 1:41; 1:31-35);
- Paul was destined for Kingdom work before birth (Gal. 1:15);
- Genesis 25:21-22 regards the unborn as children within the pregnant mother, "The children struggled together within her" (that is, Rebekah).

These doctrines are validated by established science which confirms life commences at conception, and so an unborn baby is fully human though still growing. This fact is made clear in the authoritative medical text, 'The Developing Human,' which explains, "Human development begins at fertilization… and a totipotent cell marks the beginning of each of us as a unique individual."[1] In support, Dr. Matthews-Roth of the prestigious Harvard University Medical School says, "It is scientifically correct to say that an individual human life begins at conception, and this developing human always is a member of our species in all stages of its

---

[1] Moore, K., The Developing Human, 1998, p. 18.

life."[2] As with the mother and father, a fetus has equal human rights, so the termination of an unborn child is both a religious and a human rights issue - principles disdained by identitarians.

Personhood at Conception

Through a cognitive disconnect of the scientific and biological fact that a child acquires life at conception, pro-abortion supporters argue identity as a human being is only conferred at birth. Yet the fetal person has a unique, different, genetic identity to the mother and father, despite some commonality. Even prior to six weeks, evidence indicates heartbeat and a complex human form with functioning organs.

The egregious practise of full-term abortion involves legal euthanasia of a child up to birth, and constitutes gross violence, murder in fact, against the nascent child. Similarly, in earlier term abortion should an aborted fetal infant remain alive, the child is left to die without medical intervention or basic palliative care.

Equally concerning, there is a widespread and profitable trade in aborted children's body parts sanctioned by the US Federal Government and conducted by the major abortion provider in the USA, Planned Parenthood. Administrations of the Democratic Party are the primary instigators of malignant policies like abortion until full term, with no compulsory medical care for children surviving these violent assaults upon them. In their view, abortion is essential in ensuring equal rights for women, promoting the claim that women's rights are civil and human rights. Polarity surrounding fetal right to life is stark, as some 70% of Republicans approve the June 2022 Supreme Court decision in the Dobbs

---

[2] Stark, P., Biology Textbooks, 2019.

trial, overruling Roe v. Wade, in which a national right to abortion was first legalized. On the other hand, 82% of Democrats favour abortion and disapprove of the Dobbs decision.

Abortion Policy

Policies approving abortion derive in part from hostility against a perceived patriarchal system dominating women's rights. These policies reflect a neo-Marxian class-struggle but adapted for gender equality, coupled to an ancient pagan concept of dualism between spirit and body. The position, it seems, of radical feminism is that although a fetal organism exists during gestation, it is piecemeal and undergoing a process of gradual formation. The pre-born child cannot be classified a human being during this process. Subsequently, the real, distinctive person, the true self and true persona, only comes into existence upon arrival of self-consciousness at some unknown stage after birth. Here, Paul Stark writes that "women see the path to personhood as a gradual one."[3]

Despite scientific and biological verification of individual identity of fetal humans, abortion actors insist personhood is conferred only after birth. Fetal infants are thus not entitled to the same rights, dignity, or intrinsic worth as born-alive infants. This dualist ideology provides justification for a woman's right to liquidate the life of her preborn child. It was Paul Johnson who cautioned about "the spread of ideologies based on the proposition that ideas matter more than people."[4] Abortion is a prime example of the validity of this warning.

---

[3] Stark, P., Unborn Children Aren't Constructed, May 12, 2021.
[4] Johnson, P. B., The Human Race: Success or Failure? November, 2006.

My Body, My Choice

Coexistent with the power maxim that 'women's rights are civil and human rights' and abortion is 'women's health care,' is the interconnected slogan of 'my body, my choice.' All these claims reflect the same position, namely, gestating women alone have the power and authority to make decisions regarding their physical body. In most circumstances the adage is understandable, for example, when applied to personal health care, but not when it infringes upon co-existent rights to life of a fetal child. The "my body, my choice" demand is utilised in justifying assault upon an unborn child, whose rights of existence are denied. Freedom of choice needs to be balanced with the associated rights of others, in this case, the fetus' right to life. Termination of a defenceless life is the most drastic and egregious action imaginable in a humane society but the problem is that there is no entity legally authorised to represent the unborn child except the mother. The father is unable to legally prevent a pregnant mother terminating the pregnancy.

In the 2022 Dobbs Supreme Court decision overruling a national right to abortion, the Court did not address the essential issue of whether or not a fetus constitutes a legal person. In this context, law professor Gerald Bradley comments, "Dobb's silence about whether the unborn count as constitutional persons deserves criticism. Even so, the only coherent reading of the majority opinion is that abortion kills a living human individual."[5] Nonetheless, the future of this vital question remains uncertain in U.S. law.

---

[5] Bradley, G. V., Downstream, October 2022.

Spirit, Soul, and Body

According to biblical theology, a human being carries the image of God and comprises an integrated unity of "spirit and soul and body," with importance also ascribed to the physical body as a "Temple of the Holy Spirit." The body is a container through which disciples of God are urged to worship him, "so glorify God in your body," writes the Apostle Paul.[6] Once the *imago Dei* is ignored then a secular creation is required to replace identity lost. The confused world of feminist theory is exposed when they separate component parts of the self to justify their ideological stance. The reality is that neither the dualism of the body-spirit proposition, nor the materialism of evolution theory, are rational. While the unborn child comes into being at conception, conferring personhood, there is a pre-existing eternal, ethereal, and transcendent facet of personhood, namely, the soul-spirit. This sacred spirit-soul emanates from the Divine in eternity past in accordance with his salvific purpose, but in unity with the physical body comprises the identity of a human being.

Feminist abortion theory imitates ancient Greek Gnostic body-spirit dichotomism adapted to suit by cultural Marxian and other hypothetical proposals. It therefore defeats the dualistic theories of the pro-abortion lobby that, in the face of overwhelming scientific proof, a fully human being comes into existence upon fertilisation. Resultantly, the unborn child is not to be considered human only after birth and vague arrival of self-consciousness. The mortal price of feminist claims to the creative power of their ego-centric sovereign-selves is the death of another human being, even if not yet born. In light of scientific evidence, the unborn child is not mere tissue to be discharged at will. Even allowing for purposed cognitive

---

[6] 1 Corinthians 6:19-20.

disconnect from reality, it is clear the issue of abortion is not about women's rights but about women's empowerment – power for its own sake, irrespective of the deadly cost to innocent and defenceless pre-natal and neonatal children.

Fathers' Rights

Despite a father's right to exercise parental care over his child, he cannot legally veto the mother's abortion decision. The unborn child can be destroyed without his consent. In the 1992 case of Planned Parenthood versus Casey, the majority opinion of the Court held it was not mandatory for women to notify their husbands of a pending abortion. But by 2005, the majority consensus of US public opinion was such that fathers should be notified about the prospective mother's planned abortion. The legal implication is that upon notification, the father of the fetal human could take action to protect his and the child's rights. The advance of DNA testing removes reservations concerning identity of the biological father of a preborn infant.

A decision by the Supreme Court would be necessary to define a father's rights nationally, but judicial decisions or legislation at State level could initially deal with the situation. In the interim, to the dismay of prospective fathers, they do not have the right of veto and continue to undergo deep emotional pain. Research indicates "71% of men suffer emotionally after an abortion of their child, including 33% of pro-choice men." These men, even if they fully supported their partner's decision, suffer anger, grief, and other negative emotions when thinking about their child they never got to know."[7] Remedial legislation is long overdue.

---

[7] Mayo, G., Support After Abortion Institute: Abortion's Long-Term Negative Impact on Men, April 2023, pp. 3, 6ff.

Fiction of Abortion Rights

The right to destroy an unborn child is based on secular humanist and pagan practices, briefly explained as follows:

- The secular humanist assertion of a creative imperial-self leads to a subjective stance on morality and ethical concerns;
- The neo-Gnostic dualist theory of the spirit (the true self) and the inconsequential physical body, enable the idea that personhood only manifests on advent of self-consciousness in a born child. In this view, an unborn fetus is disposable;
- At the core of abortion practices are diabolical spiritual forces intent on destroying the pinnacle of God's creation, the human beings made in his image. These evil forces empower atheistic, nihilistic, and heretical ideologies.

The first two issues are reflective of the human search for identity and meaning outside a conferred *imago Dei*. The third is the underlying Satanic force motivating all human resistance to the Creator and his dynamic redemptive program. This spiritual assault is to be expected for, after all, Satan is the "prince of the power of the air;" "the spirit that is now at work in the sons of disobedience" (Eph. 2:2); the "rulers of this age" (1 Cor. 2:8), and who is the "spirit of the world" (1 Cor. 2:12). His evil spirit does not operate in a vacuum as is evident from the Garden scenario, but through willing agents such as Judas Iscariot and numerous personages through the ages and, no doubt unwittingly, those aligned with abortion, euthanasia and eugenics in present society.

Women's Rights are Civil Rights

Feminists claim their rights are civil (and human) rights. While there is truth to this, it is simply part of a larger view for all human beings have equal civil rights. Women certainly have rights, but so do unborn humans they might be gestating as so do fathers of expected children.

All representations of human society are entitled to equal rights, the mother, child and father, but there must be a balance between the articulation of such rights and the coexistent rights of others. This is even more so with intentional euthanasia of fetal humans, euphemistically labelled abortion.

The feminist right to abortion is likewise based on women's claim to health care rights. Here, there is no hint of altruism or self-abnegation in the reasoning of a gestating mother aborting her unborn baby, despite heartbeat and other scientific factors confirming viable life. It is difficult to conceive that, other for a rare therapeutic reason where possibly the mother's life could be in danger should the pregnancy go to term – and even that exception is open to debate - the wholesale slaughter of innocent preborn infants can be designated health care, or women's reproductive health care. It is on record that during 2019, 30,000 US Medical Doctors supported the proposed 'Born-Alive Abortion Survivors Protection Act,' declaring it was never necessary to intentionally terminate a fetal human being to ensure the life of the mother. The Statement represented the stance of numerous medical practitioners' organisations such as the American College of Paediatricians. These Hippocratic oath-adherent practitioners clarified their standpoint by stressing certain truths:

- "It is an undisputed scientific fact that a distinct, living, human being exists in the womb of a pregnant mother." From the "moment of fertilization and for 20 weeks thereafter, it is never necessary to kill a fetal human being to save the mother's life, although an extremely rare possibility can exist prior thereto;"
- "Abortion is not healthcare, much less an essential part of women's health care, and abortions in the third trimester are not done to save a woman's life;"
- "No matter circumstances of their birth, infants who are born alive must be given appropriate medical care;"

- "There is no scientific or legal reason to distinguish between human beings born-alive after an attempted abortion, and human beings born after a planned live birth."[8]

Rights of the Unborn

In early 2023, certain legal events took place giving new hope to the issue of an unborn person's rights. Firstly, at national level, legislation was brought before the Senate in the form of Bill H. R. 26, named the 'Born-Alive Abortion Survivors Act.' Awaiting final enactment during the 119th Congress, the Bill "affirms that there is, after a failed abortion, a human being who has an equal right (to life)."[9] Failure to adhere to the Act brings stringent civil and criminal sanctions. Credit must be given to Professor Hedley Arkes for his sterling work in persisting with this Bill which effectively recognizes the legal personhood of those that survive abortion attempts, and thus of all unborn persons.

Secondly, at State level, the Massachusetts Supreme Judicial Court ruled, on February 14, 2023, that "an unborn baby killed as the result of the homicide of a pregnant woman is entitled to personhood rights."[10] Thirdly, although a little while back but again at State level, the Alabama Supreme Court held, "unborn children are persons entitled to the full and equal protection of the law."[11] These are important developments towards a wider acknowledgment of the unborn as persons with full legal rights, including the right of life.

---

[8] Harrison, D., A Fetal Human Being, 2019.
[9] Forte, D. F., Justice Alito, January 28, 2023.
[10] Commonwealth of Massachusetts v. P. Ronchi, February 14, 2023, SJS-13043; Kumar, A., Personhood, Feb. 20, 2023.
[11] Supreme Court of Alabama, Ex Parte J. L. Phillips, #1160403, October 19, 2018.

Emotional Damage

The emotional and psychological cost of abortion upon the well-being of women has been quantified by a US organisation, 'Advancing New Standards in Reproductive Health.' They concede 58% of women undergoing an abortion experience psychological stress, "from some level of attachment to their pregnancies;" while 64% of aborting women "feel pressure by others to abort." It is a natural physiological and neurochemical process for women to feel emotional attachment to their unborn child, with psychological damage occurring from conscious termination.

Consequently, 64% of women are concerned about "ending a potential life;" and 70% experience doubt about undergoing abortion. In short, the vast majority of aborting women, "are at elevated risk of negative emotional reactions after their abortions," including "regret, grief, loss, depression, sleep disorders, substance abuse and a host of other problems."[12] Emotional damage is understandable for studies show remnants of the child's DNA remain within the mother for some years, a factor described as "fetal microchimerism." These are perturbing discoveries especially as 25% of all American women will have an abortion before the age of 45 years," according to the world's chief abortion provider, Planned Parenthood. With the demise of federally sanctioned abortion, the onus is now on individual States to continue the struggle in eliminating this reprehensible practice.

---

[12] Reardon, D., A Minority of Abortions, 2021.

About Fathers

Studies reveal the significant emotional and psychological cost on fathers of a terminated child. Naturally, many fathers are highly distressed at the prospect of abortion, especially at their powerlessness of legal prevention. The rights and holistic well-being of fathers are completely dismissed in the abortion controversy. The US Supreme Court (in the case of Planned Parenthood of Missouri v. Danforth, 1976), overruled State laws requiring fathers to be notified in the event of a proposed abortion by the prospective mother. The situation is the same in the UK. The emotional impact on fathers remains severe. Even 40 years ago, in 1983, a study was undertaken of the psychological effects on a father of his aborted child. Research indicated that due to termination, "persecutory or depressive anxiety and psychosomatic symptoms" may manifest in fathers for, "fatherhood causes deep personal and social changes and variances."[13]

Chemical Abortion

Statistics of abortion are disturbing. In the US, in excess of 63 million unborn children were legally terminated by medical or surgical abortion during the period 1973 – 2018. Specific figures for chemical abortions are unknown as most such abortions take place in private, with drugs ordered online or purchased over-counter. It is estimated that more "than half of all abortions in the US are now performed via chemical-abortion pills."[14] Due to significant pro-life backlash, the largest pharmaceutical chain, Walgreens, undertook not to dispense abortion pills in over 20 Republican dominated States, even though it remained legal to do so.

---

[13] Benvenuti, P., Abortion and the Man, 1983.
[14] Blaff, A., AOC, Leading Democrats Call on White House to Ignore Abortion Pill Injunction, April 8, 2023.

In legal action[15] instigated by the public action group 'Alliance Defending Freedom' (ADF) in April 2023, a Federal Court ruled against FDA's (US Food and Drug Administration) approval of the two primary chemical abortion pills, thereby outlawing them nationwide. The Administration's Department of Justice immediately challenged this ruling and the legal process will continue relentlessly until it arrives at the Supreme Court. In this event, a final decision will only occur in 2024 or later. The ADF's Erin Hawley argues the FDA "never had authority to approve the two-pill chemical-abortion regiment[16] when it did so nearly 25 years ago." She explains approval was granted on the irrational grounds that the pills were to be used for "serious or life-threatening illness," neither of which describes pregnancy being a "natural biological condition."[17]

At State level, pro-life legislation in Texas known as the 'Women and Child Safety Act,' has far-reaching consequences not only for physical abortion but internet-based abortion pill distributors. The motivating basis of the law is set out in the Preamble to the Act which declares, firstly, "human life begins at fertilization;" secondly, "abortion is a murderous act of violence that purposefully and knowingly terminates a life in the womb;" and thirdly, "unborn human beings are entitled to the full and equal protection of the laws that prohibit violence against other human beings."[18] During the period of Roe versus Wade, some 48 so-called 'sanctuary cities' in Texas protected the unborn within their local districts.

---

[15] Alliance for Hippocratic Medicine v. U.S. Food and Drug Administration.
[16] Mifepristone and Misoprostol.
[17] Mills, R., Fifth Circuit Strikes Down FDA Approval, August 16, 2023.
[18] H.B. 2690, effective September 1, 2023.

With the demise of Roe v. Wade, resistance to abortion at both local and State level throughout the nation is escalating.

On the international scene, surveys reveal 75% of abortions in England and Wales are legally performed at home through chemical abortion pills, amounting to over 185,000 annual occurrences. In these instances which are conducted in private without medical supervision, it is the woman herself who is responsible for her own health. However, since 2019, over 30,000 women have "suffered complications and required medical intervention at their local state hospital." Statistically there is a "one in 20 risk"[19] of home abortion failing, resulting in essential hospital treatment.

General Abortion Statistics

From a high of 1.5 million annually, US legal abortions have decreased. In 2020, a figure of 930,000 abortions were recorded. Internationally, in the Republic of Ireland for instance, the Department of Health confirmed 13,709 unborn humans have been killed through abortion since January 1, 2019 (to June 2021), when abortion was first legalised. Between January and December 2020, 6,577 abortions took place there, the vast majority (6,455) categorised as "early pregnancy," often a euphemism for abortion as a form of contraception. Overall, it is estimated that 50 million induced abortions annually occur worldwide, some 25% of all pregnancies. Abortion is rated "the leading cause of death worldwide for a third year in a row."[20] Terminating millions of innocent and defenceless unborn human beings is a diabolical and inhumane act. This is especially so as in the UK,

---

[19] Duffy, K., At-Home Abortions Putting Women at Risk, July 14, 2023.
[20] Foley, R., Abortion Leading Cause of Death, 2022.

for instance, over 100,000 abortions annually are repeat abortions.[21] This implies abortion is used as a form of birth control. Failure to take simple precautions against pregnancy results in death of a pre-born child.

Fetal Death

The 'Journal of Medical Ethics' reveals unborn children feel pain during the termination process, even at 24 weeks and probably as early as 13 weeks when most terminations occur. The method of fetal death is described as follows, "an injection of potassium chloride directly into the fetal heart or an injection of digoxin directly into the fetus or intra-amniotically." When done surgically via a dilation and evacuation ("D & E") procedure, the "fetus is removed in pieces via several surgical manoeuvres using grasping forceps. Fetal death follows either direct feticide performed before the D & C or trauma results in the death of the fetus."[22]

Taking into account that heartbeat can be detected as early as 3-6 weeks after conception, this description of fetal termination can only be described as sanctioned torture and murder. The participants conspire against the rights of a living, sentient, human being - a child deprived of the right to life without legal or ethical consequence for the perpetrators. Such act is clearly *malum in re* (an evil, inherently wrong act), and against natural law precepts.

Whereas legislation exists in the UK and elsewhere that an animal fetus is entitled to a humane destruction, no such requirement exists for unborn human beings, the pinnacle of creation. A devastating indictment of modernist societies, influenced by atheistic nihilists. The description by

---

[21] Christian Today, March for Life UK, September 4, 2023.
[22] Derbyshire, S. W., Fetal Pain, 2020, p. 3.

Pope John Paul II of a "culture of death" well describes the "various scientific and commercial currents that, in the false name of progress, encourage hideous abuses against mankind."[23] This statement provides a graphic view of the mortal threat facing so many members of society through abortion, eugenics and euthanasia.

Trade in Fetal Bodies

Allied with abortion is the trade in fetal body parts harvested for financial reasons. Video evidence provided by investigative journalist, David Daleiden, showed the dealing in bodies of aborted infants. The videos prove even neonates, those born alive, "are vivisected for their organs" while "abortionists altered procedures to procure more commercially valuable fetal organs and parts." The "altered abortion procedures were even done with the intended result of delivering fully intact fetuses, some of whose hearts were still beating," says Daleiden. The Thomas More Society, a public interest law firm which represents Daleiden, confirms that through hidden video recordings Daleiden "uncovered evidence of infants born alive and vivisected for their organs, illegal partial birth abortions, and a host of financial and ethical violations relating to the illegal trafficking in aborted baby body parts."[24]

At the University of California San Francisco, a State institution, researchers engaged in commercial trade of body parts of aborted children, especially children's genitalia, kidneys, and bladders. Apparently in the name of science and finance, respect and dignity of the deceased is not a consideration. The lack of basic human rights, and the ignoring of all

---

[23] Cotton, T., The Pro-Life Movement, 2021.
[24] In 2022 a U.S. Court fined Daleiden $2.4 million for illegally obtaining and disclosing confidential information.

moral codes and traditional natural law precepts, is especially concerning in a seemingly civilized environment.

Similarly, at the University's affiliated 'Women's Options Centers,' "labour induction abortion techniques often resulted in live births." In a disturbing admission, the University confirmed they do not have protocols for "verifying signs of life or handling live birth scenarios," despite admitting that "live births do sometimes occur during abortion procedures."[25] In other words, the University pleads ignorance as to what to do in the case of live births due to a lack of procedures – this, in a medical facility. Consequently, neonates are left to perish without palliative care like Roman era exposure of unwanted babies, some 2,000 years ago.

Commercial trade in unborn children's body parts is unsurprising for such trade is an extension of the abortion industry, itself a commercial enterprise headed by profitable conglomerates. The ideology behind this pernicious trade originates from Eve's heretical assertion of creative license. Feminist ideologues claim primacy of women's health care and women's rights irrespective of a fetal baby's well-being and right to life.

6.9. Eugenics and Euthanasia

Due to denial of the intrinsic dignity, equality, and value of each human being made in the image of the Creator, individuals are now viewed in social, economic, and philosophical terms rather than theologically, with inherent natural rights. To dismiss the value of the individual, first the Fatherhood of God concept needs to be eradicated for only then will the ensuing *imago Dei* of humankind be invalidated. Dualist hypotheses,

---

[25] Gryboski, M., Callous Experiments, 2021.

resulting in immoral subjectivist values, are embraced by activists claiming irrelevance of the body. It is then a short step towards abortion, eugenics, and euthanasia and, by extension, assisted suicide.

Practical Eugenics

In the current 'culture of death' era, eugenical practice severely affects unborn children diagnosed with Down's Syndrome, children with an extra chromosome 21. Overwhelmingly, Down's persons lead a content and fulfilled life. A study in the 'Journal of Medical Genetics' of the self-perceptions of Down's afflicted persons aged over 12 years, indicated that 99% are well satisfied with their lives; 97% liked who they are; 96% liked how they looked; 99% declared a love for their families; 79% of parents "had a positive outlook on life because of their life" with a Down's child; 99% of parents loved their child; and 97% of parents were proud of their Downs child.[26]

Medical practitioners in most Western countries advise termination of a potential Down's child. The UK for example, permits this practice at any stage up to the time of birth - a living, fully-fledged and developed child killed at time of birth. This also applies to unborn babies suspected of any deformity such as club feet or cleft palate - hardly lethal or serious issues under normal circumstances and quite easily remediated. In Canada, sex selection is a permissible reason for abortion. If prospective parents do not desire a child of a particular binary gender, they simply destroy the child and try new pregnancies until they obtain a fetal human with the desired gender. The essential characteristics of a human being such as care, love,

---

[26] Skotko, B. G, Levine S. P, & Goldstein R., Self-perceptions from People with Down Syndrome, Medical Genetics, 2011, Part A, Vol. 155, No. 10, pp. 2360–2369.

dignity, respect, empathy, kindness, and compassion, are unimportant in the quest for a perfect, problem-free, child.

Voluntary Euthanasia

Netherlands law allows any person older than 12 years to consent to euthanasia, but plans are ahead to permit anyone between 1 and 12 years to be euthanised on grounds of terminal illness. Over 8,000 people were euthanised there during 2022, comprising 5% of all deaths, and increasing annually. In Australia, all States but one, enacted legislation permitting euthanasia and voluntary suicide. In the UK, the advance of voluntary euthanasia raises concerns among disabled persons, an imperilled fringe group whose organisations are not consulted on proposed legislation. The Scottish Daily Mail revealed a survey that showed, "Only one in five older people feel valued, while more than a third believe they are a burden."[27]

In Canada, assisted suicide and euthanasia was legalised in 2016. A report disclosed "disabled Canadians are told to kill themselves by bureaucrats and there are plans to extend euthanasia access to the mentally ill and mature minors."[28] Canada leads the world in number of persons euthanised annually. Official statistics revealed "medically assisted deaths from 2016 to 2021" came to 32,000, which number is predicted to increase by over 30% annually.[29] In the few years that physician-assisted killing has been permitted, Canadian law has "enabled the killing of the poor and the disabled precisely because they are poor and disabled."[30] A slippery slope emerges, leading to possibilities for future economic euthanasia.

---

[27] Scottish Daily Mail, September 15, 2021.
[28] Yuan Yi Zhu, The Dark Side of Canada's Euthanasia Policy, December 20, 2022.
[29] Government of Canada, 3rd Annual Report on Medically Assisted Dying, 2021.
[30] Camosy, C. C., A Glimpse into a Post-Christian Future: Public Support for Killing the Poor and Disabled, June 12, 2023.

In Belgium, the situation is equally egregious for in 2014 it became legal for persons of all ages to undergo voluntary euthanasia for the purposes of alleviate suffering - a subjective determination, albeit aided by medical indicators. Persons have been euthanised for "depression, blindness, deafness, gender-identity crisis and anorexia."[31] In 2021, it was estimated "nearly one in five people euthanised were not likely to die naturally in the immediate future."[32] Internationally, the 'culture of death' escalates relentlessly.

Dominion Over Creation

Eradicating ever-increasing categories of human beings indicates a short step from voluntary to mandatory euthanasia of those deemed a burden to society. The philosophical seeds of such immoral and unethical ideologies already exist. The practice of selective life is at its core a fresh application of Eve's desire for creative dominion, the power of life and death, 'to be like God' (*eritus sicut Deus*), in Genesis 3:5. It is also belief in irrelevance of the physical body as corrupted matter, in contrast to the essence of personhood, namely, the spirit-mind complex. The duality theory is noticeable in the grey area of dementia or mental disability where euthanasia is proposed on the understanding that once the mind-spirit ceases to function, the essence of human identity is lost and the body can be disposed of.

Contrary to Moral Law

Euthanasia and assisted suicide are contrary to the biblical doctrines upon which Western societies are founded. The Edenic influence continues in

---

[31] Mildred, J., Euthanasia, 2021.
[32] Del Turco, A., Belgium, 2022.

ever expanding measure through abortion and the eugenical adjunct of euthanasia. The evil onslaught against the nuclear family comes from the wicked strategy of the serpent to firstly, destroy the relationship of the First Couple with their Creator and to introduce mortality to humankind; secondly, to destroy the matrimonial and filial interdependent relationship between Adam and Eve themselves; and thirdly, to destroy the family unit and thus society. In such manner, have societies become ethically and morally corrupted.

CHAPTER SIX
PART SIX

THE CULTURAL REVOLUTION

"I celebrate myself, and sing myself; And what I assume you shall assume:
For every atom belonging to me as good belongs to you"
(Walt Whitman, Song of Myself, 1892)

6.10. The Issue of Transgenderism

Sex-gender ideology has led to unexpected consequences for feminists who are challenged by the political and social advantages of those persons, both male and female, identifying as transgender.[1] These advantages supersede existing women's rights and protections, resulting in feminists viewing the legal primacy of transgender persons as an "erasure of women."[2] There is much truth in that assessment for transgenderism (when biological males masquerade as women) is not only misogynous, but a prime instance of toxic masculinity. For instance, in competitive sport a biological male identifying as a female can legitimately participate in female-only events. Consequently, due to superior physical strength, biological men triumph in sports previously reserved for natural-born women.

---

[1] Transgenderism "is associated with gender dysphoria, a disabling condition in which the discordance between a person's natal sex (that assigned to them at birth) and (desired) gender identity results in distress, high rates of self-harm, suicidality and function impairment" (Joseph, Cliffe et al, The Transgender Patient, 2017, p. 144).
[2] Hartline, J., Refuse to Consent to Erasure of Women, 2022.

This anomaly is sanctioned by the International Olympic Committee ("IOC") for at the 2020/2021 Tokyo games, biological men participated in women-only events outraging competitors and spectators. In the female-only category of the London Marathon, a natural-born male (a transgender runner) won the event against 14,000 females despite competing as a man in the New York City marathon six months earlier, finishing unplaced.[3] Some 70% of the general public strongly disagree with biological men participating in female-only events, and over 25 US States prohibit this practice.[4]

The erasure of protections for women continues unabated. In female-only prisons and shelters for vulnerable women survivors of domestic violence, biological men are permitted access upon self-identifying as female. The absurdity continues, a transgender man was crowned Miss Netherlands 2023 in the national female beauty pageant. The winner is eligible to enter the Miss Universe contest. Meanwhile, in a private, female only California Spa, a transgender man paraded naked in front of women, many being mothers with young girls. When reported to the Press, the Los Angeles Times board defended the man,[5] as did the management of the Spa, arguing he was legally entitled to be there as he self-identified as female.

Transgender Irrationality

The refusal to face gender realism is evident in the UK also. Scottish Police "record alleged rapes by offenders, with male genitalia, as committed by a woman if the attacker identifies as female." Justification is provided by

---

[3] Downey, C., Trans Marathoner Defeats 14,000 Women, April 25, 2023.
[4] Foley, R., Americans Oppose Men in Women's Sports, June 14, 2023.
[5] Brown, M., Radical Transgender Activism, 2021.

the Sexual Offences (Scotland) Act of 2009 where rape is defined as "non-consensual penetration by a penis." Therefore, the official reasoning goes, it cannot be committed by someone without a penis, like a transgender, and so rape could not have been be possible. This deduction is arrived at despite the fact that transgenders are biological men, generally with full genitalia. This absurd fiction, devoid of realism, was criticised by Ken MacAskill, a former Justice Secretary, who exclaimed, "I have seen some legal absurdities but this tops it all and is dangerous... it is all about dogma overriding common sense. Women are harmed by this."

A precedent for transgender men transferring to women-only prisons was established in California when, upon promulgation of relevant civil codes, 255 biological male prisoners immediately identified as women and claimed the right to lodge in women-only facilities. Expectedly, some female prisoners were impregnated by male transgenders. In Wisconsin correctional facilities, for example, of the 161 transgender men identifying as women, 50% have been convicted of sexual abuse or assault. Overall, 47% of US "male trans-identified inmates are sex offenders."[6]

Taking full advantage, 18 biological male political candidates in Mexico registered as transgender women to meet a new constitutional political gender quota. Apparently, power is more attractive than integrity.

Judicial support for the fiction that "human sex is not limited to Biology" was recorded in the U.K. High Court when a Judge pronounced, "Biological men can become women and gain their legal protections."[7] To facilitate the process of gender self-identification, proposed Scottish legislation will allow "every single man to be just a certificate away from

---

[6] Harrington, M., The Statistic No One's Allowed to Study, September, 24, 2023.
[7] Sanderson, D., Human Sex, The Telegraph, December 13, 2022.

being a woman."[8] The British legal system has historically influenced all Commonwealth countries, generally displaying the highest ethical standards and finest legal principles. This reputation is now in serious jeopardy of ridicule.

The absurdity of transgender ideology stretches the imagination of all right-thinking persons. All at once, Hans Christian Andersen's fable of the Emperor and his imaginary clothes, publicly exposed by a truthful, naïve, child, becomes meaningful in this era of relative truth and disconnection from reality. Victor Davis Hanson describes the grave situation facing culture as follows: "The sign of a civilization in headlong decline is its embrace of absurdities."[9] Along the same lines, Rebecca Brown says "Philosophy can make the previously unthinkable thinkable."[10] Both scholars emphasize the irrationality and deficit from reality of identity theories plaguing all sectors of society, with activists demanding political, legal, and social compliance with senseless construals.

Feminism Defeated?

Feminists have succeeded in establishing equality in most areas of public life. Even so, they have lost hard-won gains to transgenders in the areas of sports, female only facilities whether private or public, and political and legal arenas, all of which give patent advantage to transgenders over natural-born females. The situation has led to righteous indignation among feminists who view society as systemically patriarchal in any event. Feminists now find confirmation of their viewpoint when a male claims

---

[8] Scotland's 'Gender Recognition Reform Bill' "removes the need for a medical diagnosis of gender dysphoria in order to receive a gender recognition certificate". (Osborne, S., Controversial Gender Legislation, December 21, 2022).
[9] Hanson, V. D., The Absurdities of our Age, May 21, 2023.
[10] Brown, R., Philosophy, January 27, 2019.

identity as female and takes full advantage of women-only protections.[11] In the opinion of feminists, such person should be categorised as a biological male for, "a male who could opt into a female identity is just another iteration of male entitlement and supremacy."[12] A reasonable assumption.

To counter growing political and legal endorsement of transgenderism, the UK 'Women's Human Rights Campaign,' launched an international effort, supported by co-ordinators in over thirty countries, demanding a multilingual Bill of Rights titled 'Women Based on Biological Sex.' The Bill includes statements like "men whose gender identity is female should not be categorised as female in the context of women's rights." David Seminara, referring to transgenders, writes "Members of the LGBT community are now often eligible for the same sort of hiring, promotion, supplier diversity, and other preferences once available only to women, non-whites, the disabled and veterans."[13] An article in the Washington University Law Review introduced the label, 'Gayffirmation Action,' in describing the preferential process available to transgenders. In the result, natural-born women are unjustly discriminated against.

Transgender Ideology

Transgender ideology is focused on an illusory neo-Gnostic dualism between the physical and the metaphysical, coupled to claimed creative authority in a contemporary version of Edenic self-deification. This

---

[11] Carl Trueman claims "transgender theory is arguably one of the most effective male confidence tricks in recent history: nothing that women can lay claim to as women is now off-limits to men" (Trueman, Liturgy, 2022). All the societal gains that women have strived for are under threat from men masquerading as women.

[12] Favale, A., Feminism's Last Battle, 2021.

[13] Seminara, D., Straight White Males Encouraged Not to Apply, December 19, 2022.

construct leads to a fabrication not unlike Harari's *homo deus* – a god-man. Radical feminist ideology endorses transgender theory, having as its objective "a metaphysical rebellion"[14] against the body conferred at birth. Trans-inclusive feminists regard female gender identity as comprising, "her innermost concept of being female."[15] This claim, being an illusory self-identification, leads to the absurd reasoning that a biological male "who identifies as a woman was never truly male in the first place, but always female." Hence, transgenders can identify as women while remaining biological male.

Legal endorsement of transgenderism is seen in the UK 'Gender Recognition Act' of 2004, authorising a 'Gender Recognition Certificate,' to those with an ideological new self-identity. Along these lines, the UK's 'University and College Union' endorses self-identification in areas of gender, race ('trans-racialism'), and disability. Support is therefore advanced for those claiming a certain ethnic origin, physical, or mental disability, or imagined gender when in reality, whether biologically, ethnically, physically or mentally, that is not the case. This situation causes complexities relating to exclusive access and participation, minority rights, financial claims, compensations and assistance, and results in special dispensations for a self-identifying cohort. Representing over 130,000 University and College staff, the Union's position is foreseeable for a survey estimates some 80% of British Academics are leftists.[16]

The prestigious UK Cambridge Dictionary compromised its fine reputation when defining a woman as, "an adult who lives and identifies as a female though they may have been said to have a different sex at

---

[14] Reno, R., Transgenderism Escaping Limits, 2022.
[15] Favale, A., Feminism's Last battle, 2021.
[16] Turner, C., Eight in Ten Lecturers are Left-Wing, March 2, 2017.

birth." The scene in Europe is similar, with Germany's 'self-declaration' law permitting a chosen gender simply upon declaration.

Gender-Affirming Surgery

In the US, the public health system provides funding for chosen gender reassignment surgery, but this benefit is under legal challenge. The list of States prohibiting harmful reassignment surgery and other medical interventions for youth numbers 22 to date and growing fast. Keen to protect children from exploitation over sex-gender, Alabama, for instance, passed legislation prohibiting, "cross-hormone treatments and destructive experimental surgeries designed to remove healthy body parts of children who are led to believe they are the opposite sex."[17] Not to be outdone, Texas published Bill 14 "outlawing gender-affirming care for minors," with Nebraska following suit with the "Let Them Grow Act' (LB 574)" passed in May 2023, and similarly with North Carolina in August 2023. Needless to say, gender activists launched legal challenges to these laws, with cases ongoing. Until the US Supreme Court intervenes on this prejudicial practice, the struggle continues. The US House of representatives passed a Bill banning trans-identified athletes from competing in women and girl sports, by amending Title IX protections.[18] However, the Bill remains stuck in the Senate where no approval is possible until moderates control the majority of votes, and even thereafter is subject to presidential veto.

Statistics indicate that during the period 2016 to 2019, 48,019 patients in the US alone underwent gender-affirming surgery, with the number

---

[17] Alliance Defending Freedom, May 24, 2023; Alabama Vulnerable Child Compassion & Protection Act (SB. 184, 2022).
[18] Protection of Women and Girls in Sports Act, Bill H. R. 734, April 20, 2023.

escalating annually. Some 57% interventions were for breast and chest procedures and 35% for genital reconstruction. Of the patients, 60% were aged 12 to 30 years.[19] Specifically, Texas-based Dr. Crane performs hundreds of non-binary surgeries whereby he combines male and female genitalia for a single individual. In plain terms, he "creates an artificial penis for a woman while retaining her vagina; or he creates an artificial vagina for a man, while retaining his penis."[20] While the insanity escalates, the vulnerable in society face increasingly deadly ideological assaults upon their birth identity and emotional health.

Research indicates 80% of children presenting with gender identity problems outgrow it by the time of adolescence. However, no "reliable mechanism exists to predict which young people will outgrow their dysphoria and which will persist."[21] This fact is perturbing for it means many children undergo drastic sex-gender surgery unnecessarily as they would, in all probability, outgrow the issue. The woke slogan that "trans kids know who they are" is defeated by convincing scientific research. The residual effect upon these children is severe mental and emotional turmoil. This is particularly so, using the UK as example, when children as young as four years of age are exposed to pro-gay propaganda. In Hull, England, parents removed their young child from school when they discovered she was exposed to a book titled, "Grandad's Pride." The gay promotional book "carries illustrations of homosexual men wearing next to nothing and women posing as men who have undergone surgical mutilation."[22]

---

[19] Wright, J. D., Chen, L., National Estimates of Gender-Affirming Surgery in the US, August 23, 2023.
[20] Rufo, C. R., Barbarism in the Name of Equality, August 24, 2023.
[21] Kaltiala-Heino, R., et al., Gender Dysphoria in Adolescence, March 9, 2018, pp. 31-41.
[22] Brown, M., Feeding Kids Garbage, September 8, 2023.

A Civil Rights Issue

In pronouncing "transgender equality is the civil rights issue of our time,"[23] President Biden signalled his narrow social and ideological priorities which have a perilous effect on society.[24] Likewise, the trans-feminist claim that gender self-identification is "this generations civil rights battle,"[25] finds support in the presidency. The issue is far more complex than a civil rights matter for it reveals a lethal threat to vulnerable persons struggling to find personal identity in a post-truth society, one with deeply flawed, atheistic, and irrational ideologies.

The civil rights issue emanates from the demand that gender self-identifiers be recognised, and their chosen identity endorsed, by mainstream society. These claims have authoritarian overtones, evident in political and legal enforcement despite objections from moderates. The articulation of claimed rights paradoxically requires extrinsic controls of some sort to protect the coexistent rights of others, necessary for the purposes of social harmony and to avoid disorder from unchecked freedom. The contest over conflicting rights of freedom is a source of much litigation.

Silencing Dissenters

Despite affirming academic freedom, it is estimated 279 academics of tertiary education institutions in the USA and Canada alone, have been cancelled to 2023. This number is fast growing, moderating the aims,

---

[23] Biden, J., Tweet on January 25, 2020.
[24] US Attorney-General William Barr, in his 2022 memoir, refutes Biden's view and counters the 'most pressing civil rights issue of our time is that of religious liberty' (Holdenreid, J., The Real Civil Rights Issue, 2022).
[25] Joyce, H., Trans: When Ideology Meets Reality, 2021.

objectives and purposes of academic freedoms such as the free exchange of ideas.

Perhaps one of the most egregious events occurred at Ohio Northern University campus when esteemed law professor, Scott Gerber tenured for 22 years, was escorted from a class he was presenting by campus security officers, with armed local police in assistance, and marched to the Dean's office. He was barred from teaching and banished from campus. The given reason was, "insufficient compliance with the school's Diversity, Equity and Inclusion (DEI) initiatives, to which he had objected publicly, in newspaper op-eds and television interviews."[26] Condemnation of the University's conduct was voiced by more than 50 other professors, and moderate groups like the US National Association of Scholars.

The Freedom of Speech Act

Stimulated by curtailment of academic freedoms on campus, the UK Parliament passed legislation to remedy the situation. The 'Higher Education (Freedom of Speech) Act 2023,' "places a duty on universities to not just protect but to promote academic freedom." The Act establishes an "Academic Freedom Director to monitor university policies," with authority of enforcement. Aside from concerns over possible State overreach into tertiary institutions, the move is commendable in enforcing traditional freedoms, not simply enacting policies and lamenting breach. In cases of continual violation of constitutional freedoms, the promulgation of statutory laws "can be vital for protecting human liberty." This policy emanates from the principle that the State has an important

---

[26] Tapson, M., Kafka Comes to College, May 26, 2023.

function in "limiting private violence in order to guarantee human freedoms."[27]

Similar developments occur in the US where the House passed the "Protection of Women and Girls in Sport Act." The Act effectively changes the Education Amendments of 1972, and thus Title IX laws, in order to "prevent men from competing against women in school sports." While the President exercises veto power over such laws, individual States enact legislation to alleviate this unjust matter.

Butler and Foucault

A miniscule sect of transgender activists dominates the narrative concerning sex and gender. Leading feminist, Judith Butler, cautions that "feminism ought not to idealize certain expressions of gender that in turn produce new forms of hierarchy and exclusion." The purpose of her remark is to ensure no solitary gender classification be advantaged over another. Even so, Butler supports the sex-gender dichotomy underlying transgenderism for she avers that, despite the intractability of biological sex, "gender is culturally constructed" and so there exists a "multiple interpretation of sex." In consequence, she says, there is no reason why genders "ought to remain as two."[28] Here, Butler is influenced by the dissolute[29] French philosopher Michel Foucault.[30]

---

[27] Kaufmann, E., Freedom Bill is Pushback Against Illiberalism, May 22, 2023.

[28] Portland Public Schools promote the "infinite gender spectrum," thereby confusing school children (Rufo, C., Portland, 2022).

[29] Foucault enjoyed sadomasochism sex, consumed illegal drugs, and frequented "gay S & M clubs" (Franks, A., Foucault's Principalities and Powers, 2021).

[30] At the time of his death in 1984 at the age of 57, Foucault was regarded as "perhaps the single most famous philosopher in the world – at least in American universities" (Kimball, R., The Perversions of Foucault, 2022).

Foucault was an important advocate of Queer theory (which rejects binary birth sex as normative) adopted by most feminists, and who claimed there exists no realistic biological sex that naturally leads to a definitive gender. For Foucault, sexuality takes on an almost transcendent quality, imparting a faux-divine concept of sacred identity. In the scathing view of Camille Paglia, Foucault is a "cheap cynic;" Derrida an "aggressive deconstructionist;" and their circle of "minor" French theorists, overrated. She claims they have had a "disastrous effect on American education" by "systematically trashing high culture, reducing everything to language and then making language destroy itself,"[31] all in the name of an idealised and unattainable social justice.

A Figurative Family

Identity activists seek a figurative family in replacement of lost familial connection. Hence importance of identity within in a LGBTQ+ family. The significance is that while personal identity is established through appropriation of a chosen gender, group membership with similar gender-identifying individuals is equally important, replacing lost filial structure and connection. Both construals lead to an illusory expression of individual authenticity, and are condemned to failure. The perpetuating of individual loss of meaning through alienation from theistically conferred identity, coupled with adverse emotional effects of a psychological dissonance between a person's natural-born sex and a claimed gender, cannot confer the desired emotional and psychological well-being.[32] The

---

[31] Smith, E. E., The Provocations of Camille Paglia, Summer, 2019.
[32] Almost 50, 000 Americans committed suicide in 2022 (Stobbe, M., US Suicides All-Time High, August 11, 2023).

result is what sociologist Peter Berger describes as modern man's "permanent identity crisis."[33]

6.11. 'Love is Love' and 'Born this Way'

After examining claims that transgender women are natural females and Gay rights are to be considered civil rights, it remains to discuss woke declarations of 'love is love' and 'born this way.' It is on the basis of 'love is love,' coupled with demands for equality, legality, diversity and inclusivity, that LGBTQ+ aims were presented to society at large. In some jurisdictions referendums were held (e.g., Australia). In other nations legislation was simply passed without consulting the populace, often in spite of a majority sector opposing same-sex marriage.[34]

Society generally agrees that 'love is love' for the slogan makes sense and thus assumed valid. Through misguided good faith and naivete, society at large publicly endorsed this claim. Popular acceptance of the cliché also occurred in many Judeo-Christian and institutions. As it turns out, the claim of love is love is simply an opening gambit for political, legal, and moral endorsement of narcissistic sexual lifestyles previously thought peculiar and immoral. Upon social acceptance, criticism of the lifestyle is regarded as hate speech. Practitioners claim the moral high ground based on a victimhood history of discrimination and persecution. Yet, their identity ideology cannot sustain a rational debate for it is based on fragile grounds detached from reality, truth, and established moral rubrics.

---

[33] Berger, P., 1974, p. 78.
[34] In South Africa, 84% of the population condemned homosexual behaviour, describing it as "always wrong" (Smith, T. W., Cross-National, 2011). Even so, Government passed legislation authorising same-sex marriage.

On the face of it, the idea of love is love appears supported in scripture for love is a biblical concept. The English lexicon, unfortunately, has severe shortcomings when describing the emotion of love for the term is imprecise in application. Biblical Greek, to the contrary, has some seven differing expressions of love but only one, *agape*, has relevance to individuals in their relationship with the Creator, being love of a divine nature. By further extension, *agape* has importance to love as between heterosexual couples in an ordained marriage. This concept originates from Adam and Eve's archetypical relationship. In every scriptural instance where love is used to describe interactions between the Messiah and his Church, or interpersonally between his 'new creations,' *agape* alone is recorded. There is one exception, however, when the Apostle Peter after his humiliating failure could not in good conscience claim his reciprocal love for the Messiah was *agape*, replying instead with *philia*.[35]

As a sacrificial, supernatural, divine love emanating from the transcendent power of the Holy Spirit, *agape* has exclusive application to sacred relationships. Unconditional, sacrificial, love says psychoanalyst Erich Fromm, "corresponds to the deepest longing, not only of the child, but of every human being."[36] It is this unique category of love that is innate to and at the core of all humanity, implanted by the Creator himself. Therefore, imitation of this love between persons of the same sex or claimed genders can only be identified as *eros*,[37] meaning, self-centred love expressed in sensual, hedonist, pleasure.

Karl Barth describes *eros*, in contradistinction to *agape*, as a love which, "does not have its origin in self-denial, but in a distinctly uncritical

---

[35] John 21:15-17.
[36] Fromm, E., The Art of Loving, 2006 (1956), p. 39.
[37] Freud considers *eros* essential "life instinct" (Marcuse, H., Eros, 1966, p. viii, p. 78).

intensification and strengthening of natural self-assertion." He continues, *eros* is a love which "man wants for himself," as a "need to express himself," or perhaps even more simply, in the "desire to find satisfaction in all his unrest."[38] In elaboration, Peter Leithart writes this heretical love means "love as enforced tolerance; love as non-judgementalism; love as unqualified acceptance and endorsement; and love enforced by cops in Rainbow uniforms." He believes "liberal love is now the established religion, the public philosophy and ethic, in the US and elsewhere."[39]

Legality and Legitimacy

It needs to be noted that legality and legitimacy are not the same concept. Despite legal and public endorsement of same-sex marriage, the legitimacy of such marriage is open to refutation. The claim that legality confers legitimacy fails in four main senses. First, approval by a public majority cannot in itself accredit legitimacy to ethereal concepts of morality. To the contrary, they require validation through a definitive, universalist, and coherent moral authority, such as those reflected in Judeo-Christian doctrine. Agent-centred, subjective, malleable, moral proposals cannot be considered equivalent to, or an improvement upon, eternal values. Moral paradigms are not able to be invented for they already exist; they therefore cannot be of "human manufacture," as Karl Barth explains.[40]

Secondly, there is the issue of truth. Identitarians embrace effectual truth as sufficient justification for their ideas. Still, the cognitive

---

[38] Barth, K., Church Dogmatics: A Selection, 1961, p. 174.
[39] Leithart, P. J., The Consuming Fire of Love, July 21, 2023.
[40] Barth, K., Church Dogmatics, 1961, p. 52.

dissonance and neo-Gnostic based dualism of a culturally construed truth[41] devoid of realism, absolutism, and rationalism has to be discounted as fanciful. The ignoring of all established biological and empirical principles underlying binary categories of gender, renders claims to the contrary irrational.

Thirdly, the prime purpose of heterosexual marriage, as the fount of nuclear families and so the source of society itself, is conveniently and unreasonably dismissed. Same-sex couples overlook the ironic fact that each of the participants are products of heterosexual relationships, as are all persons from inception of the human race.

Fourthly, all three major pillars founding Western civilization, namely, Judeo-Christian doctrine, Hellenistic philosophy and rationality, coupled with Roman law (from which emanates the Rule of Law concept which holds no one is above the law), are based on objective realism, common sense, natural justice, and fairness. These founding principles are contravened in the clichéd artifice that same-sex marriage is not only defensible, but is valid being based on natural love.

Consequently, the various Equality Acts and the Respect for Marriage Act contravene natural, moral, and legal precepts founded on biblical principles. Here, arises the question of determining which acts are considered moral or immoral, just or unjust, or acts that are *malum in re* – wrong in themselves. Thomas Aquinas wrote an "unjust law is a human law that is not rooted in eternal and natural law." He said "Any law degrading human personality is unjust,"[42] which identity laws certainly do. These laws must thus be regarded as illegitimate in natural law, moral,

---

[41] Relativist truth is a Gnostic construal assuming intellect transcends truth itself" (Montgomery, M., Metaphysical, 1993).
[42] Creech, J., The Rule of Law, January 15, 2023.

terms, being contrary to the Creator's grand design for humankind. Therefore, the practice of same-sex is *malum in re* (wrong in itself), contradicting the natural order of creation. The complex question of just and unjust law is a subject for another time, so suffice it to say that progressives deny the pertinence of natural, eternal, law as the source of all moral and ethical principles.

Eros and Philia

Reflecting personal identity crises, Alphabet zealots search for a solution to their "unrest" by embracing *eros* as the universal love language. At best, an articulation of love as between same-sex couples might additionally, but not principally, be seen as *philia*, never *agape* despite imitation. As a secular and humanist derived emotional and physical desire, *eros*[43] is contrary to scripture and hence a contravention of divine precepts, as are all carnal same-sex relationships. The universal veracity of the slogan, love is love, being *eros*, is to be rejected by right-thinking followers of God. The maxim is simply a reductionist view of a complex matter and, in light of biblical doctrine, is morally insupportably being contrary to the natural order, and thus illegitimate.

Born This Way

Alphabet tribalists claim they were 'born this way,' being subject to congenital circumstances beyond their control. They argue their sex-gender rearrangement is simply part of the order of creation. In denying personal responsibility, they point out that just as heterosexual persons are

---

[43] *Eros* is the Greek word for passionate love, sexual desire, and homoeroticism (Plato, 1994, p. xv - xx).

genetically programmed, so too are those of same-sex or self-identified gender inclination.

Biblical doctrine contradicts this justification. Human beings are formed in the image of the Creator, with members of opposite binary genders consecrated in marriage and progenitors of families and society. Scripture only justifies biological binary genders. Although the Messiah stated, "There are eunuchs who have been so from birth,"[44] the statement was made in the context of marriage and refers to those individuals unable to marry and procreate due to congenital defects affecting their reproductive organs. The statement is not relevant to those claiming genders of their own making, and especially not those rejecting established morality derived from natural law, as reflected in the Masoretic moral tradition. Same-sex attraction based on the argument that they were born this way, is a narcissistic and hyper-individualistic attempt to by-pass God's design for humanity and to validate personal immorality.

Scientific Research

To counter criticism of their sexual choices, same-sex exponents seek scientific and biological genetic verification of the claim they were 'born this way.' A 2019 research article in the prestigious 'Science Journal' involving a comprehensive scientific investigation of nearly 500,000 individuals, indicated that "all tested genetic variants... do not allow meaningful prediction of an individual's sexual behaviour." The results reveal "there is no single continuum from opposite-sex to same-sex sexual behaviour."[45]

---

[44] Matthew 19:12.
[45] Ganna, A., Verweij, K., Sexual Behaviour, 2019, p. 769.

In summary, there are no dominant or identifiable genes validating same-sex proclivity. From a theological viewpoint, humankind's original sin is the culprit, underscoring the desire for licentious behaviour, typified by sodomite inhabitants of Sodom and Gomorrah. However, socio-psychological influences in exacerbating same-sex desire are not to be underestimated.

The Gay Male Lobby

Although this section is categorised under the heading of Radical Feminism, the same ideological considerations apply equally to the vibrant male homosexual lobby. Male same-sex adherents likewise find their search for personal identity and meaning within a sectarian, Alphabet, context. In striving for the authentic self, there will also be those persons who "hope to blend in," expressing a "desire to avoid isolation as a recalcitrant, non-conforming individual."[46] In any event, issues of sex and gender whether pertinent to males or females, are so co-mingled that they cannot be considered separately. The male lobby is as zealous in the affirmation of their putative rights as that of devoted feminists.

Reminiscent of the actions of the sodomite fanatics recounted in narratives relating to Lot and his family in the town of Sodom, are actions of the San Francisco Gay Men's Choir. The choir published a video singing, "We are coming for your Children," with the refrain, "We will convert your children – it happens bit by bit, quietly and subtly and you will barely notice it…we'll convert your children: we'll make them tolerant and fair."[47] It is concerning that criticism of the Choir is viewed as unacceptable whereas their own words contain destructive intent

---

[46] Reed, L. W., Thesis on Evil, 2022.
[47] Brown, M., We're coming for your children, 2021.

towards the innocent. The prophetic characteristic of this scenario, as initially recorded in the Sodomite episodes of Genesis 18-19, has a 'fresh" application in a current setting. Fulfilment will eventually take place with an eschatological destruction of the licentious Babylon spirit of Revelation 18.

Censorship

A repressive political, legal, and social environment limits free exercise of constitutional rights such as freedom of speech and religion. The ideologues' tyrannical approach leads to a new form of censorship where no dissent is tolerated, despite claims of diversity, equality, and inclusion. These claims are misnomers, for while denying freedom of contrary views they irrationally demand compliance with their slanted version of social justice. The insanity besetting society is well condensed by Chris Rufo when he writes, "Healthy debate has been replaced by activist hysterics. Speech is declared violence while violence is excused as speech. Masculinity is condemned as regressive, while men in skirts and heels are celebrated in the public square."[48]

---

[48] Rufo, C., The Cluster B Society, September 20, 2023.

CHAPTER SIX
PART SEVEN

THE CULTURAL REVOLUTION

"When the sense of God is lost, there is a tendency
to lose the sense of man, of his dignity and his life"
(Pope John Paul II, Evangelium Vitae, 1995)

6.12. A Crisis of Doctrine

In the areas of truth, morality, ethics, virtue, personal identity and meaning in life, Judeo-Christian influence on society is becoming less noticeable. This consequence is expected for the crowds will unfailingly choose Barabbas (Matt. 27:21), rejecting truth found only in the Messiah.

Crisis in society is matched by crisis of biblical doctrine. As Francis Mair says, "many religious voices have simply defected to the surrounding culture."[1] Compromised Christians present as "progressive, while dismantling human dignity on issues ranging from abortion and physician-assisted suicide to sexual ethics and human identity." The Evangelical Lutheran Church in America ("ELCA"), for instance, capitulated to demands for cultural conformity, permitting mésalliance marriages. The Church "voted to ordain practising homosexuals," another blasphemous

---

[1] Mair, F. X., Why I Read First Things, 2021.

act. Unsurprisingly, ELCA leader, Bishop Elizabeth Eaton, appeared in a "gay pride video celebrating pride month."[2]

The situation is equally dire in other Protestant circles, the Church of England issued a guidance recommending the 5,000 schools under its oversight allow students to "play with the many cloaks of identity."[3] Here, the Church supported the UK Government educating students in gender fluidity irrespective of biological sex, totally ignoring gender realism. In April 2023, the 'Fourth Global Anglican Future Conference' of Bible-adhering Anglicans - grouped under the label of 'Anglican Communion,' was held in Rwanda, Africa. At the conference, Anglican Communion leaders, representing some 85% of Anglicans worldwide, announced their schism from the Church of England. They rejected the Archbishop of Canterbury as an 'Instrument of Communion,' due to his departure from orthodox doctrine. Accordingly, the Church of England was expelled from the Communion until its return to Apostolic doctrine. The Anglican Communion emphasized they are not leaving the Communion. To the contrary, they said, it is the Church of England that has left the Communion for that relationship is based on canonical doctrine, which the Church of England rejects. Church schisms reflect the cultural struggle for truth likewise occurring in other sectors of society.

Tax Status

To appease the LGBT+ cohort, the leftist US Administration contemplates revoking the institutional Church's tax exemption status. Financial donations to Churches constitute a tax deduction against income and such

---

[2] 'Pride Month' is described as, "a government-promoted, corporate-sponsored, 30 day celebration of LGBTQ acceptance and achievement" (De Young, K., Conscience, 2022).
[3] Klett, L., Vatical Slams Gender Fluidity, 2019.

benefit could be revoked unless the organisations, "capitulate to the spirit of the age."[4] By capitulation is meant the endorsing[5] of secular humanist ideologies, with a focus on peculiar sex and gender which will in turn eradicate the sacred message of the Church. As it is, donations to Churches have declined since 2001. Gallup Polls report 44% of Americans donated to Churches in 2021, the lowest figure for 20 years. The concern surrounding the potential demise of tax exemption status of churches and other religious-based organizations and charities, became a real possibility with the US President signing into law the Respect for Marriage Act. This Act has the potential to:

> • Deprive "non-profit, faith-based, organizations of their tax-exempt status" should they continue to enforce "religious beliefs of marriage;"
> • Subject churches and religious organizations to litigation and severe financial penalties if they persist in maintaining traditional beliefs;
> • Enable the Federal government to "recognize any State's definition of marriage no matter how far-fetched."[6]

6.13. Divergence of Values

The assault on marriage and the family continues on all fronts. Rabbi Sacks emphasises that "strong families are essential to free societies."[7] Destruction of these Judeo-Christian social concepts remain the focus of activists intent on refabricating traditional beliefs of personhood, the family unit, and society.

---

[4] Trueman, C., Church, 2014.
[5] The demand is to "Put down the Bible and pick up the Rainbow flag" (Eberstadt, M., Men are at War with God, 2022).
[6] The 2022 "Respect for Marriage Act" redefines marriage contrary to established norms and the natural law. The purpose is to entrench legality of same-sex marriage (Shackleford K., Marriage, 2022).
[7] Sacks, J., Covenant and Conversation: Genesis 1 - Family Feeling, 2009, para. 5783.

A Note Verbal

The Roman Catholic Church steadfastly maintains its opposition to the Alphabet clutch's pernicious attempts to transform church and society. In 2021, the Vatican lodged a diplomatic protest, a *note verbal,* against Italy's proposed law which would, "punish acts of discrimination and incitement to violence against gay, lesbian, transgender and disabled people." In practice, such law would effectively "curtail catholic freedoms of belief and expression."[8] The proposed law would protect Alphabet members against vocal Christian prayer and counselling against homosexual practices. In other words, the law would force all members of society to acquiesce to identitarian influence.

The Vatican earlier criticised gender ideology for "not being based on truth" but on "nothing more than a confused concept of freedom in the realm of feelings and wants."[9] The Vatican's 'Congregation for Catholic Education' issued a document titled, 'Male and Female He Created Them,' decrying the influence of gender ideology in education and its destabilising effect on families. They instead validated the biblical view of binary gender and marriage, based on Pope John Paul II's 'Theology of the Body' lectures.

In 2021, the Vatican's 'Holy See Press Office' issued a statement confirming the Church does not have divine mandate to bless same-sex unions. In this way, the Vatican officially blocked attempts by seditious Priests publicly endorsing heretical relationships on behalf of the Catholic church. These are brave efforts in resisting ideological attempts to pollute traditional dogma. Protestant evangelicals likewise resist the woke

---

[8] France 24 News Service, Note Verbal, June 22, 2021.
[9] Klett, L. M., Vatican Slams Gender Fluidity, 2019.

narrative for the largest US evangelical organisation, the 'Southern Baptist Convention' ("SBC"), passed a resolution reading, "We state unequivocally abortion is murder and we reject any position that allows for exceptions to the legal protection of our preborn neighbours."[10] The SBC represents 50,000 Churches, comprising nearly 15 million members. Nonetheless, there exists a concerning state of affairs with many doctrinally compromised Churches, Seminaries, and theological institutions generally.

Kingdom Culture

Disciples of the Redeemer-Messiah cannot acquiesce to Alphabet lobby's demands for diversity, tolerance, inclusivity and equity. The principles of Kingdom culture are based on claims by the Redeemer-Messiah that he is, "the way, the truth and the life" (Jn. 14:6). There is no other way, no path to identity, meaning, morality, emotional security and sanctity of life; and no truth apart from the absolute truth and moral legitimacy of Judeo-Christian dogma. Here alone is found guidance for sexual ethics and the template for marriage. There is no other pathway to eschatological hope. It is for this reason that believers are considered contemptuous in the current political and social environment. Biblical norms like sexual ethics, heterosexual marriage, binary gender, the sanctity of life, especially that of unborn babies, and the Fatherhood of God, remain under acute threat of eradication or irrelevancy in the prevailing post-truth humanist environment.

---

[10] Wingfield, M, SBC, 2021; Psalms 94:6; Isaiah 10:1-2; Proverbs 24:11; Psalms 82;1-4.

6.14. Conclusion

In rejecting the ways of the Creator, Adam and Eve created the ideology of secular humanism. Their actions resulted in a practical atheism ending in the malaise of nihilism for without God, the only outcome is eternal alienation from his divine presence.

The long-term impact of atheism is evident in contemporary society through identity activists who believe, "identity is the ruling ideology of the day."[11] These activists justify abortion, eugenics, euthanasia, and the right of gender self-identification by applying neo-Gnostic elitist, dualist, philosophical theories emerging from Eden. By striving for power, they disconnect from reality in favour of utopian ideals which cause immense turmoil in society. Maureen Brown is not far wrong when she attributes blame to philosophies which "can make the previously unthinkable thinkable."[12] The philosophical hypotheses of Judith Butler, Simone de Beauvoir, Michael Foucault, various existentialists and many others, certainly fit this charge.

An Enduring Theme

Numerous biblical passages prove continuity of the heretical *eritus sicut Deus* (to be like God) theme. Commencing in the archetypical Garden, the heresy continued through First and Second Testament recapitulations into an existing setting, with future eschatological finalisation. To validate this continuity scripturally, the theme requires justification through applied interpretive methods. Here, Second Temple period Palestinian Rabbinical Jewish exegesis will be essential. Specifically, the use of ancient midrashic *darash* of *haggadah* prophetic passages should show a continuous theme

---

[11] Gurri, M, How the Identity Cult Captured America, June 17, 2023.
[12] Brown, R., Philosophy, January 27, 2019.

from Genesis to eschatological finality in the book of Revelation for, in Jewish thought, "the pattern of the past is the pattern of the future."[13]

Applied Darash

While acknowledging the *peshat* (plain, literal) meaning of passages to ensure originalism and contextualisation, the goal is to "search (*darash*) the scriptures to seek light from them on new situations." James Sanders explains that this strategy is "precisely what the prophets, psalmists, and historians did, as well as their heirs who wrote early Jewish literature."[14] A limited examination of pertinent passages relating to the theme of *eritus sicut Deus* (to be like God) follows:

- Prior to Eden, the Archangel Lucifer tried to usurp authority of the Most-High God, the Creator of all things. This is explained in Isaiah 14:14 and Ezekiel 28:15, "I will make myself like the Most High." Here is the earliest instance of *eritus sicut Deus;*
- Satan's strategy to be like God in Genesis 3:5 compelled him to destroy God's pinnacle of creation, the first human couple made in his own image;
- The First Couple believed the deceitful serpent in Genesis 3. This fraud led them to anticipate a form of divinity with creative rights, leading to a self-constructed future free of *imago Dei*. Coupled with rejection of the natural law, the love, and confines of the Creator, the First Couple gave birth to secular humanism;
- In Genesis 11, Nimrod and his followers desired to be like God, *eritus sicut Deus*. They constructed a tall edifice to exalt themselves, "a tower with its top in the heavens, so let us make a name for ourselves;"
- In a Second Testament context, Satan's desire of *eritus sicut Deus* is mentioned in 2 Thess. 2:4 where he, "exalts himself against every so-called god or object of worship, so that he takes his seat in the temple of God, proclaiming himself to be God;"
- It is in the eschaton that the prophetic incident of Genesis 3:5, *eritus sicut Deus,* finds completion. Satan's deep aim is to claim the status of God,

---

[13] Russell, D. S., Jewish Apocalyptic, 1964, p. 231.
[14] Sanders, J. A., Foreword, 1993, p. vii.

of which the desires of Adam and Eve for self-deification are but a duplication. The triptych of Satan, the Dragon, and Beast of Revelation 13:4-6, worshipped as god, will be summarily destroyed. The Most-High God, the Creator of Heaven and Earth, will countenance no challenge to the primacy, glory, and worship due to him alone, "Fear God and give him glory, because the hour of his judgment has come, and worship him who made heaven and earth" (Rev. 14:7).

Finale

The spread of ideological secular humanism and neo-paganism is reflected in the abortion of innocent unborn human beings, coupled with eugenical and euthanasia practices. These motives reveal a desire for independent creative power, an attempt 'to be like God,' as explored in this chapter.

The thematic advent of *eritus sicut Deus* in early Genesis, with a fresh recreation in subsequent scenarios, has ultimate eschatological application in the mode of early Palestinian Rabbinical midrashic exegesis. Upon such finality, and in the eternal order, the disrupted utopian Garden situation is permanently restored in a setting of love, harmony, peace, fellowship, innocence, ontological security of identity and meaning. Through the sacrificial work of the Redeemer-Messiah, the eternal order reveals the glorious redemptive strategy of the Creator God.

CHAPTER SEVEN
PART ONE

POLITICS, LAW, AND SOCIAL JUSTICE

"We think it true to say that politics, in largest part,
is an expression of culture and at the heart of culture is religion"
(Richard John Neuhaus, 1990)

7.1. Introduction

The "core of common culture is religion"[1] says Roger Scruton, explaining
the inextricable connection between these two concepts. Consequently, the
cultural turmoil in society can be traced to the issue of religion, particularly
the Judeo-Christian principles underpinning the Western way of life.
Society, its culture, and its biblical principles are threatened by a synergy
of secular humanist ideology and New Age spirituality, together
comprising the atheistic nature of Identity Politics.

Society and Judeo-Christianity

Secular humanist philosophy, in all its practical articulations, has as its
deepest aim the replacement of biblical precepts with an alternative,
ideological, utopian worldview. Despite the proliferation of identity
theories and faith systems, there remains no rational, coherent,
transcendent, and sacerdotal substitution for the eternal truths of Judeo-

---

[1] Scruton, R., Modern Culture, 2005, p. 5.

Christianity. It is from these truths that Western society derives its pragmatic values relating to ethics, morality, law and justice. Theologian George Weigel summarised essential elements of Judeo-Christianity's influence on Western society along the following lines:

- The concept of family. Family is a core component of society, reflecting God's intention to create a people bearing his image, imparting to them a sacred character;
- The idea of equality of all persons. This results in the biblical principle of social justice for "justice must reflect moral equality rather than natural inequality;"
- The "desacralizing of the State." There can be no democratic project, no traditional political order, if the State considers itself omnipotent. Limiting State power gives life to principles such as personal freedoms, separation of State and Church, and "republican forms of self-government;"
- Law and justice. Through historic Councils like at Toledo, biblical doctrine influenced law and justice by insisting on evidence-based verdicts. These principles remain the norm in "21st century democratic societies;"
- The first universities. Medieval universities were established by the Roman Catholic Church in "Paris, Bologna, Oxford, Krakow, and Prague." Here, the practice of "disciplined public debate took root in the civilization soil of the West, with profound implications for Western culture and democratic public life;"
- All persons are "responsible moral agents and capable of virtue." This principle has had deep implications for personal responsibility and accountability.

In the result, Western society with its "science, economics, and democratic project, developed in cultural soil enriched by Judeo-Christian ideas, convictions, modes of life and practices" evolved into the sophisticated classic liberal political tradition of the West.[2] These biblical principles, the very foundation of society, are now under threat for, as

---

[2] Weigel, G., The Difference Christianity Made, 2021.

Hungary's Prime Minister Viktor Orbán claims, "we have entered an age of dangers, and the pillars of Western civilization once thought unshakeable, are cracking."[3] It was Niccolò Machiavelli (1469-1527) who pointed to the formative truth that, "there is no surer sign of decay in a country than to see its religion held in contempt."

Two Views of Natural Law

A humanist definition of natural law was offered by professors Kody Cooper and Justin Dyer when they wrote natural law is a "moral law known through rationally discerned moral obligations."[4] However, natural law comes from the counsel of God, not from frail human reason although it meets all tests of reason. Therefore, Thomas Aquinas' understanding of natural law origins is preferable. He explains that there is a "standard of natural justice that exists independently of human contrivance and that acts as a measure for the legitimacy of civil laws and political Institutions."[5] In contrast, atheistic, humanist, natural law proposals originate not from an independent authority but from within the human mind and the natural order. All laws must of necessity hold to a moral basis but only a theistic view of natural law can rationally defend a moral position.

The US Declaration of Independence states, "All men are created equal, they are endowed by their Creator with certain unalienable rights, that among these are the right to life, liberty and the pursuit of happiness." This declaration says Supreme Court Judge, Clarence Thomas, validates the theistic natural law foundation of the Constitution and of all U.S. laws. Understandably, the Creator's natural law principles are abhorrent to

---

[3] Roussinos, A., A Decade of Danger, 2022.
[4] Cooper, K., Dyer, J., Classical and Christian Origins of American Politics, 2022, Ch. 1.
[5] Ward, L., Natural Law, 2021.

radical identity ideologues focused on a morality of their own formula, and a biased concept of justice. As discussed in Chapter 3, the valid principles of natural law are recorded in the moral codes of Moses and the law of Christ.

Subjective Ethics

Identity activists replace established ethical principles with their own fluid, irrational, and subjective ideas of morality. Existentialist philosophers label this 'situational ethics.' By so doing, the moral principles set out in the 'Ten Commandments' are eradicated. An inclination of this sort cannot result in a beneficial moral philosophy so necessary for the good ordering of society. The simple reason is that activists confuse liberty with license. The latter concept was never part of the classic liberal democratic tradition which, despite laudable personal freedoms, held to restraints upon excess liberties. The purpose of boundaries was to acknowledge the rights of others, those with a more moderate disposition, disagreeing with unfettered freedoms, lack of modesty, decency and public immorality. The necessity of constraining licentiousness is understandable due to the Judeo-Christian roots of the Western political order.

As it was in the Edenic Garden, pride is a significant factor in the post-truth cynicism of Western society. Mary Eberstadt writes, "We moderns have bought into a seductive secular story, namely, that we are smarter and more sophisticated than the people who came before us; that we have outgrown antiquities like God, Church, and a transcendent code by which to live." She believes our arrogance may blind us to the "possibility that in some critical areas the opposite may be true."[6]

Exclusivist claims to divinity by the Judeo-Christian God makes this faith a critical target for assailment by all those adopting their own avenues to truth. Criticism of the relative morality of identity self-identifiers by those of a more centrist or conservative[7] political framework, causes offence in the secular, spiritually eclectic, culture. In particular, public utterance of the law of Christ, as set out in the Beatitudes and elsewhere, may be deemed 'hate speech' towards those with a different morality. Criticism of woke policies is considered contravention of legal codes defining scurrilous speech. These codes are based on ideological grounds, purportedly neutral but in practice biased against objective claims to truth.[8] In this manner, not only is the public practice of Judeo-Christianity under threat of marginalisation, but also the germinal doctrines upon which society is birthed.

Western Culture

A society that previously reflected biblical principles in public affairs, particularly as concerns morality, is now faced with an anti-Christian bias. In such circumstances social, political, and moral decline should be expected for, as President George Washington in his 1796 Farewell Address warned, "Religion and Morality are indispensable supports to political prosperity."[9] The current conflict of ideas, though, did not come

---

[6] Anderson, R. T., Eberstadt, M., What Plagues the West, 2021.

[7] Conservatism "honours, preserves, and renews the natural and sacred sources of authority that holds things together" (Reno, R., What We Are For, 2021).

[8] Denying absolute, objective, verifiable truths in favour of contextual reality is a core indicator of post-truth identity ideology.

[9] Washington, G., Farewell Address, September 19, 1796.

from a vacuum lacking historic context, and so the philosophical, political, social and religious background of this development needs attention.

Patrick Deneen lists broad movements that contributed to weakening of religion in public life. Firstly, early continental scholasticism of the 13-14th centuries; liberalism of 17-18th century Enlightenment era; prolific secularism of the subsequent modernist period; criticism of religion and truth in the 20th century, particularly through philosophy; and, finally, fashionable neo-Marxist theories stimulated radical social ideologies for a new world order. Through these historic movements, the foundational principle of Western political order, that of classic liberal democracy upholding personal freedoms like speech and religion, now faces severe political, legal, and social challenges.

7.2. Democracy, Liberalism, and Modernity

Without checks and balances necessary to protect rights of minorities, pure and unqualified democracy can be its own enemy. As Alexander Hamilton, a founding father of the American Constitution said, "We are forming a republican government as real liberty is neither found in despotism nor the extremes of democracy but in moderate governments."[10]

To guard against government extremism, the Greek historian Polybius (200 – 118 B.C.E.) insisted true democracy not only required "a numerical value but also a moral or even a spiritual component."[11] That is the ideal, but the reality is that a uniform and systemic moral representation in society would only be possible in a theocracy. Still, humankind is certainly capable of reflecting levels of morality as the Apostle Paul makes clear in 2 Corinthians 5:17.

---

[10] Hamilton, A., Convention, 1787.
[11] Tuckfield, B., How to Destroy Democracy, 2021.

To counter governmental tyranny, American founders demanded a representative democracy through a republican constitution. The hallmark of this system is the Rule of Law and the separation of powers restraining the three branches of government, namely, the executive, judicial and legislative, together with a traditional separation of the State and the Church. In the USA, Canada, Germany and Australia, for instance, added limitations against central government overreach are achieved through a federalist structure devolving certain powers to individual States. Within this republican order, with its necessary limitations, a classic liberalist democracy was free to develop through the period of modernity.

The idea of representative democracy is laudable but has shortcomings. The most obvious being citizens' reliance on their elected representatives in Congress to fairly represent them, they being unable to participate directly. The Federal system of government however, allows citizens to directly participate in the deliberative process at a local level, that is, in local government such as school boards. In this way, at a basic 'grass roots' level, citizens can indirectly influence future State and national elections.

Classic Liberal Democracy

From a background of the 17-18th century Enlightenment era with its revolt against religious and State authoritarianism, modernity came to be identified through a liberalist political philosophy. Simply explained, liberalism places individual freedom at the centre of political life. It can be defined by characteristics of representative democracy, republicanism, capitalism, separation of Church and state, separation of powers of government, limited government, secularism in public life, with individual rights, obligations, and freedoms balanced by the equality of all persons and religions in an open society, and enforced through the rule of law applied fairly.

The advantages of this tradition were described by 2010 Nobel laureate, Mario Vargas Llosa, when he wrote, "from its very beginnings, liberal doctrine has given expression to the most advanced form of democratic culture and, in free societies, has given the greatest impulse to human rights, freedom of expression, the rights of sexual, religious and political minorities, the defense of the environment and the participation of ordinary citizens in public life."[12] Hence, preserving biblical principles underlying Western society is essential. It is ironic that the freedoms enjoyed in a liberalist tradition have enabled identity activists to practise their counter-culture lives while at the same time those exact freedoms are under threat of extinction by the same activists. To ensure basic freedoms, there needs to be a balance between individual freedom and State authority for the public good, a principle ignored by those imposing deviant ideas on an unwilling society.

The precarious nature of freedom was highlighted by President Ronald Reagan in his so-called 'Freedom Speech' ('A Time for Choosing,' 1964) when he cautioned, "Freedom is never more than one generation from extinction." He concluded, "it must be fought for, protected, and handed on for our children to do the same..." Still, this freedom needs to be located within a definitive moral and ethical order to benefit society. Identity activists lack moral components in their ideology and so their proposals are socially detrimental. This is where biblical principles become essential in providing a sound basis upon which society and

---

[12] Vargas Llosa, M., The Call of the Tribe, 2023, p. 20.

culture need to be founded. It was Thomas Jefferson who confirmed, "people are inherently independent of all but moral law."[13]

Separation of Powers

The pivotal doctrine of separation of powers was proposal by French philosopher Charles-Louis Montesquieu in his 1748 manuscript, 'The Spirit of the Laws,' although John Locke (1632-1704) had earlier mentioned division of powers as between king and parliament. Separation of powers has a biblical precedent[14] for there was to be a permanent split between the offices of the King, the prophet, and the High Priest, excepting Melchizedek and the Messiah, Jesus of Nazareth. The doctrine has sacred political beginnings and so carries biblical authority.

Birthed through insurrections in Britain (the 'Glorious Revolution' of 1688), America (1776) and France (1789), social liberalism soon became the pervasive political philosophy of rising modernity. The purpose of this regime was to rid society of feudalism, economic bondage, authoritarianism and tyranny but, to an extent, notably in France,[15] a new despotic regime arose. Nonetheless, the worthy objectives of liberty, equality, and fraternity, occasioning the purging of distinct and prejudicial social classes, were established to some degree albeit at great social cost. Over a period of time, restrictions on political and economic freedoms became progressively relaxed and controls maintaining a level of acceptable decency, compassion, and morality in society decreased.

The rise of individualism and influence of the 16th century Reformation led to a decline in restraining factors. This evolvement was a

---

[13] Jefferson, T., Letter to Spencer Roane, September 6, 1819.
[14] Deuteronomy 18 – 21.
[15] "Liberalism originated in the French revolution and spread from there" (Rosenblatt, H., Lost History of Liberalism, 2018, p. 5).

continuum process for, assuming a dominant level of the characteristics of rights, obligations, and equality, the next evolutionary step for societal institutions was the advancement of individual freedoms and the simultaneous reduction of autocratic State controls. The situation has escalated over the centuries into the moral and ethical crisis of this postmodern environment – a contest between idealists and realists, illiberalists and conservatives, all claiming to strive for the public good of society.

Consequently, liberal[16] democracy can constitute its own enemy for an inescapable tension exists between the balance of freedoms, rights, and checks against political, moral, and ethical extremism. This tension results in a political power-struggle affecting all sectors of society. Nonetheless, moral restraints are required for, if not, then a constitutional liberal democratic political order cannot survive.

The Term, 'Liberal'

It needs clarification that in prevailing American jargon, the term 'liberal' refers to leftism,[17] not in the sense of classic English liberalism which is a moderate, conservative,[18] or centrist political conviction the principles of which established liberal democracies internationally. Furthermore, the word, 'progressive'[19] also applies to leftist identity ideologies. In this post-truth era, 'liberal' implies the "never ending search for individual

---

[16] Liberalism is the "freedom from constraint: the freedom to act according to one's conception of the good without impinging on another's right to do the same" (Mills, M. A., Liberalism, 2021).

[17] Liberals are "members of the radical left, favoring Statism in people's lives" (Powell, A. R., Liberal, 2012).

[18] Conservatism seeks to "conserve the community" with its conventional values. (Scruton, R., What, 2002).

[19] 'Leftist' and 'Progressive' are interchangeable terms in the current political context.

autonomy, dismembering the structure of civil society, and eroding bonds from which we derive our sense of personal identity."[20] In other words, extreme ego-centralism. 'Liberal' is an exasperating word with fluctuating connotations, and so the cultural framework, the context, is vital.

Liberalism and Conservatism

An aim of classic liberalism is an ordered society, and this condition can only be achieved through a level of control. In this sense, there is a convergence of conservative and classic liberal objectives for both of these political philosophies seek social stability, good order, and reasonable standards of ethics in public affairs. John Horvat describes the American political order as a "political consensus where citizens agree to certain laws and rules which allow them to get along. It includes a religious consensus loosely based on a respect for the Ten Commandments."[21] It is when the political consensus disintegrates that religious consensus meets resistance, resulting in social discord.

Political Ideology

Courageously leading his country from a totalitarian Marxist political regime into a liberal democratic order, Czech Republic president, Václav Havel, explained the concept of an ideology, "Ideology is a specious way of relating to the world. It offers human beings the illusion of an identity, of dignity, and of morality." In plain words, ideology enables people to substitute one set of values for a completely new set, and so create an alternative reality and ethical order. This concept is nothing other than neo-Gnostic dualism given new life through principles of the Marxist slave

---

[20] Bitton, M., Death of the Romantic Liberal, September 1, 2023.
[21] Horvat, J., Return to Order, 2013, p. 10.

– master dichotomy. Havel believes this concept creates an "illusion that the system is in harmony with the human order and the order of the university."[22] Explained this way, as an illusion detached from reality, it is understandable progressives are utterly committed to their system of ensuring social justice.

Conservatism

Classic liberalism is based upon the solid and timeless[23] pillars of biblical values. This is especially so in areas of law, justice, ethics, truth, and morality. Combined, the values lead to a conservative political outlook necessary in the exercise of personal freedoms and ensuring an acceptable standard of distributive justice, ethics, morality, and social harmony. Russell Kirk describes the aspirations of conservatism as "concerned with the regeneration of spirit and character – with the perennial problem of the inner order of the soul; the restoration of the ethical understanding; and the religious sanction upon which any life worth living is founded. This is conservatism at its highest."[24] A valiant objective, but one which cannot be achieved politically. The reason is that Kirk's idea of "regeneration of spirit and character" is dependent upon an inner work of the Holy Spirit at an individual level, not corporate. Politically speaking, Italian intellectual Giuseppe Tomasi di Lampedusa points out a paradoxical truth of conservatism when he says, "If we want things to stay as they are, things will have to change."[25]

---

[22] Havel, V., The Power of the Powerless, 1985, pp. 28-29.
[23] Conservatism has eternal values beyond any era, remaining valid (Giubilei, F., European Conservative Thought, 2019, p. 3).
[24] Kirk, R. S., The Conservative Mind, 1953, p. 414.
[25] Giuseppe Tomasi di Lampedusa, The Leopard, 1911, p. 31.

Cultural Biblical Principles

The influence of cultural Judeo-Christianity has decreased in the public square. In its place is rising secularism which creates a moral vacuum. This is in contrast to the earlier situation when Americans enjoyed "an establishment of religion in the life of the nation," where "an agreement about morals" existed whether explicit or implicit. In such period, Judeo-Christianity set the tone for the culture.

Europe also reflects a secular trend for "Protestantism is essentially gone from Europe now."[26] Likewise in the polar opposite hemispheres of the Antipodes and the Nordic countries, once bastions of Protestantism. Secularism is very visible around sexuality (especially LGBT issues) and bioethics."[27] Oswald Spengler (1880-1936), would not have been surprised for he perceived that the primary cultural struggle would be "between diverse human identities and the cultural symbols that represent them".[28] The confrontation between truth, morality, and religion in a resistant culture ultimately results in a secular milieux. Always heretical through the ages, secular humanist ideologies and paganist spirituality have had opportunity to expand in the post-truth moral vacuum, to become socially normative rather than remaining of limited influence.

A Neutral Justice

An established legal principle is that justice should be ideologically neutral. To the contrary, the social justice version of cultural engineers is not neutral. Despite claims of egalitarianism, their version of justice has resulted in politically biased laws forcing compliance with heretical

---

[26] Bottum, J., Death of Protestant America, 2008.
[27] Forster, J., Role in Society, 2021.
[28] Rose, M., World After Liberalism, 2021, p. 20.

ideologies promoted by a minority sect. Their ideas are morally and socially unacceptable for they ignore the need for a virtuous society. Instead, activists scorn principles of truth, decency, dignity, restraint, virtue, and manners inherent in a biblically founded social order.

Marginalisation of Judeo-Christianity

Society has entered a post-truth stage in which an anti-Christian narrative has become widespread. This indicates a civilisational crisis through deconstruction, the eradication, of conservative biblical principles, and the humane order upon which the culture is instituted. Professor Joshua Mitchell believes leftists force society to "return to the pre-liberal condition of tribalism."[29] This view has much merit for the politics of identity, the new civic religion[30] with its compromised freedoms, are not to the public advantage despite protestations to the contrary. In actuality, identity concerns divide the populace along tribal lines while striving for an elusive concept of diversity, equality and inclusion in the name of social justice. Professor Hadley Arkes believes the US domestic situation can best be described as "the gravest crisis of the regime since the Civil war."[31] Strong words indeed.

Tribalism

The Nobel Laureate for literature of 2010, Mario Vargas Llosa, criticises the "call of the tribe," by which he means the 'call,' the allegiance, to "fanaticism, tribalism, and intellectual conformity in a variety of forms."[32]

---

[29] Mitchell, J., Politics, 2021.
[30] Barr says the "secular project has become a religion, pursued with religious fervor. (Barr, W., Notre Dame, 2019).
[31] Arkes, H., Hammer, J., A Better Originalism, 2021.
[32] Vargas Llosa, M., The Call of the Tribe, 2023 (Mahoney, D. J., Breaking the Spell of Marxism, March 13, 2023).

The "call of the tribe" is evident in the so-called Rainbow Flag concept (the "Pride Reich"), the banner under which the Alphabet fringe gather to distinguish their sexually atypical clan from the remainder of society, the conventional heterosexual majority. This expression of tribalism, whether based on race or sexuality, demands passionate ideological commitment by all members. Purpose, meaning, and identity is found in a fake-familial identity providing a veneer of sociological connection and meaning through integration. Striving in vain for a sacred identity, activists reject the fact that a solution to their quest can only be found in their Creator, not through a clan identity.

The Common Good

This concept was initially developed by Aristotle in his work 'Politics' (350 B.C.E.); enhanced by Machiavelli in 'The Prince' (1513); and further developed by French philosopher Jean-Jacques Rousseau in the 18th century. From there, the principle was adopted by American founding fathers for inclusion in seminal documents, and later influenced the Western order generally.

In 1943, Charles De Koninck described the concept by saying this "supreme good, is a common good that rests on the proper good of each," and for the benefit of all.[33] This is correct, only a common good founded on moral and ethical biblical parameters benefitting society as a whole, can lead to an equitable form of justice. The biblical idea of equality, fairness, and justice demands a moral and ethical underlay to benefit society. It was this understanding that the American Founders endorsed. In the current social climate, the idea of a common good has been replaced

---

[33] Roy, C., Moral, 2014.

by a hyper-focus on individualism, meaning the well-being of an inner-self which is an ego-centric therapeutic theory stimulated by Freud and his psychoanalytic hypotheses.

Internal Decline

The moral decline of ancient Roman Society eventually led to the nation's destruction by invading Visigoth barbarians (410 C.E.). Western societies face a similar dilemma through diminution of foundational precepts sustaining the legal, moral, and ethical basis of the culture. The 'Barbarian hordes' threatening the stability of contemporary society comprise ego-centric visionaries, functioning in the name of distributive justice but in actuality polarizing the populace along lines of identity.

In this context, the term 'justice' is a grave misnomer for 'injustice' is what transpires socially and legally. Constitutional freedoms are compromised to appease the utopian tribe, for denial of the right to publicly disagree, to hold a contrary view in the public sphere despite rights of speech and religion,[34] is under critical threat through restrictive laws mislabelled as 'Equality Acts.' Importantly, rejection of a specific freedom inescapably compromises other freedoms for all freedoms are inextricably linked. As an example, freedom of religion in public life is not possible without freedom of speech and freedom of association. Freedom is an inalienable human right, derived from the natural law concept of free will - the right to personal choice – graciously assigned to the Edenic couple who represented all future generations. Even so, true freedom can only be realized within certain limits in order to protect the overlapping rights of others, for with rights come obligations.

---

[34] Freedom of Religion is "a natural inalienable right," not a "privilege granted by governments" (Farr, T., Freedom, 2022).

Government Overreach

Intrusion of the State into the private lives of its citizens is the antithesis of a classic liberal democratic political framework. In this manner, human rights with codified civil and social freedoms and established constitutional principles are diminished. Escalating interference by the State, markedly in the areas of sex and gender, is evidence of authoritarianism. State control over citizens' personal concerns has long existed in jurisdictions with collectivist economic and social arrangements such as Marxist-Leninist China, Cuba, and North Korea.

In Western societies, despite exposure to authoritarianism through feudalism and monarchical dictates of the past, similar practices increase. To counter this threat, a number of European political parties bandied together to oppose dictatorial attempts of the European Union Parliament (EU) to enforce identity ideology rules and regulations upon Europe as a whole. The parties allege the EU[35] seeks a "cultural revolution that will destroy social structures, starting with family and traditions," in order to create something new. The defiant group claims the EU has become a "tool of radical forces" and intends to "carry out a civilization transformation of Europe." The replacement would "create a superstate devoid of European traditions, social Institutions or moral principles." In so doing they "abandon Judeo-Christian values and, instead, align themselves with leftist positions for political gain."[36]

As in most EU member countries, UK culture has succumbed to the avalanche of political identity policies emanating from the US. Despite cultural differences between the two countries, "Abortion and same-sex

---

[35] The "EU is a kind of secular papacy" (Badewnas, J. Christendom, 2022).
[36] Kern, S., New Political Alliance, 2021.

marriage have been quickly accepted into the British mainstream (and) for is not surprising that events on one side of the Atlantic should affect the other."[37] The same sentiments apply to other Western jurisdictions. American promotion of secularist and neo-pagan leftist ideologies such as abortion, same-sex marriage and similar, is in stark contrast to the directive of the 18th President, Ulysses Grant. It was President Grant who, in 1878, publicly recommended to students that they should "hold fast to the Bible as the anchor sheet of your liberties; write its precepts in your hearts, and practise them in your lives. To the influence of this Book, we are indebted for all the progress made in true civilization and to this we must look as our guide in the future."[38]

Ordered Society

A well-functioning society requires both internal and external peace and order. As Russell Kirk pointed out, "Order is the first need of all. One finds happiness in restoring and improving the order of the soul and the order of the republic."[39] While shrinking in influence, a renaissance of cultural Christianity can arise again. Chief Rabbi of the UK, Jonathan Sacks, addresses this issue, "without a return to the shared commitment of a common good, liberal democracy will fail."[40] Unfortunately, a uniform concept of the common good leading to a consensual social justice, has little realistic chance of implementation in the present social atmosphere due to determined ideological assaults upon freedom and truth.

---

[37] Cowan, D., Britain's Culture War, 2021.
[38] Federer, W., Ulysses S. Grant, 2021.
[39] Kirk, R., The Roots of American Order, 2003 (1974), p. 475.
[40] Sacks, J., Rabbi, 2020.

A New Civilization

A cultural void cannot exist, the demise of a dominant culture inexorably leads to replacement by another. Identity idealists seek a new form of global civilization to replace the traditional ethos. To defeat this cultural radicalism, society "needs to be rebuilt on the noble habits and practices of previous generations of conservative thought."[41] Attempts of this nature necessarily "originate in our homes, our neighbourhoods, our communities, our cities, our schools, and should guide our national debates."[42] Western culture should again reflect established biblical precepts for the common good and well-being of all members of society. It is incumbent upon citizens to bring this about.

---

[41] Roberts, K. D., Future of Conservatism, 2022.
[42] Dawson, C., The Crisis of Western Civilization, 1961, p. 3.

CHAPTER SEVEN
PART TWO

POLITICS, LAW,
AND SOCIAL JUSTICE

*"The farther a society drifts from the truth,
the more it will hate those who speak it"*
(George Orwell)

7.3. Social Justice

Prior to the present social friction, ideas surrounding the concept of social justice were advanced by scholars like John Stuart Mill (1806-1873), Roscoe Pound (1870-1964), Friedrich Hayek (1899-1992), John Rawls (1921-2002) and many others. The slogans of the French revolution (1789) relating to concepts of liberty, equality and fraternity, and the subsequent imitation of those principles in the Communist inspired Bolshevik uprising (1917), were motivated by a social justice concept, for the common good.

Claiming victimhood and seeking remedial justice is likewise the war cry of radical actors pursuing a metamorphosis of contemporary society. In his study of the French Revolution, the great English statesman Edmund Burke (1729-1797), perceived the civil war in France was powered purely by ideological motives under a façade of social justice. Bearing in mind that Burke was a contemporary of that period, he wrote "it is a war between partisans of the ancient civil, moral, and political order of Europe against a sect of fanatical and ambitious atheists with intentions to change them all."[1] The motivation underlying this "war" was again seen in the Russian revolution of 1917, and repeats itself in current Western society through identity anarchists fomenting civil and political discord to cement a neo-Marxist version of social justice.

Governing authorities invariably seek to dominate and control the populace as Karl Popper emphasised in 'The Open Society and its Enemies.' Popper well understood that totalitarian tendencies "belong to a tradition which is just as old or just as young as civilization itself."[2] Along the same lines, philosopher Roger Scruton agrees that Marxism, under the pretense of social justice, disguises the fact that "it is not a truth-directed but a power-directed system of thought," and that explains the "willingness of intellectuals to believe it."[3] Although definitions of social justice may vary according to the particular age and the agenda of its proponents from time to time, a social justice not benefitting society as a whole cannot be a regarded as justice but, instead, a sectarian ideology resulting in injustice through a power grab.

Social Divergence

There are three primary reasons for the ideologically-based current social disorder: firstly, the idea of a common good needs to be founded on biblical principles like equality, freedom, fairness and the rule of law applied equally. However, these principles are understood quite differently by social activists. Secondly, despite avowals to the contrary, the woke agenda is not to accomplish a consensual social justice for the good of all

---

[1] Burke, E., Letters on the Proposals for Peace, Letter II, 1841 (1796), p. 104.
[2] Popper, K., The Open Society, 1945, p. xxxv.
[3] Scruton, R., Political Philosophy, 2006, p. 150.

but for power – political, legal and social power.[4] This power is necessary to impose an atheistic identity ideology upon society at large. The desire for power was well explained by Thomas Hobbes when he said, "the general inclination of all mankind is a perpetual and restless desire of power after power that ceases only in death."[5] Thirdly, the abstract ideal upon which secular ideology is based cannot give life to an objective, utilitarian, ethical and moral definity so necessary in achieving a multi-lateral common good. Resultantly, without a settled understanding of common good no true, fair, or enduring social justice is possible.

A Solution

The political history of the US indicates no one party governs for indefinite periods. As the identity brigade hardly represents the majority of the populace, change from the present regime stimulating social discordance will be forthcoming. In the interim, though, immense damage occurs to vulnerable sectors of society such as the unborn, the youth and the aged. It is incumbent upon Judeo-Christian believers to bring 'salt and light' to society, especially the political class. In this manner, reinstatement of traditional laws will ultimate reflect a common good expressing public virtue, indicative of the historic biblical basis of society.

Influence of Ancient Heresy

In striving for social justice, the Alphabet sect seek purpose and identity outside the established principles upon which the culture relies. Their aims are reminiscent of ancient actors such as the rebellious Edenic First Couple and their descendants like Nimrod. The Tower of Babyl episode reflects

---

[4] Wokeness "is not about kindness, equality, fairness or morality (Hanson, V. D., Wokeism, 2022).
[5] Hobbes, T., Leviathan, 1651, Part 1, Ch. 11, p. 77.

Nimrod's attempt to create a secular humanist and pagan utopia, as do present identity actors.

Therefore, the struggle for social justice can be understood as a confrontation between the Creator God and ancient serpentine spirituality, as it was in the Garden. The primeval origins of this heresy, reiterated through all ages, has led to the contemporary contest surrounding truth, personal identity, meaning, and the purpose of life.

Divine Purpose

The Redeemer-Messiah, on his first advent, did not come for the primary purpose of establishing political and social justice, much to the chagrin of the Jewish nation. His mission was to proclaim the good news of redemption and to advance the Kingdom of God on earth. Still, there are many instances where the Messiah expressed compassion for the poor (both materially and spiritually poor), the downtrodden and outcasts of society. He reacted to poverty in society, not to attain social justice but, rather, as a demonstration of higher purpose through compassion, mercy, and love.

Contrarily, the woke brigade has as their higher purpose an idealistic form of social justice. A report from the 'National Association of Scholars' in New York reveals, "Social Justice activists in the Universities subordinate higher education towards the goal of achieving social justice." This action has led to mandatory registration for students in social justice courses like "Native Sexualities and Queer Discourse," in order to graduate.[6] In this way, the social justice concept has become sacred, a form of religion, for identity activists.

---

[6] Macdonald, H., Cost of America's Revolution, 2019, p. 18.

7.4. Radical Secular Humanism

Practical atheism, an expression of secular humanism, drives the ethical, moral, religious, and cultural decay within present-day society, upsetting its social order and established values. In an attempt to create a progressive humanist utopia and to force upon society an ideological monopoly, activists attempt destruction of the prevailing moral and social framework which they deem obsolete. Their intention is to relegate existent culture to a pre-civilization era for, in anarchist jargon, *res delenda est* – everything is to be destroyed - and recreated with a loftier idealistic identity.

A Long March Through the Institutions

Although the seeds of practical atheism were sown long ago, in ancient times, they persisted throughout subsequent history manifesting in forms like the neo-Gnostic heresy of present times.[7] Even so, the rather rapid emergence of institutionally compelled secularism in the last few decades is cause for great concern.

It was during the 18th century Enlightenment period that the important intellectual, Baruch Spinoza, proposed truth is found only through philosophy and reason. This forceful argument eventually led to the personalised truth and ethical enquiry typical of secular humanism in the postmodern period. Not only absolute truths but freedom itself, are the first victims of a social revolution for narrow ideologies cannot bear competitors of any kind. Consequently, postmodernism is reflected in power politics, replacing reason and debate in governance while not emphasizing primacy of good conscience for the public good but, instead, favouring priority of the ideological self.

---

[7] "Neo-Gnosticism plays a decisive role in the process of Western secularization" (Del Noce, A., 2014, p. xviii).

The main onslaught of postmodern secularism has occurred in the educational field of liberal arts. Professor Virgil Nemoianu explains that the "humanities were born of a Judeo-Christian religious tradition," the goal of which is the "reconciliation between human solidarity and the dignity of individual persons."[8] Social activists, through neo-pagan identity concepts, have exploited these broad, accommodating, disciplines in the liberal arts tradition.

In a strategy to advance Marxism, Antonio Gramsci (1891 - 1937) had to overcome the social obstacle of established, biblically founded, truth, freedom and virtue. He therefore encouraged his followers to infiltrate the vulnerable fields of the liberal arts. Gramsci's words were as follows, "Socialism is precisely the religion that must overwhelm Christianity. In the new order, Socialism will triumph by first capturing the culture through infiltration of schools, universities, Churches and the media by transforming the consciousness of society."[9] Roger Kiska commented on this strategy by saying, "the problem with this type of Marxism is that an attack on the family, and the Judeo-Christian values that sustain it, leads to catastrophic economic and social effects."[10] These adverse effects are evident in all societies dominated by Marxist thought such as North Korea, Cuba, and Venezuela. Communist regimes, while claiming a laudable motive of liberating citizens from oppression, actually enslave them to a new master – the hardline State with its nihilist, atheist, dogma and compromised individual freedoms.

---

[8] Nemoianu, V., Teaching Christian Humanism, 1996.
[9] Gramsci, A., Prison Notebooks, 1971, p. 118.
[10] Kiska, R., Long March Through History, 2019.

The principles behind Gramsci's proposals[11] were endorsed by Marxist philosopher Herbert Marcuse,[12] himself inspired by radical leftist Rudi Dutschke's[13] ploy of an infiltration through all categories of Western education. Dutschke termed this strategy "the long march through the institutions," which Marcuse explained as "working against the established institutions while working in them, not simply by 'boring from within' but rather by 'doing the job,' learning how to teach at all levels of education, how to use the mass media..."[14] The eventual outcome was predictable, "Universities allowed political activists to commandeer the humanities, social sciences and in some cases, even the sciences." In the revolutionary view of social engineers, "everything must be thrown into the great cause of social justice."[15] This is classic Marxist revolutionary strategy, having collectivism as its aim through an idealized social justice theory.

Secular Education

Apart from the neo-Marxist influence through Gramsci, Marcuse and Dutschke, the principal catalyst for 20th century secularisation of the US education system was influential reformer, Professor John Dewey (1859-1952). A founder of the atheistic American Humanist Association's 'Humanist Manifesto' of 1933, Dewey's secular approach was a turning point in US education. Dispensing with biblical values as a basis of

---

[11] Gramsci's theory of a "passive revolution" (1971, p. 106), is akin to Dutschke's, "long march through the institutions."

[12] Herbert Marcuse (1898 – 1979), of the Frankfurt School of Critical Theorists, advocated social justice along Marxist principles. Critical theorists created ideologies like Critical Race Theory and Social Justice theory (Farr, A., Marcuse, 2021).

[13] Rudi Dutschke (1940 – 1979), greatly influenced by Critical Theories and cultural Marxism (Zündorf, I., Bibliography, 2021).

[14] Marcuse, H., Counterrevolution and Revolt, 1972, p. 55.

[15] Reno, R., What We're For, 2021.

education, Dewey implemented a secular, sociological, approach where "nationalism replaced Christianity as the centre of *paideia*." Thomas Sowell predicted the dire outcome of these policies in the following terms, "Ours may become the first civilization destroyed – not by the power of our enemies – but by the ignorance of our teachers and the dangerous nonsense they are teaching our children."[16]

In the end, Dewey was responsible for "turning public schools from largely Protestant Christian academies into secular indoctrination centers."[17] Within such environment, religious symbols and activities like biblical studies and public prayer were prohibited. Predictably, society itself eventually reflected Dewey's ideology and this in turn influenced politics, government, religious institutions, and the ethos of the justice system.

Legal Authority

Attention must be given to the 1963 Supreme Court case of Abington School District versus Schempp which compromised First Amendment rights of freedom of religion. The Court held that, in public affairs, one religion cannot be preferred to another. The State itself was prohibited from recognising religious principles in public affairs. Instead, the Court decided the State should be neutral towards all religions (including atheism), and therefore instances of Judeo-Christianity (such as Bible readings) in Public schools were forbidden. The Court insisted it was not attempting to entrench a religion of secularism, but was promoting neutrality towards all religions. And that is the central issue, for proclaimed neutrality inescapably has a default position of secularism,

---

[16] Sowell, T., Controversial Essays, 2002, p. 308.
[17] Clay, B., Failure of John Dewey, 2021.

which caters for a pluralistic culture. To deny religious input in the public sphere is to enforce secularism, the exclusion of God, an atheistic position not a neutral one. Practical atheism has therefore become the default position in a vacuum of religious participation. In actuality, secularism constitutes a religion of its own, being a rival faith to Judeo-Christianity.

The 'secular purpose doctrine' of the Abingdon case was affirmed in the 1971 Supreme Court matter of Lemon versus Kurtzman. Yet, in striving to be neutral, State sponsored secularism promotes an environment without God, without definitive, value-based, precepts. While State neutrality appeals as an equal, just, and fair position to all parties, the reality is quite the contrary for neutrality is a contextual concept that can be manipulated. For instance, Court decisions can reflect an actual bias against religious freedom rights, despite claimed neutrality.

In 2022, some 50 years later, the Supreme Court effectively overruled the blanket Lemon precedent when it upheld the principle of religious liberty in Kennedy versus Bremerton. In this case, the Court affirmed the right of a public high school football coach, a Christian, to openly pray on the field after the game, thereby reintroducing religious freedom, albeit of a limited nature.

The Issue of Religion

Supported by earlier U.S. Supreme Court decisions, the totality of Western culture developed over preceding centuries is under threat of abolishment through a reconstitution of fundamental values.[18] The key target for destruction is the religious basis of the culture with its long-standing

---

[18] These values are biblical and include "human dignity, the rule of law, separation of powers, democracy, civil liberties and inviolability of private property" (Bintsarovskyi, D., Misconceptions, January 6, 2023).

values. In the method of classic revolutionary strategy, socio-anarchists endeavour to negate rights such as freedom of religion and speech. In consequence, the influence of religious principles in public life is side-lined in favour of a 'neutral' secular humanism. By so doing, reliance is placed on situational ethical concepts validating subjective values. Gene Veith surmises that "whereas modernism sought to rid the world of religion, postmodernism spawns new ones. Unconstrained by objectivity, customs, reason, or morality, these new faiths differ radically from Christian principles. Instead, they draw on strains of ancient and primitive paganisms."[19] Paganism is an instance of practical atheism, itself a secular humanist offshoot.

Hate Speech

In the post-truth era, biblical values are rejected as discriminatory and judgemental towards those holding their opposing ideas of truth. Even so, the concept of discrimination is necessary to some degree. All right-thinking societies need to discriminate between decency and barbarianism and to identify principles and practices unacceptable in such society. In denouncing criticism of their sectarian practices, radicals reveal that their true objective is not the advance of democracy but hegemonic power. For these social idealists, true representative democracy does not suit their intentions as they wish to impose a refabricated social structure upon a dissenting majority populace.

Emphasizing traditional values is now considered 'hate speech' under ideologically slanted legislation. This legislation generally consists of an 'Equality Act' enacted under the guise of political correctness and fairness,

---

[19] Veith, G., Postmodern Times, 1994, p. 198.

yet forcing compliance in the public arena. An Equality Act is therefore used to repress sensible debate. The majority populace is required to condescend to identity ideologies exemplified by the Rainbow flag - the Pride flag - and not to the rights and obligations represented in the US National flag, the 'Stars and Stripes.' Mary Eberstadt points out the "new intolerance is a wholly owned subsidiary of a neo-Marxist social revolution. Thus, no revolution, no new intolerance."[20] Protected by favourable legislation, activists have no hesitation in promoting a different morality.

Civil Freedoms

Nonetheless, society cannot "permit any product, no matter how depraved its content, to be created, sold, promulgated, procured or kept," says Professor David Bentley Hart. He elaborates, "a society that refuses all censorship is in some very crucial sense extremely unjust."[21] Fairness, equality and justice are not, in actuality, the concern of leftists for they seek a form of skewed distributive justice subjugating others to their unconventional ideas.

Civil freedoms encompass a balance, through restraint, of competing public rights to ensure the smooth and harmonious operation of society. It is within mutually beneficial boundaries that decency, modesty, tolerance, and virtue are promoted. Civilisation has not been hindered but, instead, benefitted through certain controls over decades. An example is the age restriction imposed on visual media to protect the childhood of the innocent.

---

[20] Eberstadt, M., The New Intolerance, 2015.
[21] Hart, D. B., Freedom and Decency, June, 2004.

Balance of Rights

Society faces conflicting demands for freedoms relating to ethical and moral expression in the public square. On the one hand there are demands for restraint and, on the other, demands for less or no restraint. The latter typically strive to dispense with traditional ethical and moral limitations and the balance of competing rights necessary for the public good. Calls for restraint by moderates provoke vociferous resistance by activists. This contest indicates a deep and irreconcilable political and religious divide reflecting competing worldviews. Yoram Hazony refers to this situation as a "contest between two powerful movements, a 'liberal' (leftist) movement that has been dominant for some time, and a nationalist movement that openly seeks to resist it."[22] The latter movement is a conservative counter-revolution for re-establishment of the traditional way of life.

To bring about peaceful change, to revert to the 'old' order of civilization established upon timeless biblical precepts, the obligation predominantly falls upon a conservative sector of the populace to influence those in authority. Authentic Judeo-Christians are mandated to bring truth to society while striving to make disciples of all men, and this mandate is crucial to the good order of society. Respected historian, Arnold Toynbee, stressed that to counter mounting secularism, the West's biblical heritage "in all its forms has to be reintroduced."

New Social Religion

In seeking distributive justice, events of the 1790 French revolutionary period led to a major weakening of society's Judeo-Christian ethos. There

---

[22] Hazony, Y., Conservative Democracy, 2019.

are similarities between the French uprising and the current agenda of identity radicals, for they also attempt to replace biblical principles with a secular and neo-pagan creed.

Russell Hittinger writes that "the human person is a domestic (matrimonial-familial) animal, a political animal, and an ecclesial animal."[23] All three categories of the person are under stress from revolutionaries through firstly, challenges to traditional ideas of marriage, family, and personal well-being coupled with hostility against the Fatherhood of God concept. Secondly, the totalitarian agenda of controlling the political narrative in relation to identity. And, thirdly, the eradication of established biblical principles sustaining ethics, morality and the rule of law. Lamenting secularism in society, Matthew Arnold in his 1867 poem, 'Dover Beach,' described the "Sea of faith" as receding with a "melancholy, long, withdrawing roar."[24] These emotive words indicate the growing demise of an established culture through severe social upheavals.

The refabrication of society is a cultural Marxist agenda to create a new order for, as Antonio Gramsci explained, Marx desired a "single culture, a single religion, a world-wide conformism."[25] Nonetheless, Judeo-Christianity cannot easily be eliminated from society. The enduring truth of ancient moral and ethical precepts always reasserts itself in various forms. Hence, the public practice and influence of biblical precepts will continue to thrive despite a mounting secular context for, as the Redeemer-Messiah emphasized, "I will build my Church and the gates of hell shall not prevail against it" (Matt. 16:8).

---

[23] Hittinger, R., Societies, 2017.
[24] Arnold, M., Dover Beach, 1867.
[25] Gramsci, A., Selections, 1971, p. 374.

7.5. Pluralism and Syncretism

In Charles Taylor's view, escalating secularisation of civilization reflects the transition of a society, "where belief in God is unchallenged, to one in which it is only one option among others and frequently not the easiest to embrace."[26] A perceptive view, for secular humanism synergized with neo-pagan New Age ideologies strive to dominate established culture.

Church Decline

Compromised churches are in decline for they have nothing different to offer a sceptical populace, being indistinct from the secular culture. Progressive Christians focus on a utopian version of social justice, embracing Darwin's evolutionary materialism. Compared to creationist doctrine, Darwin's ideology escalates in popularity as an alternative avenue to meaning and personal identity. Around 54% of college educated Americans agree with the statement that, "Human beings as we know them, developed from earlier species of animals."[27] In so doing, they deny the created *sui generis* and *imago Dei* identity of humankind – the unique personal identity of all individuals made in the image of the Creator.

---

[26] Taylor, C., A Secular Age, 2007, p. 3.
[27] Blair, L., Relationship with God, 2021.

CHAPTER SEVEN
PART THREE

POLITICS, LAW,
AND SOCIAL JUSTICE

"We have placed too much hope in political and social reforms, only to find out that we were being deprived of our most precious possession: our spiritual life"
(Aleksandr Solzhenitsyn, 1978).

7.6. A Clash of Civilisations

In 1996, Harvard University's Samuel Huntington predicted an external clash of the world's leading civilizations. In particular, a confrontation between Western civilization, with its Judeo-Christian principles, and those nations holding to Islamic fundamentalism, eastern religiosity, and Marxist dogma. Huntington's prophecy became dramatically valid in October 2023 when the fundamentalist Hamas organisation attacked the Jewish nation of Israel, threatening its very survival.

James Kurth perceives that in the West there exists an internal confrontation of civilisations.[1] Kurth's view is likewise valid for an internal cultural battle for social dominance between biblical orthodoxy and secular, neo-pagan, ideology also amounts to a collision of civilisations. During early 2023, in Israel, an internal clash of values occurred with mass social turbulence between the secular, progressive,

---

[1] Kurth, J., The Real Clash, 1994.

cultural elites of Tel Aviv and the religious, orthodox, conservative leaders in Jerusalem. The catalyst was government implementation of democratic principles correcting an imbalance in the classic liberal separation of powers, as between judiciary and legislature. This contest reflected anarcho-secularists pitted against citizens embracing established religious and democratic values,[2] just as is taking place in Western jurisdictions.

Deities of Blood and Soil

The Nazi-era conflagration of ideologies was a macro-indicator of the postmodern crisis over truth, freedom, and the liberal democratic tradition. Yet German novelist Thomas Mann, in a 1940 radio address, confirmed that the Third Reich's program in purging European Jews was "nothing else but the ever-recurrent revolt of unconquered pagan instincts, protesting against the restrictions of the Ten Commandments." In Mann's view, the basis for war in Europe was "more than politics, it was about theology." Specifically, it was the Judeo-Christian faith in a mortal contest with neo-paganist Nordic ideology, embracing "deities of blood and soil."[3]

The Nazi agenda was to "replace Christianity with a religious faith that was more authentically German," meaning, "Ario-Germanic paganism and Indo-Aryan Spiritualism."[4] A study[5] by History Professor Eric Kurlander of the spiritual heritage of Nazi ideology confirms its occultist basis.[6] For instance, Deputy Führer Rudolf Hess was fascinated with the occult and "sponsored astrology, cosmic-biology and other

---

[2] Fleisher, Y., The Civilization Clash: Tel Aviv and Jerusalem, February 26, 2023.
[3] Levenson, D., The God of Abraham, 1991.
[4] Kurlander, E., Hitler's Monsters: Supernatural History of the Third Reich, 2017, Ch. 6.
[5] Kurlander, E., *ibid.*
[6] Nazi ideology is a neo-Gnostic idea, "revealed by the very symbol of the Third Reich and the idea of the thousand years" (Del Noce, A., 2014, p. 303).

esoteric medical practices." Heinrich Himmler, Chief of the SS, encouraged research on the "Holy Grail, witchcraft, and medieval devil worship."[7] Nonconformity to Nazi ideology justified liquidation of dissenters. Not only Jews were regarded as mortal enemies of the desired new ethnicity (of which Nietzsche's *Übermensch* was an unwitting contributor), but Christians too, as critics like Dietrich Bonhoeffer, Thomas Mann, and Paul Tillich experienced.

In more contemporary times, the 2023 existential battle between the Jewish nation of Israel and the jihadist Islamic fanaticism of Hamas terrorists is, likewise, a lethal clash over religious truth: the Judeo-Christian faith against heathen Islamism. The Israeli Minister of Defense, Yoav Gallant, explained that "the war here is the war of the sons of light against the sons of darkness."[8] And, just as the Nazi-era battle was Nordic pagan ideology against Mediterranean Jewish religious truth and ethnic identity (and by extension, Christian truth and identity), so the present Israeli Jewish – jihadist Islamic struggle is a battle for faith and identity. Occurring in a common geographical arena, this amounts to both an internal and external clash of civilisations. As in the Nazi-era, neither religious culture can compromise with the other for they hold diametrically opposing views of truth, values, and faith. Therefore, there can be no expectation of peace with ideological heathen zealots determined to eradicate all believers of the Judeo-Christian faith from the region.

Ideological Dominance

Aggressive race and sexual identity concepts, long energised by academics

---

[7] Kurlander, E., Hitler's Monsters, 2017, p. 2.
[8] Fabian, E., Gallant Vows to Find and Kill Every Last Hamas Terrorist, October 15, 2023.

and elites through vulnerable conduits of the humanities, clash with society's biblically founded principles for cultural dominance in society.

Using educational disciplines of the humanities as a tool for promoting utopian ideals is unsurprising for, as educator John Agresto explains, the "liberal arts, properly understood, are both the depository of civilization and the engine of its advancement."[9] Here, Irving Horowitz lamenting ideological capture of US sociology writes, "sociology has largely become a gathering of individuals who have special agendas. Any idea of a common democratic culture or a universal scientific base has become suspect." He explains that the "aim of sociology is now to retool human nature and effect a systematic overhaul of society."[10]

The outcome of ideological infiltration in tertiary education was described by Pierre Ryckmans in his Australian 1996 'Boyer Lecture' when he said, "The main problem is not so much that the University, as Western civilization knew it, is now dead but that its death has hardly registered in the consciousness of the public, and even the majority of academics."[11]

The Cause

Woke ideologies, emerging from critical theories, comprise the following: race theory (ethnic hierarchy); radical feminist theory (abortion, euthanasia, eugenics); the Gay agenda (the Alphabet sect with its sex-gender theories and same-sex marriage); and multiculturalism (emphasis on minorities, secularism, religious pluralism and an unattainable cultural unity).

---

[9] Agresto, J., The Death of Learning: Preface, 2022.
[10] Horowitz, I. V., The Decomposition of Sociology, 1994, p. 12.
[11] Ryckmans, P., Boyer Lectures, 1996.

Despite defensible, rational, ethical codes founding the laws, rules, and the moral order of Western societies for centuries, biblical principles are to be refabricated by social engineers in the name of social justice. To attain this result, activists seek autocratic powers through political, corporate, media and legal endorsement. Simultaneously, they insist on downgrading entrenched Constitutional rights of freedoms available to society as a whole.

Two Competing Views

The main issue between views of conservatives and leftists concerns differences in moral and religious viewpoints arising from their respective creeds. While biblical moral codes reflecting a sacred tradition are rationally defensible, they are contrary to the neo-Marxist order proposed by social utopians. In this context, G. K. Chesterton remarks that, "Christianity is at one with common sense; but all religious history shows that this common sense perishes except where there is Christianity to preserve it."[12]

To exacerbate matters, drastic ideological propositions are supported by an overreach of Federal organs. But apart from state and juridical endorsement, the adoption of identity ideologies as official corporate policy by large multinational commercial entities in the US and Europe, brings a serious social and economic dimension to both public and private life. Employees are bound by policies imposed by the corporate elite, failing which their livelihoods are threatened. In conjunction with a statist administration, unelected nomenklaturas, politicians, academia, mass

---

[12] Chesterton, G. K., The Everlasting Man, 1925, p. 85.

media, and sundry supporters, a powerful corporate elite has emerged in the name of political correctness and social justice.

The Archbishop of Los Angeles, Jose Gomez, explains the elite are "in charge of corporations, governments, universities, the media, and the cultural and professional establishments." They desire a "global civilization, built on a consumer economy and guided by science, technology, humanitarian values, and technocratic ideas about organizing society." Gomez adds that in this "elite worldview, there is no need for old-fashioned belief systems and religion. In fact, religion as they see it especially Christianity, only gets in the way of the society they hope to build."[13] These are powerful words but Gomez's findings apply also to the public education system, now detached from biblical principles in favour of an ostensible neutrality which, inescapably, leads to enforced secularism. Educators no longer seek or teach objective truths but, instead, rely on slanted understandings of social justice (through conduits like CRT and DEI), to achieve outcomes that accord with popular ideology.

This theme finds support in Alan Bloom's study of the U.S. education ethos, 'The Closing of the American Mind.' He writes, "the one thing a professor can be absolutely certain of is that almost every student entering the university believes, or says he believes, that truth is relative."[14] Here, again, the caution of prophet Isaiah rings true for not only has truth "stumbled in the public squares,"[15] the inalienable right of intellectual freedom has been curtailed. The youth, the future leaders of the free world, suffer unceasing propaganda and, in time, will be affected by the current anti-truth ethos. The situation does not bode well for a society founded on

---

[13] Gomez, J., Reflections on the Church, 2021.
[14] Bloom A. D. The Closing of the American Mind, 1988, p. 25.
[15] Isaiah 59:14.

traditional values. The Greek philosopher, Diogenes (412-323 B.C.E.), warned "the foundation of every state is the education of its youth" – sound advice, but ignored in the clamour for ideologically based education.

Political Correctness

Activists apply a power tactic known as 'cancel culture,' depriving notable speakers from public platforms, while incongruously avowing diversity, equality, and inclusiveness in seeking a beneficent social justice for all. Dissenters are silenced verbally, politically, and economically, whether individuals (academics, public figures, or politicians), or businesses. Gomez highlights the fact that "often what is cancelled and corrected are perspectives rooted in Christian beliefs – about human life, and the human person, about marriage, the family, and more."[16] And that is the basic truth of the matter, for human identity, the *imago Dei* of humankind, is under threat of refabrication in favour of the heretical *eritus sicut Deus* (to be like God), which results in Yuval Noah Harari's idea of a *homo deus* (mangod), the self-deified person.[17] As is to be expected, underlying the assailment on personal identity is the evil spirit of the ancient serpent, the alter ego of his master, acting through compliant social radicals.

Multiculturalism

The issue of multiculturism is a complex one, markedly in Canada where the term denotes a firm leftist agenda. The Canadian State aims to create a new polyethnic national identity diluting the homogeneous white ethnicity of society, under the guise of ethnic diversity.

---

[16] Gomez, J., Reflections on the Church, 2021.
[17] Harari, Y. N., Homo Deus: A Brief History of Tomorrow, 2016, p. 21.

Multiculturism means the offsetting of dominant national and ethnic culture, and the religious roots of its liberal democratic polity. The purpose is to socially reflect revered components of all alien immigrant cultures.[18] Nathan Pinkoski describes the situation this way, "Multiculturalist progressivism demands the subjugation and destruction of traditional forms of life, particularly in the West."[19] Unmitigated migration brings about multiculturism but has had adverse effects upon the nations of Scandinavia and Europe, especially France and Sweden with ongoing social discord. Studies show the effect of multiculturalism is fragmentation into ethnic social enclaves, not integration with the majority populace as intended. This factor "tends to reduce social solidarity and social capital" and leads to significant absence of community cooperation and friendship with those of differing ethnic groups.[20]

Ethnic and Religious Factors

Shortcomings of multiculturalist policies are evident in the Swedish social situation where diversity agenda has led to Muslim majority in the 3rd largest Swedish city, Malmö. A report by sociology professor, Erica Righard, refers to the current status as a praiseworthy "superdiversity."[21] On the other hand, Bruce Bawer denies merit in a cultural "superdiversity," claiming it amounts to a "great replacement" of Sweden's culture with its Lutheran background.[22] Bawer's view is accurate for he refers to a sermon by Malmö's Imam Basem Mahmoud

---

[18] The "great replacement of culture is happening in America and throughout the West" (Anton, M., Unprecedented, 2021).
[19] Pinkoski, N., Spiritual Death of the West, May 2023.
[20] Putnam, R. D., Diversity and Community in the 21st Century, June 15, 2007.
[21] Righard, E., Integration, Malmo Institute for Studies of Migration, Diversity and Welfare, June 1, 2022, p. 11.
[22] Bawer, B., Superdiversity in Malmö, January 6, 2023.

who declared in 2022, "Sweden is ours. It is ours whether they like it or not. In 10-15 years, it will be ours."[23] This result implies eventual implementation of Sharia law, thus compromising Sweden's classic liberal democratic order with its human freedoms long based on Protestant principles. Sweden's culture is in danger of being subsumed by alien religious principles for the sake of fostering unattainable ideological objectives, such as diversity through an enforced pluralism.

A diverse society naturally reflects the view of all sectors of society including atheists, agnostics and competing religious tenets, yet multiculturalism is a naïve and impractical concept for there is no compelling factor, no *asabiyah*,[24] consolidating a diversified populace other than living in the same territory. Religious, ethnic, cultural differences do not bind citizens together, quite the contrary as is clear from historic wars and genocides. This fact is noticeably so with regard to certain expressions of Islam which view Judaism and Christianity, in particular, as false religions to be eradicated. In a study of multiculturalism, Jens Kurt Heycke concludes that without the binding component of *asabiyah,* "multi-ethnic societies can easily descend into discord and violence,"[25] a situation seen in Sweden, France and Germany with their large multiculturalist communities. Due to cultural, religious and ethical divergence, there can never be an *asabiyah* in these nations.

Diversity, Equality, and Inclusion

Even though Judeo-Christianity is fast becoming a minority faith in an environment of pluralistic faith, it persists as the repository and purveyor

---

[23] Bawer, B., Sweden is a Big Step Forward for Islam, August 24, 2022.
[24] An Arabic term meaning "a unifying feeling that binds a group and makes collective action possible."
[25] Heycke, J. K., Out of the Melting Pot into the Fire: Multiculturalism, 2023, Ch. 1.

of crucial truths and principles. In Canada, the State engages in authoritarian efforts to achieve vague objectives of equality, diversity, cultural freedom and authenticity. This raises questions like does equality mean "equal opportunity or equal outcomes, egalitarian distribution, equality before the law, sexual equality, racial equality, or cultural equality and so on?"[26] The basic issue is, as always, that of religion for if all persons are reasoned equal so all religions are to be considered equal repositories of truth. Therefore, one religion cannot claim to represent truth to the exclusion of others for this amounts to hostile speech under Equality laws.

The Canadian State, as in the USA, enforces a stance of secularism necessary to ensure a neutral common ground in binding people together. Canada's strategy is the practice of *Laïcité*, that is, the establishment of a "secular state that vigilantly guards against the incursion of religious convictions into the public square."[27] Just as in the USA, religion in Canada is to be removed from the public square.

Cultural Judeo-Christianity in the West is under grave threat of marginalisation due to pluralistic claims of truth. With this understanding, atheist philosopher Douglas Murray penned an article titled, "Would human life be sacred in an atheist world?" Murray believes a post-Christian society has only three alternatives. The first, "to abandon the idea that all human life is precious." Secondly, to adjust to an atheist "version of the sanctity of the individual." thirdly, if the previous two "do not work, then there is only one other place to go, which is back to faith whether we like it or not." He concludes that "sanctity of life as a biblical notion, might not survive the disappearance of Judeo-Christian civilization."[28]

---

[26] Yenor, S., Lament for the Nations, 2021.
[27] Koyzis, D., Canada Divided as Ever, 2021.
[28] Murray, D., Would Human Life be Sacred, 2014.

Multiculturalism exacerbates the demise of established Judeo-Christian principles in the very societies founded upon them. Phillip Shannon refers to this phenomenon as "the dismemberment of Western civilization before the high altar of multi-cult diversity."[29]

Churchill and King David

Faced with the imminent Battle of Britain for survival of the Isles, Winston Churchill warned, "If we fail, then the whole world, including the United States, including all that we have known and cared for, will sink into the abyss of a new Dark Age made more sinister by the lights of perverted science."[30] Couched in theological terms, a post-Christian civilization will result in an atheist fabrication intersected with a neo-paganist spirituality of sorts. The consequence, says theologian David Hart, will be a "sordid service of the self, of the impulses of the will, of the nothingness that is all that the withdrawal of Christianity leaves behind...a conscious nihilism, with its inevitable devotion to death."[31]

The decisive challenge facing Western civilization is recounted in King David's rhetorical question from Psalm 11:3, "if the foundations are destroyed, what can the righteous do?" Here is the motivation for all Judeo-Christian disciples to rise up against malevolent forces threatening their civilization and the eternal principles upon which it is founded.

7.7. Conclusion

Emerging from a primeval background, secular humanism finds validation through deconstruction of established biblical doctrines underlying Western culture. Secularism combines with pluralistic and eclectic neo-

---

[29] Shannon, P., A Woke Word, 2022.
[30] Churchill, W., House of Commons, 1940.
[31] Hart, D. B., Christ and Nothing, 2003.

pagan spiritual New Age belief systems in challenging the moral, just, and religious order of society. In effect a state religion, secular humanism is enforced through legal directives of the highest juridical authorities.

Ideological Challenges

The ideological confrontation centers on the issue of identity, specifically the Fatherhood of God. Once this pivotal doctrine has lost effect, all ensuant dogma is likewise compromised. The offensive against the Fatherhood doctrine is actually aimed at repudiating the likeness of God in human beings. Subsequently, annulment of the binary gender identities of individuals, and the heterosexual format of their marriage regime, can be eradicated. Ideological justification for an alternative matrimonial bond then takes place. Upon removal of the Fatherhood of God idea, activists adopt feminine, intersex, or androgenous deities as replacement thereby validating their own sex-gender fabrications. In this way, fatherhood and the traditional nuclear family arrangement can be refabricated. Even so, scripture confirms humankind only finds meaning in the Most-High God where, "we live and move and have our being" (Acts 17:28).

Future of Western Civilization

Russian intellectual Konstantin Kisin explains the current situation, "Today, the fate of Western civilization hangs in the balance once again. The tomb of discord and division has been forced open by a small group of ideological zealots. Retreat is no longer an option."[32] Concerningly, the preservation of established, traditional, culture seems almost impossible to recapture. This dilemma is explained by Frank Meyer, "the delicate fabric (of the past) can never be recreated in its identical form, for its integral

---

[32] Kisin, K., An Immigrant's Love Letter to the West, 2022, Preface.

character has been destroyed."[33] Nonetheless, citizens accept that because they "live in the midst of a terrible revolution," they will have to "struggle to form a new, intelligible, responsive, and responsible conservatism to preserve the most precious things against those who wish to tear and rend and ruin."[34] The "precious things" that need preserving are the dignity, nobility, and inherent value of the sacred identity of human beings.

A Spiritual War

Social activists justify extreme nihilist practices, "a culture of death," such as unmitigated abortion; reconstruction of binary sex to suit gender acolytes; the euthanasia and eugenical termination of vulnerable persons; the ideological neutering of heterosexual males and social emasculation of males generally; the destruction of women's rights in favour of transgender identifiers; and the marginalisation of the white ethnic group in favour of minorities. These issues are central to the upheaval besetting Western societies, and reflect the Edenic search for unconstrained freedom and a subjective, fabricated, ideal of truth. This search has never ceased through the ages, simply articulating itself in differing guises.

The struggle for orthodoxy is not ultimately against gender self-identifiers, social justice activists or feminists in conjunction, but essentially, "against the rulers, against the authorities, against the cosmic powers over this present darkness, against the spiritual forces of evil in the heavenly places" (Eph. 6:12). It is a spiritual battle for the salvation of souls, using divine, supernatural, weapons such as prayer, *agape* love, faith, and the Word of God. Still, the visible line of battle is against human agents, as agents of darkness, who doubtlessly act unwittingly on behalf

---

[33] Meyer, F. S., Freedom, Conservatism, Modern Age, 1960, Vol. 4, pp. 366-363.
[34] Snell, R. J., How Should Conservatives Respond to Revolution, April 4, 2023.

of the fallen angel, Lucifer. Satan does not operate in a vacuum but through unwitting representatives like world rulers and leaders of society, who conspire against the Most-High God and his Kingdom purposes, as did Nimrod and his tribe in ancient times.

CHAPTER EIGHT
PART ONE

FINAL THINGS

"The duel of Christianity and atheism is the most important battle in the world"
(William F. Buckley, 1951)

8.1. Overview

The First Couple's rebellion in the Garden of Eden, stimulated by the demonic serpent's deceptive arguments but enabled by their own license of contrary choice, resulted in a severe disruption to the serene utopia planned for humanity.

Eritus Sicut Deus (To Be Like God)

Adam and Eve's rejection of their divinely conferred identity, the *imago Dei* (image of God), in favour of a Gnostic-like, occultist, search for knowledge affected all future generations. Their new independence would enable them to satisfy their desires to be like God (*eritus sicut Deus*), knowing good and evil, and to create a future free of boundaries. Their exile forced them to explore alternative pathways to meaning and identity, but one free of the Creator's paradigms. In so doing, they rejected the fatherhood role of the Creator, instead seeking a form of divinity like *homo deus* (god-man), the imperialism of self. Yet, their attempt was destined for failure for God will not share his glory with another (Isa. 42:8). This very human objective continued throughout subsequent history, to manifest in the fierce ego-centralism and hyper-individualism of a post-truth environment.

From time immemorial, spreading world-wide, occultist practice metastasising into assorted ideological and spiritual expositions. The medium through which this heresy emerged so strongly in the Aquarian New Age of postmodernity is that of ancient Gnostic dualist theory, inherent in conduits like astrology, eastern religions, and various philosophical and spiritual theories. The result, according to commentator Gerald Baker, is that we are "in the grip of an ideology that disowns our genius, denounces our success, distains merit. If Western civilization dies, put it down as a suicide."[1]

Creative Authority

As an outcome to Edenic events, "humanity is now at war with God over a question that reaches back to the beginning of time" says Mary Eberstadt. She reveals the root question of all secular humanism through the ages, "who, exactly, should have power over creation?" Eberstadt concludes the "culture dominant in the West today teaches that the creation of life is ours to control – more precisely, that it is for women to control."[2] The maelstrom over identity and meaning, causing much disorder, validates the veracity of Eberstadt's claim.

Through an illusionary belief in creative powers over their own bodies, individuals lose their sense of the sacred[3] in favour of a forged identity. Denial of the sacred element of humankind leads to a naturalist, instead of a supernaturalist, worldview. This belief is simply that of

---

[1] Baker, G., If Western Civilization Dies, Put It Down as a Suicide, April 17, 2023.
[2] Eberstadt, M., At War with God, 2022.
[3] Rowan Williams, Archbishop of Canterbury, calls transgenderism a "sacred journey."

atheism, without a transcendent meaning of life, amounting to an empty, nihilist, endgame. However, there is no alternative pathway to truth other than through biblical principles. A meaningful transcendent order, a blessed and eternal life, cannot arise from a humanist ideology offering no future hope. To gain a true identity, a "new creation," as sought by ideologues, a divine transaction involving the Messiah and the regenerating power of the Holy Spirit in required - all of which cannot occur in a secular operation.

Moral Cynicism

Historic influence of biblical principles on laws resulted in restrictions on public immorality, benefiting all members of society. These restraints now face a process of social and political demolition[4] to accommodate fashionable post-moral cultural refabrication. Instead of definitive moral guidelines, activists fabricate their own versions of acceptable moral practice. Judicial decisions and statutory laws reflect this trend.

The era of hedonistic moral cynicism is a contemporary repeat of the rebellious spirit first manifest in Eden. The conflict between Judeo-Christian values and atheist, neo-pagan, ethical standards produce confusion and uncertainty. The current cultural contest, while dividing society on ideological, political, and social grounds, reflects an attempt to establish truth, life, meaning, and purpose free of biblical traces.

A Culture of Life

Dualist Gnostic idealism birthed notorious concepts like Marx's dialectical materialism; the absurdist existentialism of Sartre and his

---

[4] Demolition or Deconstruction involve "interrogating, re-evaluating, and often shedding Christian doctrines, values and practices that are outdated, problematic or just plain harmful" (Henry, A., Deconstruction, 2022).

cluster of writer-philosophers; Nietzsche's nihilism; Jung's psychoanalysis; and Freud's sexual hypotheses with a therapeutic focus on the repressed 'inner-self.' The wide popularity of these concepts eventually caused marginalisation of cultural Judeo-Christianity in the public arena.[5] Although biblical precepts sustain what Pope John Paul II refers to as a "culture of life,"[6] these principles are vigorously repudiated by the identity cohort. In turn, this necessitates an existential struggle for truth which, in the words of the prophet Isaiah, "has stumbled in the public squares" (Isa. 59:14).

Perhaps poet Matthew Arnold best describes the precipitous nature of the desperate battle over truth and reality when he writes, "Fires will be kindled to testify that two and two make four. Swords will be drawn to prove that leaves are green in summer."[7] In plain language, there is no middle-ground, no compromise over absolutist truths and reality for it is a spiritual war between death and life eternal. Faced with many challenges, citizens of the West can identify with the words of Charles Dickens describing the state of affairs confronting his society when he writes, "It was the best of times, it was the worst of times, it was the age of wisdom, it was the age of foolishness, it was the epoch of belief, it was the epoch of incredulity, it was the spring of hope, the winter of despair."[8]

8.2. Legal Concerns

Exacerbating the social and political discord is an ideological bias common to all three branches of government, the executive, legislative and

---

[5] Christendom "has fought for two centuries not to die" (Delsol, C., End, 2021).
[6] Pope John Paul II, Evangelium Vitae, 1995.
[7] Arnold, M., Heretics, p. 305, 1905.
[8] Dickens, C., A Tale of Two Cities, 1859, p. 35.

judicial. The governmental leftist ideological penchant is likewise conditioned within a vast array of powerful but unelected public-civil servants, ostensibly accountable to the Executive. This army of 'deep state' activists constitute what political science professor, Charles Lipson, labels a "4th branch of government." As a consequence, says Professor Helen Krieble, "Americans accused of violations are now ten times more likely to be tried by an unelected bureaucrat than by a Federal judge."[9] This situation is contrary to basic principles of democracy and justice.

White House lawyer Peter Wallison, addresses the issue of a 'deep state' in his work 'Judicial Fortitude,' where he warns, "we risk losing our democracy unless we can gain control of the agencies of the administrative state."[10] His proposed solution is an enforcement of the non-delegation principle for "it is difficult if not impossible to defend the separation of powers without a viable non-delegation doctrine."[11]

The Administrative Branch

The rise of an administrative-centric state results in a quandary as to exactly who is "making laws and what laws are being made." Religious and other freedoms are casualties of this situation and so is justice, both social and due process. To worsen matters is the administrative state's "increasing reliance on the private sector to deliver service for various federal social-welfare policies."[12] This tendency amounts to delegation of governmental tasks to private agencies, and has adverse effects on personal and constitutional freedoms. The US Federal Trade Commission ("FTC") comes to mind here. Supposedly accountable to the executive

---

[9] Krieble, H. E., The Things We Believe In, December 10, 2022.
[10] Some 400 Federal agencies exist in US (Watts, L., Unchecked Power, May 15, 2023).
[11] Wallison, P. J., Judicial Fortitude, 2018, pp. 1ff., 109.
[12] White, A. L., Overseers of American Religion, October 3, 2022.

branch, the FTC acts independently, contrary to Constitution parameters, effectively endorsing the claim of a fourth branch of State. Corbin Barthold claims the FTC, "defies, sidesteps and subverts all three branches of government."[13]

The significant increase in 'deep state' activity is a result of excessive authority delegated to low-ranking employees, coupled with judicial deference to the agencies themselves on interpretation of regulatory language. David Bernhardt believes this situation allows "administrative agencies to wield increasing power in a way that is insulated" from executive oversight. Bernhardt urges political leaders to "reassert control of administrative agencies."[14] Widespread concern of a powerful administrative state exercising autocratic and independent authority, while undermining Constitutional obligations and citizens' rights, is quite warranted. The culminative effect on society of 'four' branches of ideologically interconnected branches of government, leads to what veteran politician Newt Gingrich describes as "American despotism." As he perceives the situation, "we are faced with a totalitarian cancer that will have to be confronted and defeated at every level."[15]

A Constitutional Balance

There is great difficulty in remedying legal judgements reflecting distinct ideological slants. Law professor Russell Hittinger foresaw this tendency developing, explaining that the "Court's motivational analysis first emerged in connection to religion but now spreads to other matters of legislation informed by substantive moral purposes."[16] In a similar

---

[13] Barthold, C. K., Thumbing Their Noses, April 13, 2023.
[14] Bernhardt, D., You Report to Me, 2023, pp. 10, 20.
[15] Gingrich, N., American Despotism, September, 6, 2023.
[16] Hittinger, R., A Crisis of Legitimacy, 1996.

approach, Professor Patrick Garry criticised nuanced juridical outcomes when he testified, "for the past sixty years the progressive left has used the Courts to enforce its vision of how society ought to look and function."[17] These are concerning averments, going to the heart of democracy, for the Court's function is to interpret existing laws and administer justice, not to create laws and "invent rights" in order to define public moral order.[18]

The judicial situation in Israel, the sole democracy in the middle east, is a prime example of imbalance between the three branches of government. There, the unelected judicial branch appropriated powers unto itself, a scenario described as follows: "The Supreme Court President has transformed the Court into a super-legislator, empowered to dictate the terms of laws to the people's elected representatives, based on the values of the Justices." The democratically elected government, in its efforts to restore constitutional balance to the three branches, faced mass protests stirred up by a disgruntled leftist opposition. Caroline Glick brings attention to the fact that Supreme Court president, Esther Hayut, "cast the Court on a course of ideological radicalism and politicization that has no parallel anywhere in the world."[19]

In short, the Supreme Court of the United States made landmark judgements in certain seminal cases in which the majority Bench favoured a populist reading of the Constitution. The outcomes have proven alarming for a society based on established democratic traditions. Three germinal cases need mentioning in this context: Roe versus Wade[20] in 1973,

---

[17] Garry, P. M., Religious Freedom, 2022.

[18] Prof. George says "laws cannot make men moral" for "only men can do that" (George, R. Making Men Moral, 1993, p. 1).

[19] Glick, C., War Against Democracy, January 22, 2023,

[20] Rated 2nd worst Supreme Court decision ever (Franck, M. J., Supreme Failures from the Court, January 26, 2023).

permitting non-therapeutic termination of a fetal human being on demand; Obergefell versus Hodges[21] in 2015, empowering same-sex marriage and forcing all States to recognise such marriages; and Bostock versus Clayton County in 2020, prohibiting discrimination on the basis of sexual identity (including homosexual and transgender identifiers) in any public sphere.

Pro-Choice Churches

A disconcerting feature of legal challenges to a Texas Bill restricting abortion, was that a coalition of 25 Churches opposed the pro-life law, with 70 other Churches applying to join the pro-choice opposition. A reporter commented, "Anyone who supports abortion already gave up on scripture."[22] A correct remark, for denial of the validity of scriptural precepts is a chief indicator of alignment with popular culture.

The assault on living, pre-born, fetal children is far from over. Moves are afoot to codify abortion rights into Federal law. Federal Bill H.R. 3755, deceptively labelled 'Women's Health Protection Act of 2021' is, according to a statement by the 'Council for Biblical Manhood and Womanhood,' an "Orwellian-termed Bill that has nothing to do with health or protection for women, but everything to do with pushing the very limits of human depravity, and intends to legalized abortion up to the second before birth."[23] Although the Bill was passed by a majority in the House of Representatives but defeated in the Senate, the intent for similar laws remain. At State level, many States still permit abortion until birth.

---

[21] Rated 5th worst Supreme Court decision ever (Franck, M. J., *ibid.*).
[22] Stonestreet, J., Texas Heartbeat Bill, 2021.
[23] Smothers, C., A Dark Day in America, 2021.

Eisegesis (Subjective Interpretation)

A pivotal facet of Constitutional interpretation is consideration of the original context, the intent, of pertinent documents. Just as a literal and historical interpretative view of the scriptures results in an orthodox comprehension, so too a contextual, historical-literal, exegesis of the Constitutional Founders' intentions results in a sustainable and justifiable judgement.

Dobbs versus Jackson

The 1973 Roe against Wade abortion ruling was founded on an eisegetical view of the Constitution (interpretation from a biased viewpoint), while ignoring the original, literal, context[24] which did not provide a right to abortion. The judgement in Roe therefore amounted to a form of judicial activism by the Court, being contrary to the intent of the Founders. As a result, many millions of fetal deaths unnecessarily occurred.

A pertinent question regarding abortion is why the Supreme Court in the Dobbs matter delegated decision making to the individual States, once it ruled there was no Constitutional justification for abortion. Be that as it may, the solution lies at national level. Federal legislation banning the practice would resolve the issue. Alternatively, the Supreme Court's recognition of personhood of the unborn child will effectually terminate abortion throughout the nation. Abortionists would then face criminal charges such as homicide or murder, in various degrees.

---

[24] Court decisions in Roe (1973), Casey (1992), Texas (2003), and Windsor (2013) are judicial activism" (Lawler, P. A., Absolutes, 2014).

The Obergefell Case

It is in the area of same-sex marriage, arising from the Obergefell[25] ruling, that no short-term opportunity appears to exist for an appeal. Threats to cohesiveness of the nuclear family unit and to residual principles defining marriage will continue for the foreseeable future. To codify the Obergefell principle into law, the US administration passed the 'Respect for Marriage Act.' On December 13, 2022, the Act was signed into law by President Biden who personally tweeted, "Our nation has reaffirmed a fundamental truth: Love is Love."[26]

Here again is misconstrual of the biblical concept of *agape* love. Although the Act does not compel individual States to legalize same-sex marriage, they are obliged to recognize those marriages validly performed in compliant States. Needless to say, the prior definition of marriage as between a man and a woman was repealed through the new Act. In the result, the Act enables authorities to prosecute those who refuse to condone same-sex marriage, believing it to be a mésalliance due to religious views which condemn such marriage as heretical and illegitimate.

Bostock and Title VII

As with the Obergefell decision, there seems to be no realistic short-term prospect of overturning the 2020 Bostock decision for it is inextricable connected to Statutory law, Title VII of the Civil Rights Act of 1964. This law makes it unlawful for any employer to, "fail or refuse to hire or to

---

[25] In his minority dissent, Justice Roberts wrote, "the Court is not a legislature. Whether same-sex marriage is a good idea should be of no concern to us. Today the Court takes the step of ordering every State to license and recognize same-sex marriage. For those who believe in a government of laws, not of men, the majority's approach is deeply disheartening" (Roberts, J., Hodges, 2015).

[26] Cook, M., Respect for Marriage Act, December 1, 2022.

discharge any individual or to otherwise discriminate against any individual because of race, colour, religion, sex or national origin." The broad principle here is that any discrimination against a person because of their sex (including assumed gender) is unlawful.[27] The result is a meteoric rise in institutionalised transgender rights causing much consternation. The rulings indicate more irrational decisions can be expected, particularly when the Court adopts a populist eisegetical interpretation rather than an originalist, textual, approach.

The Abington Case

Pivotal Supreme Court decisions in Abington School District versus Schempp (1963) and in Lemon versus Kurtzman (1971),[28] are what created the post-Christian secular milieux in which the same-sex and abortion rulings were decided. Fortunately, due to sterling efforts by conservative public interest legal action groups, challenges are brought against Court rulings contravening Constitutional safeguards. Hope remains that these decisions will eventually be remedied.

In essence, eisegetical judicial rulings from the 60's and 70's amount to what Professor Ryan Anderson calls "Alien Jurisprudence," meaning judges read into the Constitution ideological "expressive individualism," giving vent to unrestrained freedom of speech rights like pornography. On this basis they struck down laws "against contraception and abortion, marginalizing religion by relegating it to the private sphere."[29]

---

[27] In December 2022, The U.S. Appeals Court, in Soule v. Connecticut Assoc. of Schools, ruled that male transgender identifiers may participate in girl's events without infringing individual Civil Rights under Title IX.

[28] Rated 16th worst Supreme Court decision in U.S. judicial history (Franck, M. J.).

[29] Anderson, R. T., To Defend True Freedom, We Need to Know the Truth, Fall 2023.

8.3. Ideological Authoritarianism

Repressive actions by the State are aimed at entrenching power to expand identity ideology. The transition of the State into a somewhat one-party entity with all three branches of government endorsing a common ideology is part of this process. In so doing, governments engage in flagrant acts of interbranch relationship, circumventing Constitutional checks and balances necessary for the separation of powers.[30] Limits to State power are essential for a healthy democracy, for they lead to "ordered liberty."[31] State interbranch cohesion, supported by powerful corporates and a vast media ecosystem, amounts to a form of ideological nationalism in antithesis of liberal democratic policies.

Cultural activists, in order to defeat conservatism, continually force social change to justify their proposed new identity order, an order they call 'progress.' As N. S. Lyons points out, to these "change merchants stability means death," for society is a work in progress and needs to continue evolving for the better. To achieve this aim, idealists control the language and the political narrative, changing everything to their advantage and causing much turmoil in the process. Lyons describes this strategy as follows, "if abstract theory is truth, then reality must be false, subject to change by sheer will." This philosophical dichotomy, an idealized construct, is none other than neo-Gnostic dualism. In the result, social damage will only cease when citizens "stop buying it," for there is

---

[30] French philosopher Montesquieu proposed this idea in his 1748 manuscript, 'The Spirit of the Laws.' John Locke had earlier mentioned division of powers between king and parliament (1632-1704). Separation of powers has biblical precedence for there was to be a permanent dichotomy between the authority of the King and that of the prophet and also between the office of the King and the High Priest (Rieders, C., Separation of Powers, January 30, 2023).

[31] Kling, A., A Better Regulatory State, 2022.

a limit as to "how much change and instability people can tolerate in a short span of time."[32]

The Political and Legal Arena

The struggle against deviant cultural change needs to be fought, not only at a social level, but in the political and legal domain. Should aberrant identity ideologies not be challenged at this level, then demise of traditional culture surely follows. Social theorist, Philip Rieff, is convinced that "unless a culture is defeated politically… it will reassert itself politically later if not sooner."[33] The current social revolution is described by Rieff as "Deathworks," meaning "an all-out assault upon something vital to established culture." An apt description of the precipitous nature of the crisis over essential Judeo-Christian principles founding the culture.

---

[32] Lyons, N. S., The Change Merchants, June 24, 2023.
[33] Rieff, P., My Life, Among Deathworks, 2006, p. 1.

CHAPTER EIGHT
PART TWO

FINAL THINGS

*"Ours may become the first civilization destroyed – not by the power
of our enemies – but by the ignorance of our teachers and
the dangerous nonsense they are teaching our children"*
(Thomas Sowell, 2002)

8.4. Future of Woke Ideology

In light of growing public resistance to identity ideologies, the question is
whether or not woke influence is on the wane. Identity ideology appears
to be at its peak,[1] firmly entrenched socially, politically, legally and
theologically (in some religious institutions). This situation reflects an
incredible achievement by a parochial, numerically minor, fringe group of
cultural revolutionaries. Some continental scholars, like Chantal Delsol,
already mourn the demise of cultural Christianity. In Delsol's opinion,
"the civilization built as a support for Christian belief over the last sixteen
centuries, since the conversion of Constantine, has finally been dismantled
by its enemies."

But many others like Harvard's James Hankins, disagree Christianity
has lost credence in the public square.[2] Christianity has survived many

---

[1] Progressives are "re-writing American history. They take aim at God, believers, and the
nuclear family. There is no area of human endeavour that they have not politicized" (Glick,
C., Progressive, 2022).
[2] Hankins, J., Among the Infidels, December 14, 2022.

challenges throughout history and, through the Divine's unassailable dynamic agenda, has overcome every obstacle. The Messiah-Redeemer will "build his church,"[3] come what may. Defiance of practical wokeness is actioned through legal challenges and political opposition, with moderate individuals becoming more vociferous and open. Mounting public resistance encourages lovers of freedom, especially religious freedom, to clamour against restrictive ideologies plaguing society. Public interest law firms like 'First Liberty Institute' witnessed the "greatest resurgence of religious freedom in the last 50 years." Evidence is provided not only through success of two pivotal Supreme Court hearings in this field, but the cumulative effect of ongoing legal success at other levels.

Go Woke, Go Broke

Media corporates suffer huge financial loss due to their woke policies. Reports indicate that "Disney, Netflix, and other giants lost over $500 billion in market value," a loss directly attributed to their strong LGBT+ policies.[4] Anheuser Busch, producers of the popular beer Budweiser Light, experienced substantial loss of sales after appointing Dylan Mulvaney - a transgender adult male masquerading as a teenage girl - as the brand's icon. 'Bud Light' customers were horrified, boycotting the brand which led to an immediate $16 billion deficit in market share. Other major corporations also experience consumer pushback, such as the Target group with 2,000 stores, losing $10 billion in market share within a few days after promoting a Pride range of clothing.

---

[3] Matthew 16:18.
[4] Giatti, I. M., Disney, January 2, 2023.

The Heart of Society

Chris Rufo refers to the cohort of resistant citizens, nuclear families especially, as the "Quiet Right" - the 'silent majority' – those intent on reclaiming conservative values in public life. After all, it is the family, "Burke's little platoons," the grass-roots movement, that is the driving force behind societies "intending to remain free."[5] The Heritage Foundation indicated that in response to the Left's "sex and gender policies, parents and kids flexed their muscles in opposition to schools that are all in on 'Pride.'"[6] Families are finding their voice, opposing destructive identity ideologies in their social and relational circles.

The heart of society is the family unit. This social nucleus, with its home and hearth, is where members can interact, can enjoy peace, love, warmth, comfort, and find sanctuary in turbulent times. Traditionalists emphasize the comforting atmosphere of the family home for, as Alexander Gauland president of Germany's 'Alternative für Deutschland' political party explains, "We do not seek to defend Christianity in any religious sense but as a traditional way of life, as a traditional sense of home."[7] The latter idea is likewise pivotal to Jewish life. Rabbi Jonathan Sacks emphasizes that the "concept of family and home is absolutely fundamental to Judaism."[8]

It was Cardinal Joseph Ratzinger who explained the biblical concept of home when he wrote, "the free man is one who is at home, that is, one who really belongs to the household. Freedom has to do with being given a home."[9] The idea of the family unit, with its home, is a transcendent

---

[5] Roberts, K. D., Burkean Nationalism, May 24, 2023.
[6] Perry, S. P., Families Clash with Schools over LBGTQ Propaganda, June 22, 2023.
[7] Cremer, T., The Godless Crusade, 2023, p. 75ff.
[8] Sacks, J., Covenant and Conversation: Genesis 1 - Family Feeling, 2009, para. 5783.
[9] Reno, R. R., Sacrificing the Young, August 2023.

biblical principle as all persons long for a home, long for connection. James Matthew Wilson describes this concept as "fidelity to place," explained as "fidelity to God, family, and country," all of which contribute towards a sense of social order, security, harmony and well-being. Fidelity to place is "not merely one virtue among others, but a foundational and formative source of our character."[10]

Even so, real belonging, finding a true home, commences with a sacred vertical relationship with the Creator from which flows meaningful horizontal, interpersonal, connections. The great English poet John Donne (1573-1631) acknowledged this theme when he wrote, "No man is an island, entire of itself; every man is a piece of the continent, a part of the main."[11] The staple requirement of "fidelity to place" is what creates right-thinking and emotionally secure individuals, those determined to conserve virtues enjoyed for generations within the freedoms of a classic liberal democratic environment.

Secretly Conservative

Professor Tyler Cowen believes "numerous U.S. institutions have maintained or even extended a right-wing stance." There is truth in his view for a Gallup poll indicates, "US conservatism is the highest in about a decade," with only 29% of the population "very liberal or liberal."[12] In support, a Pew Research survey reveals decreasing public support for identity cohorts like Black Lives Matter, which reflects a drop to 51% from a high of 70% a short time ago.[13]

---

[10] Wilson, J. M., Fidelity to Place, June 6, 2023.
[11] Donne, J., Devotions Upon Emergent Occasions, 1623, 17th Meditation, p. 108.
[12] Justice, T., Poll Debunks Myth, June 9, 2023.
[13] Horowitz, J. M., Support for BLM Drops Considerably, June 14, 2023.

International Resistance

A demonstration similar to that of Canada's truckers protest against woke policies occurred in Canberra, Australia's capital city. In this case, citizens rebelled against the leftist government's over-reactions to Covid-19 and other ideological controls. Mass objection to woke policy is evident in the area of abortion when thirty-seven pro-life nations committed to the "Geneva Consensus Declaration on Promoting Women's Health and Strengthening the Family." The manifesto declared "there is no international right to abortion."[14] In opposition, the Biden Administration considers countries like Finland, the U.K., and Sweden to be "human rights abusers." The reason? These countries, renowned for their admirable human rights record, refused to enforce drastic prohibitions on "conversion therapy" which might have the effect of dissuading individuals to proceed with gender transition.

Gender Surgery

Sweden has "banned gender surgeries for minors,"[15] with other Europeans countries following suit. At least sixteen U.S. States have prohibitions or limitations on using public funds for gender reassignment procedures, with the number of States steadily growing. In June 2023, as an example, Texas extended protection rights for minors by promulgated laws prohibiting sex-change surgery and associated interventions like puberty blockers, mastectomies, cross-sex hormones.[16] However, the reality is that "the U.S.

---

[14] Foley, R., Pro-Life Countries, November 18, 2022 (CP Politics).
[15] Sapir, L., America Exporter of Gender Revolution, 2022.
[16] Texas Legislature, Senate Bill 14, Effective September 1, 2023.

is the most permissive country when it comes to legal and medical gender transition of children."[17]

The resistance of European nations, and an increasing number of U.S. States, to woke policies adversely affecting vulnerable youth indicates a deep opposition to leftist policies. These policies are fostered upon an unwilling majority populace concerned about the unborn, the youth, the innocent and vulnerable. Leftist politicians overlook the fact that they are elected to serve the people, to do their bidding as it were, but in countries like the USA, Canada, Australia, New Zealand and in Europe, politicians and bureaucrats exercise powers not allocated to them constitutionally, nor by the majority of the electorate. While purporting to act for the common good of all, leaders continue their ideological schemes, their 'culture of death.' Consequently, progressive politicians increasingly get elected out of office for "reacting to protestors with such contempt."[18]

Africa

Very few countries in Africa have legalized same-sex marriage, most banning it outright with various degrees of criminal penalties. Homosexuality is contrary to African culture as it is to Western culture. The difference is that identity ideology has mostly been rejected in Africa, with many countries holding to Judeo-Christian roots inaugurated by missionaries of long ago. Mainland African countries legally permitting same-sex relationships comprise South Africa, Botswana, and Mozambique, with the rest criminalizing such practice.[19]

---

[17]'The U.S. is the Most Permissive Country for Children's Gender Transition,' Epoch Times, USA, January 19, 2023.
[18] Miller, S., Modern Leftism and Fascism, 2022.
[19] Matabeni, Z., Being Queer in Africa, May 29, 2023.

Tertiary Institutions

Probably bearing in mind Diogenes' proverb (300 B.C.E.) that "the foundation of every State is the education of its youth," Harvard professor Niall Ferguson purposed to "start a new college because higher education is broken." He claims institutions "dedicated to the search for truth have ossified into havens for liberal intolerance and administrative overreach."[20] Ferguson and partners then launched the University of Austin, Texas, offering traditional modules not generally available at progressive institutions.

Similar developments occurred in Florida with reorientation of the left-wing public university, New College, into a conservative classical liberal arts college, offering, "a distinctly traditional brand of education and scholarship."[21] In February 2023, the newly appointed conservative Board terminated services of the incumbent college President. Likewise, moves are afoot at University of North Carolina-Chapel Hill to, "challenge the prevailing progressive ideological monoculture." At State level, Texas, Florida, Arizona, and Missouri among others, with reference to existing CRT and DEI programs in education,[22] published new rulings "prohibiting state colleges and universities from enforcing discriminatory ideology based on race, colour, religion, sex, gender, ethnicity, national origin, or ancestry." In this manner commences the "long counter-march through the institutions,"[23] a conservative movement sorely needed to re-establish the true concept of education. Still, there is a long way to go before DEI ideology is attenuated. The University of Alabama, for instance, employs

---

[20] Ferguson, N., A New College, 2021.
[21] Rufo, C., Recapturing Higher Education, January 12, 2023.
[22] Gonzalez, M., Leading the Charge, March 7, 2023.
[23] Weingarten, B., The Long Counter-March through the Institutions, March 1, 2023.

31 dedicated DEI personnel and its Dean is on record declaring, "DEI is the whole purpose of the university."[24]

Education is central to the Western traditional order, accumulating knowledge and wisdom through centuries for the benefit of all citizens. G. K. Chesterton mentioned this idea in 1924 when explaining, "education is the soul of a society as it passes from one generation to the next,"[25] so continuing the West's great heritage. Ancient philosophers like Aristotle recognised this point, holding that the primary purpose of education was, simply stated, to prepare citizens to partake in politics. In so doing, they would impart good character and democracy for the public good of society. In his magisterial work, 'Politics,' Aristotle wrote the "educator should direct his attention above all to the education of the youth for the neglect of education does harm to states, as the better the character, the better the government."[26] Leaders of society in this post-structuralist era should heed this advice for, "no nation can endure when the elite prosper atop a disintegrating body politic."[27]

Academic Freedom

Organizations like the Heterodox Academy, a 5,300 strong collection of conservative-centrist academics and intellectuals opposed to radical leftism of tertiary colleges, have a stated goal to positively influence education. Members resist ideologically slanted, parochial, academia while endorsing the following statement, "I support open enquiry, viewpoint diversity, and constructive disagreement in research and

---

[24] Randall, D., Identity Politics is the Whole Purpose, August 29, 2023.
[25] Chesterton, G. K., The Observer, London, July 6, 1924.
[26] Aristotle, Politics, 1908, Book VIII, p. 300, para. 1.
[27] Reno, R. R., Deneen's New Deal, August 2023.

education."[28] This commitment is necessary as a survey indicated 62% of students "agreed that the climate on their campus prevented them from saying things they believed in."[29] Ergo, far from being under-represented in education, fair-minded students and educationalists are increasingly revealing themselves, with names of Heterodox Academy members for example, publicly identifiable on the website.

Nevertheless, as the situation currently stands, and using the prestigious Harvard University as example, a survey among academics revealed that "very liberal and liberal" professors constitute 80%" of staff; while conservative professors amount to some 20%."[30]

To add insult to injury, in the Foundation for Individual Rights and Expression's '2024 College Free Speech Rankings,' "Harvard University obtained the lowest possible score."[31] To counter the University's endemic ideologically-based education, a cohort of over 50 Harvard professors formed a "Council on Academic Freedom" emphasizing free speech." Freedom of expression is "essential to human progress,"[32] the Council proclaimed. True academic freedom, the free exchange of ideas, is contrary to identity policies but crucial to ensure merit-based intellectual and educational excellence.

Freedom of Speech

The constitutional right of free speech was confirmed by the Supreme Court in the 2023 matter of 303 Creative v. Elinis where it was held:

---

[28] Heterodox, Membership, 2021.
[29] Heterodox, Campus, 2020.
[30] Bikales, J., Harvard, 2022.
[31] Foundation for Individual Rights and Expression, 2024 College Free Speech Rankings, September 2023.
[32] Editorial, Wall Street Journal, April 12, 2023.

- The State cannot force someone who "provides expressive services to abandon her conscience and speak its preferred message instead;"
- The "impermissible abridgement of First Amendment right to speak freely," was confirmed;
- The First Amendment "extends to all those engaged in expressive conduct;"
- The Court has an "enduring commitment to protect speech rights of all comers, no matter how controversial the message at hand;"
- The minority Judges' dissenting opinion is "emblematic of some to defend First Amendment values only when the speaker's message is sympathetic;"
- The First Amendment "envisages the US as a place where all are free to think and speak as they wish, not as the government demands;"
- The right of free speech is "one of our most cherished liberties and part of what keeps our Republic strong;"
- "Public accommodations laws are not immune from the demands of the Constitution," whose principles "must prevail."[33]

The fundamental right to free speech, whether in the context of education or in public life generally, was endorsed at the highest possible judicial level. Inherent Constitutional rights were upheld, in effect condemning actions of cancel culture ideologists in restricting the public narrative.

Freedom of Religion

The primary reason for the founding of America by immigrant pioneers was that of religious freedom. President Ronald Reagan confirmed freedom as a feature of American exceptionalism when he proclaimed, "America's particular calling is the triumph of human freedom, the triumph of human freedom under God."[34] A Rasmussen Reports poll

---

[33] Fleetwood, S., Gorsuch's Defense of Free Speech in 303 Creative, June 30, 2023.
[34] Public Papers of the Presidents of the US, Ronald Reagan, 1987, p.p. 1040-43.

revealed "82% of Americans believe religious freedom[35] is key to a healthy society."[36]

Despite inroads by the State and activists into this inherent human right, important changes are occurring at judicial level due to the present composition of the Supreme Court Judges (the majority are conservative). In the case of Carson versus Makin, for instance, the Supreme Court nullified the State of Maine's ban on public funding for religious schools. Chief Justice John Roberts ruled the "State pays tuition for certain students at private schools – as long as the schools are not religious. That is discrimination against religion." Although somewhat limited in context, the decision clarifies public funding for religious schools does not necessarily violate Constitutional establishment and neutrality clauses.[37] The general principle of free speech, enunciated in the 303 Creative matter, which includes the inherent right to expression of religious belief, creates obstacles by administrators insistent on curtailing dissenting views in educational institutions.

Resisting Transgenderism

Feminist resistance to the ascendent power of transgender theory is growing. Feminists allege historic social gains have been lost to biological men irrationally identifying as women. Author Hadley Freeman writes that "debates about (trans)gender rights are also debates about women's rights, because activists are asking, essentially, for the abolition of women's (biological) sex-based rights." In her opinion, "the clash between gender-

---

[35] Religious freedom is "a cornerstone in the edifice of human rights" (Witte, J., 2022, Liberty, p. 7).
[36] Gryboski, M., Freedom, 2021.
[37] Carson v. Makin, SCOTUS, 20-1088, June 21, 2022.

based rights and women's rights"[38] will accelerate as the transgender minority attempt to further capture the media narrative on gender. State objections to transgender primacy is seen in the example of Alabama's ban on transgender men participating in female-only collegiate sports events. State prohibitions are becoming prevalent as statistics show 65% of Americans believe "there are only two gender identities."[39]

The only gender clinic in the UK, Tavistock, a primary sponsor of transgenderism, was forced to close by independent reviewer, Dr. Hilary Cass. During her investigation into "transgender medicine for children,' Cass acknowledged the protocols were not "a safe or viable long-term solution." Later, some 1,000 families on behalf of their children, entered litigation against the Clinic claiming medical negligence.[40] Complications also beset gender clinics in "Sweden, Finland and France."[41]

Professor Cowen predicts that "wokeism is likely to evolve into a sub-culture that is highly educated, highly white, and feminine" but will probably not "vanish from public life." He believes it will prevail in universities despite being, "even more out of touch with mainstream America."[42] Similarly, Victor Davis Hanson believes, "Canada is now governed by absurdism, symptomatic of an ailing Western elite."[43]

Effect on Military

When Russia invaded Ukraine in 2022, President Putin divulged his reason for this opportunistic action, "prosperous leading powers have other pressing social problems, challenges, and risks in ample supply, and many

[38] Freeman, H., Good Girl, 2022.
[39] PRRI Research, The Politics of Gender, Pronouns and Public Education, June 8, 2023.
[40] Berrien, H., Gender Clinic, 2022.
[41] Cook, M., Castle, 2022.
[42] Cowen, T., Peaked, 2022.
[43] Hanson, V., Storm, 2022.

among them are no longer interested in fighting for influence since, as they say, they already have enough on their plates."[44] This view reveals the West's focus on contentious internal social issues while neglecting to protect its great civilization, the home of classic liberal democratic political culture.

Resistance in Europe

Internationally, political leaders like Spain's Isabel Diaz Ayuso, President of the Community of Madrid, together with Italian prime minister, Giorgia Meloni, bring common sense to the woke political dynamo. For instance, Ayuso condemned legislation permitting 16-year-olds to change gender without parental approval. Meloni herself is averse to woke policies, while France's Marine Le Pen (who won 41% of the vote in 2022 elections), is critical of mass immigration and subsequent increase in gender-based violence that follows sudden social freedom for illegal migrants.

In Sweden, Member of Parliament Ebba Hermansson, publicly supported Le Pen's sentiments. In Germany, leader of the 'Alternative for Germany' party Alice Weidel, criticised "gender idiocy and early sexualization classes." Interestingly, Weidel opposes same-sex marriage although she remains in a same-sex relationship herself. It can be claimed, then, that "many of Europe's right-wing politicians are united by an aversion to woke ideology and many of them are women."[45] Professor Hanson is correct when he predicts much of "wokeism will disappear because it is inherently nihilistic and cannibalistic."[46] In plain language, wokeism might implode upon itself. This end can be expected for, as

---

[44] Putin, V., Speech, 2021.
[45] Starkey, L., Spain Leading Europe's Feminine Swing to the Right, March 2, 2023.
[46] Hanson, V. D., The Woke Wreaking Machine, March 26, 2023.

George Orwell sardonically quips, "One has to belong to the intelligentsia to believe things like that for no ordinary man could be such a fool."[47]

A Premature Death

Although polls indicate "75% of Americans claim the transgender movement has gone too far," the demise of wokeism has not yet arrived. To the extent desired by moderates, it might never fully arrive even though over 70% of Americans want woke abortion rights significantly curtailed.

Something New

Rabbi Jonathan Sacks anticipated this turmoil when he wrote, "something new is taking shape but we do not know precisely what."[48] Perhaps Elon Musk could have enlightened him when he quipped, "the most likely outcome is the most ironic outcome - a Christian precept in which 'the first shall be last' - for the opposite of what you think is going to happen, happens so often."[49] Understandably, citizens are anxious about their society's future. Matthew Arnold's poem describes the complexity, polarity, and anxiety of an uncertain future about to descend upon society:

> "*Wandering between two worlds,*
> *One dead the other powerless to be born.*"[50]

---

[47] Orwell, G., Notes on Nationalism, October 1945.
[48] Sacks, J. On Creative Minorities, 2014.
[49] Elon Musk, Fox News Interview with Tucker Carlson, April 18, 2023.
[50] Arnold, M., Stanzas from the Grand Chartreuse, 1852.

CHAPTER EIGHT
PART THREE

FINAL THINGS

"Believing there is a God means we are not the centre of our world. God is"
(Rabbi Jonathan Sacks, 2016)

8.5. The Judeo-Christian Tradition

With its essential Jewish heritage, the Church is God's designated vehicle on earth - what Puritan John Winthrop in 1630 referred to as the "City upon a Hill,"[1] charged to "make disciples of all men" (Matt. 28:19). In turn, disciples would foster biblical values throughout society. Devout followers of God are obligated to influence the culture, ensuring just and equitable laws for the common good of all. There exists no feasible alternative. Permeating society with traditional values is fundamental to the welfare of citizens for, as Winston Churchill said, "when there is no enemy within, enemies outside cannot hurt you."

Although Identity Politics has significantly infiltrated much of the Church and Synagogue, tempering their message, God has his committed representatives as seen in 1 Kings 19:18. For example, in March 2023, Congresswoman Mary Miller of Illinois announced formation of the Congressional Family Caucus, a group which aims to "defend the natural family from attempts by the radical left to erode this core foundation of

---

[1] Winthrop, J., A Model of Christian Charity, 1630, p. 47.

our society." The intention of the Caucus is "to initiate legislation favourable to American families for the natural family, ordained by God, is essential for a nation to prosper."[2] To this end, Montana State Representative Kerri Seekins-Crowe, declared she is "here to fight for that which is true, noble, right, pure, lovely, admirable, excellent, and praiseworthy."[3] These words highlight the virtuous characteristics of Western civilization, now under mortal threat by malignant forces determined to rob it of its beauty.

At the end of the day, the pivotal question is whether "we seek to live in accord with the idea of a Christian society, or will we accept the tutelage of a pagan society?"[4] In other words, does Western society desire a bible-based future as before, or a new arrangement reflecting secularism and primitive pagan practices. The latter concept results in a culture lacking the timeless precepts of love and grace, law and justice, mercy and forgiveness, transcendence and eternal redemption.

Russell Reno makes the telling point that while our 'open society' has "dissolved the anchoring institutions, man is not made to tread water in a liquid world."[5] A society without foundational precepts is subject to the whim of populist ideologies, including plastic morality, shifting values, and subjective fabrications of reality. The result is, inevitably, one of nihilism - an end game without hope or future.

A Gospel for All

While Ayn Rand decided the "Upper classes are a nation's past; the middle

---

[2] Congresswoman Mary Miller, Press Release, Washington, D. C., March 7, 2023.
[3] The Heritage Foundation, 50th Anniversary Gala, April 20, 2023.
[4] Reno, R. R., Resurrecting the Idea of a Christian Society, 2016, p. 3.
[5] Reno, R. R., Deneen's New Deal, August 2023.

class is its future,"[6] truth should nonetheless be directed at all spheres of society. All sectors require truth and hope, not only the poor, the marginalized and disadvantaged, but also the middle class and the *intelligentsia*, the leaders and shapers of society. Paul also ministered to the latter class as recounted in Acts 17:12 (Berea) and Acts 17:22-23 (Athens). Paul's disciples penetrated the highest echelons of authority in Rome, "All the saints greet you, especially those of Caesar's household."[7] In Corinth, Erastus the City Treasurer was a disciple.

The mandate to bring hope to all, including those in authority, is exemplified in the Book of Esther when Mordecai encouraged her to approach the King. Mordecai's words were, "And who knows whether you have not come to the kingdom for such a time as this?" (Est. 4:4). In such circumstances, remaining silent was not a feasible option as the destiny of Esther's tribe, the Jewish people and their sacred faith, was at stake. Hilary of Poitiers (310-367 C.E.) highlighted this test when he wrote, "If sacred truth be met by silence, then that silence is construed as consent."[8] Likewise, the Russian writer, Alexander Pushkin (1799-1837), implies at the very end of his play 'Boris Godunov,' that remaining silent results in surrender to revolutionaries for it indicates conformity. His main character, Masalski, outraged at the crowd's apathy in the face of gross injustice demands to know, "Why are you silent?"[9]

Inaction during times of political and ideological war is inexcusable for there are serious casualties: individuals emotionally and psychologically crippled by assaults upon their identity, purpose, and

[6] Rand, A., The Dead End: Middle Class, Ayn Rand Letter, 1986 (1971), p. 297.
[7] Philippians 4:22.
[8] Schaff, P., 1955, Nicene & Post-Nicene Fathers Hilary of Poitiers, Vol. IX, p. 56.
[9] Pushkin, A. S., Boris Godunov, 1953 (1831), p. 151.

emotional well-being. President Franklin D. Roosevelt is attributed with the distressing words, "War is young men dying and old men talking." In the face of acute threats to vulnerable citizens, this is not the time for simply talking by those who, like Esther, have "come to the kingdom for such a time as this."

William Graham Sumner (1840-1910) describes the 'vulnerable citizen' as the "forgotten man, the victim of the reformer, the social speculator and philanthropist, who has many burdens laid upon him."[10] It is the average family, the forgotten ones, who suffer most from reprehensible actions of social idealists seeking an unattainable utopia, causing much emotional and spiritual damage in the process.

Recovering a Biblical Worldview

Wanting nothing of 'Caesar's kingdom' but, instead, striving to fulfill their kingdom mandate, Judeo-Christians are called to live authentic lives building credibility among outsiders. Credibility, integrity, and reputation will generate access to the political arena which determines laws affecting and reflecting the values of society. The late evangelist Billy Graham is a prime example of this point, having access to a number of US Presidents, world leaders, and politicians. To this end, the sage advice of Yoram Hazony, President of the Herzl Institute in Jerusalem, is that "we need to recover the biblical view of human action in public affairs if we are to restore a culture of political responsibility."[11]

Immanuel Kant's view of the interconnectedness between politics and morality highlights the necessity of biblical influence on the political landscape. As Kant correctly perceived, "true politics can never take a step

---

[10] Sumner, W. G., The Forgotten Man, 1919, p. 466.
[11] Hazony, Y., Miracle of Esther, 2016.

without homage to morality." He emphasized, "everything evil that stands in the way (of peace) derives from the fact that the political moralist begins where the moral politician would correctly leave off."[12] This view is quite valid for without moral principles, a politically engineered society results in a secularised and amoral concoction of values with no ability to upgrade the culture. The consequence is evident in the current political landscape for not only is there an absence of peace, there is cultural turmoil.

The challenge is that society rejects objective or consensual standards of morality. Hence, forgiveness of sin is redundant as sin itself is non-existent. In a context with no boundaries, each person determines their own standard of behaviour. Believers cannot remain silent in the face of this heresy without risking the same warning made to the Church in Sardis, "Wake up, strengthen what remains and is about to die, for I have not found your works complete in the sight of my God" (Rev. 3:2).

Moral Intensity

It is in the area of personal morality that Judeo-Christians can stand out from the secular culture. The novels of Yiddish writer, Chaim Grade, are renowned for displaying a "moral intensity."[13] Rightly so, for without an authentic display of "moral intensity," there is little to differentiate disciples of the true God from non-believers. Grade warns there are many religious imitators, as exposed in his work, 'The Yeshiva.' He writes, "They make their bellies their gods, their clothes their Torah, and their desires their moral codes."[14] Within this framework, the words of the Messiah-Redeemer caution inauthentic disciples, the cultural believers,

---

[12] Kant, I., History, 1957, pp. 124-128.
[13] Wisse, R. R., Writings of a Notable Yiddish Novelist, February 6, 2023.
[14] Grade, C., The Yeshiva, 1967, p. 83.

that they will be exposed "by their fruits,"[15] that is, by their actions and character, as will the duplicity and moral convenience of identity activists.

Influencing Society

Families are the focal point of society, and they are at the forefront of ideological attacks in areas of race, sex-gender, abortion, pornography and similar. To ensure an essential biblical ethos in the culture, a counter-revolution is needed, starting with families and individuals at 'grass roots' level so local politicians can eventually modify insidious laws. Of elected voting members in the mid-term 118th US Congress, 88% could be considered Christian, while thirteen identified as gay, lesbian or bisexual (2%)."[16] With a strong Judeo-Christian representation, hope exists for fresh legislation mitigating deviant policies imposed on society by progressive politicians.

The Counter-Culture

The 14th century Italian scholar, Petrarch, urged Christians to familiarise themselves with literature and philosophy to influence society for its advantage. The result was a spread of "virtue and eloquence among the future leaders of society."[17] Bearing in mind its transcendent calling, the perpetual function of Judeo-Christianity is to create an alternative culture, a counter-culture, reflecting eternal values distinct from prevailing culture. Rabbi Sacks frames the obligation this way, "Judaism is a protest against the world, in the name of a world that ought to be."[18]

---

[15] Matthew 7:15-16.
[16] Schaeffer, K., 118th Congress, January 11, 2023 (Pew Research).
[17] Hankins J., Guide, 2021.
[18] Sacks, J., From Despair to Hope, #5783, Covenant and Conversation.

The result of cultural biblical influence in politics can be seen through the defence of customary values by lawmakers in many US States, passing legislation contrary to woke dictates. For example, arising from pressure on School Boards by irate parents, the teaching of Critical Race Theory is prohibited in the public education system of more than 20 States. Relatedly, the State of Louisiana requires "In God We Trust" signs to be prominently displayed in classrooms of public Universities, colleges and schools State-wide.[19] Louisiana joins Texas, Florida, South Dakota, and Arkansas who published similar laws.

In the public domain, long-suffering citizens reclaim the nation's heritage. President Abraham Lincoln predicted success of this kind when he said, "With public sentiment, nothing can fail; without it, nothing can succeed. Consequently, he who moulds public sentiment goes deeper than he who enacts statutes or pronounces judicial decisions. He makes statutes and decisions possible or impossible to be executed."[20]

Healing the Land

The wisdom of King Solomon, in Proverbs 24:11, touches on the heart of the matter, "Rescue those who are being taken away to death and hold back those who are stumbling to the slaughter," like a "brand plucked from the fire" (Zech. 3:2). God's assurance applies here for "if my people who are called by my name humble themselves and pray and seek my face and turn from their wicked ways, I will hear from heaven and will forgive their sin and heal their land." (2 Chron. 7:14-20).

---

[19] Weismann, S., 'In God We Trust' in Every Louisiana Classroom, June 29, 2023.
[20] Lincoln, A., Debate, 1858.

The inferno affecting society cannot fully be understood in secular terms. This is because it reflects a demonic spiritual[21] assault by a combination of secular humanism and pagan spirituality, born in the Edenic Garden and continuing through into the contemporary era.

Dangers of Authoritarianism

The greatest challenge to freedom in any society is big government, for it presumes to represent public life. Therefore, the State poses a danger to freedom when it allows a situation in which the "people can no longer publicly express their obligations to the Creator." As a result, says Richard Neuhaus, "it is to be feared that they will no longer acknowledge their obligations to one another – nor to the Constitution in which the obligations of freedom are enshrined."[22] Still, believers should remain confident that "the romantic realism of our faith can overcome the Equality Act, and other assaults on families, sanity and culture."[23] "Romantic realism" is indeed a fitting description for it reflects biblical principles of faith-love-hope in God's salvation purposes.

In the end, biblical realism is the only counter-revolutionary movement that can defeat revolutionary idealism. Eric Patterson makes the point that "Christian realism stands in stark contrast to the violent idealism of revolutionary ideologies seeking to conform the world to their fantastical blueprints." Patterson finds that in contrast to idealism, the biblical tradition of "realism emphasizes political order and justice"[24] and, moreover, ordered morality and ethics. The concept of biblical realism, he

---

[21] The "woke revolution is a spiritual disease and our deepest resistance must be spiritual" (Reno, R., Gnostic Politics, 2021).
[22] Neuhaus, R., Order, 1992.
[23] Arrington, L., Romantic, 2021.
[24] Patterson, E., The Danger of Revolutionary Idealism, November 2, 2022.

says, "remains a vital and crucial source for the next generation of diplomats, scholars, warriors, public servants, and political officials" to counter endemic "political ideologies or racist programs."[25]

Obligations of Priests

Notwithstanding their divine mission, Judeo-Christians face being immobilized by the domineering influence of secular humanism, esotericism, and eroticism in the anti-truth setting. At this crucial time for society, leaders are perceived as failing in their duty to adequately equip others in confronting a potent offensive against their created identity and faith. Believers are called to be both scholars and warriors for otherwise, "their thinking will be done by cowards and their fighting by fools," to paraphrase Thucydides (460-400 B.C.E.). Knowledgeable warriors, zealous for the truth, is required of all disciples. Henry Kissinger, in a secular context but no less pertinent, refers to true leadership as a purposed "strategy of the will," coupled to a "strategy of humility."[26]

The divinely mandated task of bringing truth to society requires determination, an attitude described in Isaiah 50:7, "Because the Sovereign Lord helps me, I will not be disgraced. Therefore, have I set my face like flint, and I know I will not be put to shame." Persecution is a natural consequence of boldness, is to be expected, and embraced as an honour for "Blessed are you when others revile you and persecute you and utter all kinds of evil against you falsely on my account" (Matt. 5:11). The rewards are eternal.

---

[25] Patterson, E., Folly of Wishful Thinking Idealism, October 31, 2022.
[26] Kissinger, H., Leadership: Six Studies in World Strategy, 2022, Ch. 1-2.

Christendom

The UK intellectual, Douglas Murray, describes himself as an "uncomfortable agnostic who recognises the virtues and values the Christian faith has brought." Murray criticises denominal Churches saying, "the Church is not doing what so many of us on the outside want it to do, which is preaching the Gospel, asserting its truths and its claims. When one sees it falling into all the latest tropes, one thinks 'well, that's another thing gone just like absolutely everything else in the era.' I am a disappointed non-adherent."[27] A sorry view of the Church from an agnostic viewpoint. In the USA, Charles Murray also believes "the American republic is unlikely to survive without a resurgence of Christianity."[28] He refers to the necessity of a virtuous common good derived from Judeo-Christian norms.

Secularism Entrenched

It is clear that in this anti-Christian era, the New Age of Aquarius, the institutionalised Church has lost much of the battle of ideals. The battle originates from the intensifying secularisation of society, the rise of pluralistic and syncretistic pagan,[29] spiritual, non-religious systems, and veneration of the narcissistic inner-self.[30] Despite diminishing influence of the formal Church, the empowering of new generations of unbelievers needs to continue unabated for the Church has, for too long, been relying on the comfortable momentum of institutionalized Christendom to change

---

[27] Murray, D., Identity, 2021.
[28] Murray, C., Reality, 2021.
[29] The "world's future depends on a face-off between Christ and the Greeks" (Girard, R., 2010, Battling, p. xxii).
[30] The "era of the psychological man" is the period when "psychology, psychoanalysis, and psychiatry are the means whereby we understand meaning and purpose of our existence" (Satinover, J., Psychology and Abolition of Meaning, 1994).

society. Jacques Ellul criticised this concept, claiming it promoted efforts to "achieve objective conduct without reference to the spiritual life, without the knowledge of God in Jesus Christ...resulting in a perversion of revelation."[31] Its demise is therefore not to be greatly lamented.

No Compromise

The true Church cannot compromise its Apostolic mandate in favour of 'seeker friendly' and fashionable religious trends. Comprise leads to tolerance of heresy, ultimately leading to moral decline. The contest is for the human soul and believers need to prepare for spiritual warfare in fulfilling their calling. A Latin phrase describes this challenge, *Si vis pacem, para bellum* – 'if you want peace, then prepare for war.' War it is, a war for humanity, for humans are made in the image of God with an eternal future and not as proposed by identity activists.

The Hollow Men

Pastor Shane Idleman explains when "pastors lack boldness, it affects all areas of preaching for, as a result, the gospel they preach is often a watered-down, non-offending, powerless message," unsuitable for invoking in others the "difficult truths of salvation." Here, the haunting words of T. S. Eliot describe feeble leaders:

> "*We are the hollow men*
> *We are the stuffed men*
> *Leaning together*
> *Headpiece filled with straw...*"[32]

---

[31] Ellul, J., The Subversion of Christianity, 1986, p. 46.
[32] Eliot, T. S., The Hollow Men, 1925.

Those who lack conviction, the "hollow men," find judgement in Eliot's conclusion when he writes, "The wind shall say, 'Here were decent godless people.'"[33]

Moses' encouragement to Joshua prior to entering the promised land, "Be strong and courageous" (Deut. 31:7), remains highly relevant for leaders today. All leaders have a duty to execute their divine task fearlessly and to embrace that role, unlike the cowardly General Barak in Judges 5 who demurred at his appointed task. Boldness is crucial for, as Shane Idleman asserts, "Only the pulpits have the power to change America."[34] This statement needs qualification for it is only the spiritual power and sovereign purposes of the risen Lord that can "change America," and the world, through his people proclaiming truth of the gospel.

A Spiritual Divide

Undoubtedly, the existential threat to Judeo-Christianity, as it is of all major monotheistic religions, is the accelerating corruption of a secular culture. Mary Eberstadt explains that the "religious divide of our time is between those who think they can compromise with the sexual revolution without compromising their faith."[35] Appeasement with identitarian ideology inescapably results in moral failure.

An apathetic Church comprising cultural Christians – those claiming Kingdom values but lacking personal morality and a supernatural relationship with God - is liable to lose its credibility. Despite the malignant spiritual origins of secular humanism and its continuation through many millennia, the Church has regularly understood this heresy

---

[33] Eliot, T. S., Choruses from the Rock, 1934, Part 1., p. 30.
[34] Idleman, S., Power, 2022.
[35] Eberstadt, M., Men at War with God, 2022.

as a fleeting phenomenon. Like other heresies from time to time, it was perhaps hoped that it would fade away, but history reveals the ongoing presence and ever-increasing potency of secularism and paganism.

Authors Van Den Broek and Hanegraaf write that "we witness a new interest in historical alternatives to the dominant components of Western culture. It is only natural that the study of Gnosis and hermeticism profits from this widespread reorientation."[36] The "dominant components" are Judeo-Christian values while the "historical alternatives," on the other hand, are Enlightenment rationality intersecting with ancient Gnosticism to become the underlying spiritual structure of the culture.

Mourning Traditional Values

Prominent non-believers mourn the expiration of biblical influence, especially in the area of ethics and absolute truths, ordered liberty, and uniform morality. They desire a return to the constancy of age-old norms. Scottish philosopher Niall Ferguson, who refers to religion as "magical thinking," lamented that atheism does not have "an evolved ethical system." He continues, "evolution alone does not get us to be moral." The solution, in his opinion, is to "adopt the inherited wisdom of a two-millennia old religion." In Ferguson's view, society cannot be based on atheism for it has a "very dangerous metaphysical framework."[37]

It is the natural law basis of Judeo-Christianity that alone imparts values, meaning, and order to society. Concerning the natural law, C. S. Lewis believes "it is not one among a series of possible systems of value. It is the sole source of all value judgements. If it is rejected, all value is

---

[36] Van Den Broek, R., Hanegraaf, W. J., Gnosis and Hermeticism from Antiquity to Modern Times,1998, p. viii.
[37] Ferguson, N., Doom, 2021; Van Maren, J., Men, 2021.

rejected. If any value is retained, it is retained. There never has been and never will be a radically new judgement of value in the history of the world." It is for these reasons that Russell Kirk encourages each generation to "take up defense of the moral order and the social order, the order of the soul and the permanent things," for these are "instruments of freedom"[38] worth conserving for future citizens.

An Indestructible Program

Come what may, hope remains for God will build his Church according to his insuperable providence. He has continually demonstrated the indestructability of his redemptive program in face of powerful evil forces. The Messiah's bodily resurrection affirms this fact. Here, G. K. Chesterton remarks that "Christianity has died many times and risen again for it had a God who knew the way out of the grave."[39] From a theological viewpoint, humankind will continue to seek God for eternity has been instilled into their hearts (Ecc. 3:11).

8.6. Applied Jewish Interpretive Methods

The application of Second Temple period, Palestinian Rabbinical interpretive methods particularly that of midrashic *darash,* prove that far from being a novelty, the contemporary identity crisis originated in the ancient Edenic Garden. These methods validate the fact that ancient Judeo-Christian doctrine is the sole purveyor of truth, providing meaning through a grounded and practical relationship with God, not in abstract theories of Greek Gnosticism. Nevertheless, in this anti-truth era, the futile search for alternative purpose and meaning continues unabated through convoluted

---

[38] Kirk, R., The Politics of Prudence, 1993, p. 24.
[39] Chesterton, G. K., The Everlasting Man, 1925, p. 290.

secular humanist, philosophical, neo-pagan spiritual identity hypotheses detached from rationality and realism.

The *eritus sicut Deus* ('to be like God') heresy remained alive through the ages in a variety of expressions until manifesting in a potent fresh demonstration, a re-creation, in the current milieux. Repetitions will continue until an ultimate application, the final recapitulation, at the end of time when the lawless will again arise in futile rebellion against God and the Redeemer-Messiah of humankind. That episode will reflect fulfilment of prophetic passages initiated in early Genesis, at the very commencement of the human story. In this dramatic manner, the Creator's redemptive program for his universal Church will be complete and the eternal order inaugurated. The desecrated Garden will be reconsecrated, and God will once again fellowship with his children in paradise, as originally intended.

The Garden Theme Demonstrated

The enduring truth of Garden events irrefutably confirms the theme that identity confusion facing contemporary civilization does, in fact, have roots in the rebellious events of Genesis chapter 3. This claim is supported by the Messiah-Redeemer when he explained that the narrative of redemption and restoration commenced in the earliest times of human history, "beginning with Moses and all the Prophets, he interpreted to them in all the Scriptures the things concerning himself" (Luke 24:27).

The Darash

The *darash,* an exploration of the Garden theme, is as follows:

- It was God, the living Word, who gave life to Adam and Eve in the Garden; and, it is he who still gives life to his people through crucifixion in a Garden (Jn. 19:41). At the end of time, the Redeemer-Messiah will be found in the eternal Garden as, "the throne of God and of the Lamb will be in it (the Garden), and his servants will worship him" (Rev. 22:3).

- Testing of the First Couple took place in the Edenic Garden when confronted by Satan's evil agent, the serpent. In this way, the Redeemer-Messiah, Jesus of Nazareth as the second Adam, was tempted and tested by Satan in the wilderness garden (Matt. 4:1-11); and, again, when confronted by Satan's evil forces, acting through human agents, in the Garden of Gethsemane (John 18:1);

- The punishment of death was exacted on the sinful First Couple in a Garden (Gen. 3:16-17). So too was the punishment of death for vicarious sin exacted on the Messiah in a Garden (John 19:41);

- The First Couple was sentenced to exile from the Father's presence in a Garden (Gen. 3); and, in the same fashion, the Redeemer-Messiah experienced exile from the Father's presence (Matt. 27:46) in a Garden, where he was buried (John 20);

- In the Garden of Genesis 3:5, the First Couple was promised eternal life through the coming Messiah, just like the Church was promised eternal redemption through the Messiah's resurrection in a Garden (Jn. 19:41);

- The sin of the First Adam in the Garden is defeated by the resurrection of the Second Adam in a Garden (John 19). In the Garden of the new heavens and new earth, paradise is restored for all eternity;

- The emblem of immortality in the Garden of Genesis 2:8 ("in the middle of the Garden was the Tree of Life"), finds thematic fulfilment in the Garden of perpetual paradise for, "on each side of the river stood the Tree of Life" (Rev. 22:2);

- From the beginning, the Creator was with the First Couple in the Garden for "they heard the sound of the Lord God walking in the Garden in the cool of the day" (Gen. 3:8). In like manner, the Messiah-Redeemer dwelt among his people, "the Word became flesh and dwelt among us…" (Jn. 1:14). He will continue to do so forever, "Behold, the dwelling place of God is with man. He will dwell with them, and they will be his people…" (Rev. 21:3);

- The complete, thematic, typological, and symmetrical pattern of salvation, from the beginning of human history (Gen. 3:15) to its eschatological completion, is to be expected for after all, the Redeemer-Messiah is "the Alpha and the Omega, the first and the last, the beginning and the end" (Rev. 22:12-13).

Through the deep love and redemptive work of the Redeemer-Messiah, humankind's alienation from the Creator finds eventual restoration in the Garden of eternal paradise. The central questions of human existence, those relating to personal identity, purpose of life, meaning in life, deliverance from sin and the transcendence of temporal life, are finally resolved.

8.7. Finale

In the interim, the concerned people of God's household may rightly feel they are despised by society and overcome by the challenges of this world, as did the Psalmist who exclaimed, "My foot is slipping" and, "anxiety was great within me."[40] Nonetheless, the romantic realism of God's eternal love overcomes all challenges for the Redeemer-Messiah emphasizes, "If the world hates you, keep in mind that it hated me first. If you belonged to the world, it would love you as its own. As it is, you do not belong to the world, but I have chosen you out of the world."[41] Similarly, Jewish brethren are comforted by the words of the Prophet Isaiah, "Behold, God is my salvation; I will trust and not be afraid for the Lord God is my strength and my song, and he has become my salvation" (Isa. 12:2).

The Promise

Wherefore, the words of the Messiah-Redeemer, the Great Creator of all humankind, ring out the promise to his expectant people at times of great distress, "Behold I am coming soon, bringing my recompense with me." He reassures the faithful that they will "have the right to the Tree of Life and that they may enter the city by the gates." And, as been the practice

---

[40] Psalm 94:18-19.
[41] John 15:18-19.

for millennia, the desperate righteous of the universal church of the risen God cry out for their Saviour's return, "Come, Lord Jesus," "the Spirit and the Bride say 'Come,'"[42] for "O Lord, our hearts are restless until they rest in you."[43]

****

Ipse se nihil scire id unum sciate

---

[42] Revelation 22:12-20.
[43] St. Augustine, Confessions.

QUOTATIONS

"All men are by nature free and equal for no one has the right to authority over another without his consent" (James Wilson, 1775).

"A sign of civilization in headlong decline is its embrace of absurdities" (Victor Davis Hanson, 2023).

"Freedom is never more than one generation away from extinction" (Ronald Reagan, 1964).

"Freedom of speech is meaningless unless you allow people you don't like to say things you don't like" (Elon Musk, 2023).

"God is dead. God remains dead. And we have killed him" (Friedrich Nietzsche, The Gay Science, 1910).

"Humankind cannot bear very much reality" (T. S. Eliot, 1943).

"If liberty means anything at all, it means the right to tell people what they do not want to hear" (George Orwell, 1903-1950).

"If the whole world is against the truth, then I am against the world" (Athanasius of Alexandra, 298-373 C. E.).

"If we want things to stay as they are, things will have to change" (Giuseppe di Lampedusa, The Leopard, 1911).

"Jesus Christ came to reveal to men that they have no enemies but themselves" (Blaise Pascal, 1623).

"Justice is turned back and righteousness stands far away, for truth has stumbled in the public squares" (Isaiah 59:14)

"No weapon formed against you will succeed" (Isaiah 54:17).

"Philosophy can make the previously unthinkable thinkable" (Rebecca Brown, 2019).

"Proclaim liberty throughout the land to all its inhabitants" (Lev. 25:10).

"Restlessness and brooding, rebellion against authority, interchange with nature, the power of the visionary imagination and of poetry, the pursuit of ideal love and the untamed spirit ever in search of freedom" (Romanticism, 1780-1850).

"The first effect of not believing in God is that you lose your common sense, and can't see things as they are" (G. K. Chesterton, Oracle of the Dog, 1926).

"The forces of evil always return, like a fungus, to feed on the fallen fabric of the world" (Joseph Pearce, 2023).

"The foundation of every State is the education of its youth" (Diogenes, 300 B.C.E.).

"The search for meaning, not pleasure of power, is mankind's central motivating force" (Viktor Frankl, 1946).

"The strength of the Constitution lies entirely in the determination of each citizen to defend it" (Albert Einstein, 1879-1955).

"There are things so ridiculous only an intellectual can believe them" (Ronen Shoval, 2023).

"To fight against untruth and falsehood, to fight against myths, to fight against an ideology which is hostile to mankind, to fight for our memory of what things were like, that is our task. A People which no longer remembers, has lost its history and its soul" (Alexander Solzhenitsyn, 1976).

"Tolerating grave evil within a society is itself a form of serious evil" (Charles Chaput, 2009).

"Truth is treason in the empire of lies" (Ron Paul, 2008).

"Visionaries work everlasting evil on earth. Their utopias inspire in the mass of mediocre minds a disgust of reality and a contempt for the secular logic of human development" (Joseph Conrad, Under Western Eyes, 1911).

"War is nothing but a continuation of politics" (Carl von Clausewitz, 1832).

"We are faced with a totalitarian cancer that will have to be confronted at every level" (Newt Gingrich, 2023).

"We have forgotten God and we have vainly imagined, in the deceitfulness of our hearts, that all these blessings were produced by some superior wisdom and virtue of our own" (Abraham Lincoln, 1863).

"When mortal men try to live without God, they infallibly succumb to megalomania or erotomania or both (Malcolm Muggeridge, 1952).

"Woe to those who call evil good and good evil; who put darkness for light and light for darkness" (Isaiah 5:20).

"Woke culture is the intellectual plague of our times" (Robert Leroux, 2021).

SELECT BIBLIOGRAPHY

Adler, Y. 2022, *The Origins of Judaism: An Archaeological-Historical Reappraisal*, Yale University Press, New Haven, USA.

Anderson, R. T., Eberstadt, M. 2021, *Mary Eberstadt on What Plagues the West*, Public Discourse Journal, December 26, 2021, Princeton, USA.

Anderson. R. T. 2022, *The Promise and Peril of the Political Common Good*, New Criterion Journal, January 2022, Vol. 40 (5), USA.

Anderson, R. T. 2022, *There is no Escaping Natural Law*, Ethics and Public Policy Center, May 23, 2022, Washington D. C., USA.

Anderson, R. T. 2023, *To Defend True Freedom, We Need to Know the Truth*, Fusion Journal, Fall 2023, American Institute for Economic Research, USA.

Arkes, H., Hammer, J., Peterson, M. 2021, *A Better Originalism*, The American Mind, March 18, 2021, Upland, USA.

Bachiochi, E. 2021, *Rights of Women: Reclaiming a Lost Vision*, Notre Dame Press, USA.

Bastiat, F. 2007 (1850), *The Law*, Ludwig von Mises Institute, USA.

Benedict XVI, His Holiness, Pope. 1990. *In the Beginning*, Eerdmans Publishing, USA.

Benvenuti, P., Borri, P. 1983, *Abortion and the Man: Psychological and Psychopathological Manifestations in the Face of Lost Fatherhood*, 104(6):255-68, Bethesda, USA.

Berger, P. L. 2014, *The Many Altars of Modernity*, De Gruyter Digital, August 19, 2014.

Berger, P. L., Berger, B., Kellner, H. 1974, *The Homeless Mind: Modernization and Consciousness*, Vintage Books, New York, USA.

Bernhardt, D. 2023, *You Report to Me: Accountability for the Failing Administrative State*, Encounter Books, New York, USA.

Bloom, A. D. 1988, *The Closing of the American Mind*, Touchstone, USA.

Bowker, J. 1979, *The Targums and Rabbinic Literature*, Cambridge University Press, UK.

Brock, S. P. 1990, *Ephrem the Syrian, Commentary on Genesis 2-3, Hymns on Paradise*, St. Vladimir's Press, Crestwood, NY, USA.

Bruns, G. L. 1987, *Midrash and Allegory: The Beginning of Scriptural Interpretation*, Harvard University Press, Massachusetts, USA.

Buck, S. 2018, *Hiding in Plain Sight: Jung, Astrology and the Psychology of the Unconscious*, Journal of Analytical Psychology, 2018, Vol. 63.

Bunch, T. E., LeCompte, M. A. 2021, *Tunguska sized airburst destroyed Tall el-Hammam a Middle Bronze Age city in Jordan Valley near Dead Sea*, Scientific Reports Journal, Rep 11, 18632 (2021), UK.

Burke, E. 1993 (1790), *Reflections on Revolution in France*, Oxford University Press, UK.

Butler, J. 2007, *Gender Trouble: Feminism and Subversion of Identity*, Routledge, USA.

Camus, A. 1955, *Myth of Sisyphus and Other Essays*, Penguin, UK.

Camus, A. 1956, *The Rebel: Essay on Man in Revolt*, Vintage Books, USA.

Carlyle, T. 1898, *The Works of Thomas Carlyle,* Vol. 1, Sartor Resartus, Book II, Chap. IX., Scribners & Sons, New York, USA.

Charlesworth, J. H. 1985, *The Old Testament Pseudepigrapha and the New Testament,* Cambridge University Press, UK.

Chesterton, G. K. 1984 (1926), *The Oracle of the Dog: The Incredulity of Father Brown,* G. K. Hall & Co., USA.

Cohen, M. Z. 2020, *The Rule of Peshat: Jewish Constructions of the Plain Sense of Scripture*, University of Pennsylvania Press, USA.

Cooke, M. 2001, *Critical Theory and Religion*, Philosophy of Religion in the 21st Century, Palgrave Macmillan, London, UK.

Couliano, I. 1992 (1990), *The Tree of Gnosis: Gnostic Mythology from Early Christianity to Modern Nihilism,* Harper Collins, USA.

Cowen, T. 2018, *The Five Most Influential Public Intellectuals,* January 23, 2018, George Mason University, Fairfax, USA.

Daly, M. 1973, *Beyond God the Father: Toward a Philosophy of Women's Liberation,* Beacon Press, USA.

Darwin, C. 1871, *The Descent of Man,* Vol. 1 & 2, John Murray, UK.

Darwin, E. 1794, *Zoonomia, or, the Laws of Organic Life, Vol. 1,* J. Johnson, London, UK.

Dawson, C. 1991 (1958), *Religion and the Rise of Western Culture*, Image Books, Doubleday, New York, USA.

Del Noce, A. 2014, *The Crisis of Modernity*, McGill-Queens University Press, Canada.

Delsol, C. 2021, *The End of Christianity,* Hungarian Conservative Journal, Vol. 1, No. 3, Budapest, Hungary.

Deneen, P. J. 2018, *Why Liberalism Failed: Politics and Culture,* Yale University, USA.

Derbyshire, S. W., Bockmann, J. C. 2020, *Reconsidering Fetal Pain*, Journal of Medical Ethics, Vol. 46, London, UK.

De Tocqueville, A. 1835, *Democracy in America,* Vol. 1, Mises Institute, Auburn, USA.

Dostoyevsky, F. 1963 (1880), *The Brothers Karamazov,* Modern Library, New York, USA.

Dworkin, R. W. 2023, *Ideology and Terror,* Law and Liberty, March 8, 2023, USA.

Eberstadt, M. 2012, *Adam and Eve After the Pill,* Ignatius Press, USA.

Eberstadt, M. 2022, *Men are at War with God,* First Things Journal, January 2022, USA.

Eberstadt, M. 2015, *The New Intolerance,* First Things Journal, March 2015, USA.

Edersheim, A. 1993 (1883), *The Life and Times of Jesus the Messiah*, Hendrickson Publishers Inc., Peabody, USA.

Eliot, T. S. 1932, *Selected Essays: Thoughts After Lambeth,* Faber, UK.

Elliot, R. 1989 (1947), *Invisible Man*, Vintage Books, New York, USA.

Elliot, R. 1978, *The Little Man at Chehaw Station*, The American Scholar, Vol. 47 (No. 1, Winter 1978), Washington D. C., USA.

Ellul, J. 1986, *The Subversion of Christianity*, Eerdmans, USA.

Favale, A. 2021, *Feminism's Last Battle*, Public Discourse Journal, July 17, 2021, USA.

Ferguson, N. 2018, *The Future of the Anglosphere: Roger Scruton Memorial Lecture*, October 18, 2021, Oxford, UK.

Firestone, S. 1970, *The Dialectic of Sex: The Case for Feminist Revolution*, William Morrow, New York, USA.

Fletcher, J. 1954, *Morals & Medicine: The Moral problems of the Patient's Rights, Contraception, Artificial Insemination, Sterilization, Euthanasia*, 1979, Princeton University Press, USA.

Fletcher, J. 1966, *Situation Ethics: The New Morality*, Westminster John Knox Press, UK.

Franks, A. 2021, *Foucault's Principalities & Powers*, First Things, March 2021, USA.

Freud, S. 1961, *Civilization and its Discontents*, Norton & Co., USA.

Fromm, E. 1962, *Beyond the Chains of Delusion: My Encounter with Marx and Freud*, Simon and Schuster, New York, USA.

Fromm, E. 1966, *You Shall Be as Gods. A Radical Interpretation of the Old Testament and Its Tradition*, Holt, Rinehart and Winston, USA.

Galbreath, R. 1971, *Introduction: The Occult Today*, Journal of Popular Culture, Vol. 5, Issue 3, Michigan State University, USA.

Garry, P. M. 2022, *The Rise of Common Good Conservatism*, The Imaginative Conservative, February 13, 2022, Houston, USA.

Gecewicz, G. 2018, *New Age Beliefs Common Among Both Religious and Non-Religious Americans*, Pew Research, 1st October, USA.

Geisler, N. L. & Clark, D. K. 1990, *Apologetics in the New Age*, Wipf & Stock, USA.

George, R. P. 1999, *A Clash of Orthodoxies*, First Things Journal, August, 1999, USA.

George, R. P. 1993, *Making Men Moral: Civil Liberties and Public Morality*, Oxford University Press, New York, USA.

George, R. P. 2022, *Performing the Ritual of a Religion Does Not Make You a Member of That Faith*, July 1, 2022, Deseret News, USA.

Gingrich, N. 2023, *American Despotism*, The American Spectator, Sept. 6, 2023, USA.

Girard, R. 2009, *Battling to the End: Conversations with Benoit Chantre*, Michigan State University Press, USA.

Glick, C. 2023, *Democracy Must be Restored to Israel*, Jewish News Syndicate, January 12, 2023, Tel Aviv, Israel.

Goldenberg, N. R. 1979, *Changing of the Gods: Feminism and the End of Traditional Religions*, Beacon Press Books, Boston, USA.

Gramsci, A. 1971, *Selections from the Prison Notebooks*, International Publishers, USA.

Green, S. K. 2022, *Separating Church and State: A History*, Cornell University, USA.

Greene, J., Persily, N., Ansolabehere, S. 2011, *Profiling Originalism*, Columbia Law Review, 356 (2011), New York, USA.

Gregg, S. 2021, *The Essential Natural Law*, Fraser Institute, Canada.

Halivni, D. W. 1991, *Peshat and Derash: Plain and Applied Meaning in Rabbinic Exegesis*, Oxford University Press, New York, USA.

Harari, Y. N. 2016, *Homo Deus: A Brief History of Tomorrow*, Harvill Secker, UK.

Harding, S. (ed.). 2004, *The Feminist Standpoint Reader: Intellectual and Political Controversies*, Routledge, New York, USA.

Harrington, M. 2022, *Return of the Cyborgs*, First Things Journal, January 11, 2022, USA.

Hart, D. B. 2013, *Jung's Therapeutic Gnosticism*, First Things Journal, Jan. 2013, USA.

Hayek, F. A. 2017, *Individualism: True and False*, December 17, 1945, Foundation for Economic Education, Atlanta, USA.

Hazony, Y. 2022, *Conservatism: A Rediscovery*, Regnery, USA.

Hazony, Y. 2019, *Conservative Democracy*, First Things Journal, January 2019, USA.

Hazony, Y. 2016, *The Miracle of Esther*, First Things Journal, March 2016, USA.

Hittinger, R. 1996, *A Crises of Legitimacy*, First Things Journal, November, 1996, USA.

Horkheimer, M. 1972, *Critical Theory: Selected Essays*, The Continuum Publishers, USA,

Horowitz, I. V. 1994, *The Decomposition of Sociology*, Oxford University Press, USA.

Horvat, J. 2013, *Return to Order: From a Frenzied Economy to an Organic Christian Society*, York Press, New York, USA.

Huntington, S. 1996, *The Clash of Civilizations: Remaking of World Order*, Simon & Schuster Inc., New York, USA.

John Paul II, Pope. 1984, *Redemption of the Body and Sacramentality of Marriage (Theology of the Body)*, Encyclical Letter, November 28, 1984, Vatican City.

Johnson, P. 2018, *Feminism as Radical Humanism*, Routledge, USA.

Johnson, P. E. 1993, *Creator or Blind Watchmaker*, First Things Journal, Jan. 1993, USA.

Johnson, P. E. 1990, *Evolution As Dogma: The Establishment of Naturalism*, First Things Journal, October 1990, New York, USA.

Johnson, P. E. 1993, *Nihilism and the End of Law*, First Things Journal, March 1993, USA.

Kass, L. R. 2003, *The Beginning of Wisdom: Reading Genesis*, Free Press, Simon & Schuster Inc., New York, USA.

Kimball, R. 1993, *The Perversions of Michael Foucault*, New Criterion Journal, Vol. 40 (5), January 2022, New York, USA.

Kirk, R. A. 1985 (1953), *The Conservative Mind: From Burke to Eliot*, Gateway Editions Publishers, 7th Edition, Washington, D. C., USA.

Kirk, R. 1993, *The Politics of Prudence*, ISI Books, Delaware, USA.

Kirk, R. A. 1974 (2003), *The Roots of American Order*, ISI Books, USA.

Kiska, R. 2019, *Antonio Gramsci's Long March Through History*, Journal of Religion and Liberty, Vol. 29 (3), December 12, 2019, USA.

Kissinger, H. A. 2022, *Leadership: Six Studies in World Strategy*, Allen Lane, Dublin, U.K.

Klavan, S. 2023, *How to Save the West – Ancient Wisdom for Five Modern Crises*, Regnery Publishing, Washington D. C., USA.

Kurlander, E. 2017, *Hitler's Monsters: A Supernatural History of the Third Reich*, Yale University Press, USA.

Kurth, J. 1994, *The Real Clash*, September 1, 1994, National Interest, Washington, USA.

Legutko, R. 2018, *The Demon in Democracy: Totalitarian Temptations in Free Societies*, Encounter Books, New York, USA.

Leithart, P. J. 1993, *Athens and Jerusalem Again*, First Things Journal, June 1993, USA.

Lewis, H., V. 2023, *Myth of Left and Right*, Oxford University Press, UK.

Longenecker, R. N. 1999, *Biblical Exegesis in the Apostolic Period*, W.B. Eerdmans Publishing, Grand Rapids, USA.

Lyons, N. S. 2021, *The Upheaval*, April 8, 2021, Substack, Washington D. C., USA.

MacIntyre, A. 1981, *After Virtue: A Study in Moral Theory*, Gerald Duckworth, U.K.

Magnet, M. 2020, *About Those Self-Evident Truths*, March 15, 2020, City Journal, USA.

Malvasi, M. 2022, *Cancel Culture and the Great Men of the West,* The Imaginative Conservative, May 31, 2022, Houston, USA.

Marcuse, H. 1972, *Counterrevolution and Revolt*, Beacon Press, USA.

Marcuse, H. 1966, *Eros and Civilization: Philosophical Inquiry into Freud,* Beacon, USA.

Markham, I. S. 1994, *Plurality and Christian Ethics*, Cambridge University Press, U.K.

Masterson, P. 1979, *The Concept of Resentment*, Studies: An Irish Quarterly Review, Vol. 68, No. 271, Dublin, Ireland.

Mayo, G. 2023, *Support After Abortion Institute: Abortion's Long-Term Negative Impact on Men*, Simpsonville, USA.

Mills, M. A. 2021, *Liberalism is Not Enough*, National Affairs, Summer 2021, Vol. 50, American Enterprise Institute, USA.

Mitchell, J. 2019, *Why Conservatives Struggle with Identity Politics*, National Affairs Journal, Vol. 50 (Winter, 2022), USA.

Moore, K., Persaud, T. V. N. 1998, *The Developing Human: Clinically Orientated Embryology*, W. B. Saunders Company, 6th Edition, Philadelphia, USA.

Nadler, A. L. 2013, *Strident Defense of Faith*, Forward Jewish Journal, Jan. 16, 2013, USA.

Neuhaus, R. J. 1992, *A New Order of Religious Freedom*, Feb. 1992, First Things, USA.

Nietzsche, F. 2002 (1886), *Beyond Good and Evil: Prelude to a Philosophy of the Future,* Cambridge University Press, UK.

Nietzsche, F. 2006 (1910), *The Gay Science,* Dover Pub., New York, USA.

Nietzsche, F. 2010, *Thus Spoke Zarathustra*, Love of Fate Series.

Nietzsche, F. 1998, *Twilight of the Idols*, Oxford University Press, UK.

Norris, P. 2021, *Cancel Culture: Myth or Reality?* Political Studies, Aug. 2021, UK.

Pagels, E. 2000, *Adam, Eve and the Serpent in Genesis 1-3,* Images of Feminine in Gnosticism, Trinity Press International, Harrisburg, USA.

Pagels E. 2004, *Revisioning Christianity: New Perspectives from the Gospel of Thomas*, Polebridge Press, Stanford University, USA.

Pearce, J. 2022, *The Seven Pillars of Western Civilization,* The Imaginative Conservative, December 10, 2022, Houston, USA.

Pecknold, C. C. 2021, *Imago Dei as a Political Concept*, November 23, 2021, The Post-Liberal Order, Washington, D. C., USA.

Pinkoski, N. 2021, *The Irreligious Right*, First Things Journal, December 2021, USA.

Pluckrose, H., Lindsay, J. 2020, *Cynical Theories: Activist Scholarship made Everything About Race, Gender & Identity*, Pitchstone Publishers, Durham, USA.

Popper, K. R. 1962 (1943), *The Open Society and its Enemies,* Vol. 1, The Spell of Plato, Princeton University Press, USA.

Prasch, J. J. 2002, *More Grain for the Famine,* Moriel, Australia.

Prasch, J. J. 1999, *Final Words of Jesus*, St. Matthew Publishing Ltd., UK.

Putnam, R. D. 2007, *E Pluribus Unum: Diversity & Community in the 21st Century*, Scandinavian Political Studies, Vol. 30. #2, Norway.

Reno, R. R. 2021, *Gnostic Politics*, First Things Journal, April 202, USA.

Reno, R., R. 2022, *Greetings from Rainbow Reich,* First Things Journal, June 21, USA.

Reno, R. R. 2023, *Sacrificing the Young,* First Things Journal, August 2023, USA.

Rieff, P. 2006, *My Life Among the Deathworks: Illustrations of the Aesthetics of Authority, Vol. 1*, March 14, 2006, University of Virginia, Charlottesville, USA.

Robertson, D. G. 2022, *Gnosticism and the History of Religions*, 2022, p. 3, Bloomsbury Academic, London, U.K.

Rose, M. 2021, *A World After Liberalism: Philosophers of the Radical Right*, Yale University Press, New Haven, USA.

Rosenblatt, H. 2018, *The Lost History of Liberalism: From Ancient Rome to the Twenty First Century*, Princeton University Press, USA.

Royal, R. 2014, *Camus Between God and Nothing,* First Things Journal, Jan. 2014, USA.

Rufo, C. R. 2023, *Barbarism in the Name of Equality*, August 24, 2023, City Journal, USA.

Rufo, C. F. 2021, *Battle Over Critical Race Theory*, WSJ., June 27, 2021, USA.

Rufo, C. F. 2021, *Critical Race Theory: What it is and how to Fight it,* Imprimis Journal, # 50, No. 3, March 2021, Hillsdale College, USA.

Russell, D.S. 1964, *The Method and Message of Jewish Apocalyptic: 200 BC - A.D. 100,* SCM Press, London, UK.

Ryckmans, P. 1996, *Are Books Useless: Extract from the 1996 Boyer Lectures*, Australian Humanities Review, Vol. 4, December, 1996, Melbourne, Australia.

Sacks, J. 2015, *Counting Time: Reflecting on the Mitzvah of Counting the Omar,* The Rabbi Sacks Legacy, May 7, 2015, London, UK.

Sacks, J. 2009, *Genesis: The Book of Beginnings*, Covenant and Conversation, Vol. 1, Maggid Books, Jerusalem, Israel.

Sanders, J. A. 1993, *Foreword*, Anti-Semitism and Early Christianity (Evans, C. A., Hagner, D. A. [eds.], Fortress Press, Minneapolis, USA.

Sartre, J. P. 1956, *Being and Nothingness: An Essay on Phenomenological Ontology*, Philosophical Library Inc., New York USA.

Sartre, J. P. 1957, *Existentialism and Human Emotions*, Wisdom Library, New York, USA.

Satinover, J. B. 1994, *Jungians and Gnostics*, First Things Journal, October 1994, USA.

Satinover, J. B. 1995, *Jung Love*, First Things Journal, Oct. 1995, USA.

Satinover, J. B. 1994, *Psychology & Abolition of Meaning*, First Things Journal, Feb, USA.

Scheler, M. 1915, *Ressentiment*, Marquette University Press, USA.

Schweigerdt, B. 1982, *Gnostic Influence on Psychology: The Effects of a Common Heresy*, Journal of Psychology and Theology, Vol. 10, No. 3, La Mirada, USA.

Scruton, R. 1980, *Meaning of Conservatism*, Penguin Books, USA.

Sharpe, M. J. 2015, *Camus, Philosophe: Return to our Beginnings*, Brill, Netherlands.

Skotko, B. G, Levine S. P, & Goldstein R. 2011. *Self-perceptions from People with Down Syndrome,* American Journal of Medical Genetics, Vol. 155, No. 10, American College of Medical Genetics and Genomics, Bethesda, USA.

Smith, R. 2021, *Deconstructionist, Deconstruct Thyself,* December 22, 2021, Public Discourse Journal, Princeton, USA.

Stepman, J. 2021, *Princeton Drops Standards in Name of Equity*, The Daily Signal, June 9, 2021, Washington, USA.

Strack, H. L. and Stemberger, G. 1992, *Introduction to the Talmud and Midrash*, Fortress Press, Minneapolis, USA.

Sumner, W. G. 1919, *The Forgotten Man and Other Essays,* Libraries Press, USA.

Taylor, C. 2007, *A Secular Age*, Harvard University Press, USA.

Taylor, C. 1989, *Sources of the Self: The Making of Modern Identity*, Harvard Uni., USA.

Tierney, J. 2023, *The Misogyny Myth*, Summer 2023, City Journal, Manhattan Institute for Policy Research, New York, USA.

Tim, A. 2012, *Kant and Categorical Imperative*, April 27, 2012, Journal of Philosophy and Philosophers, London, UK.

Toynbee, A. J. 1946, *A Study of History: Abridgement of Vols. 1 – 6*, Dell Publishing Co. Inc., New York, USA.

Trueman, C. R. 2020, *Rise & Triumph of Modern Self: Cultural Amnesia, Expressive Individualism & Sexual Revolution*, Crossway, USA.

Van den Broek, R., Hanegraaf, W. J. 1998, *Gnosis and Hermeticism from Antiquity to Modern Times*, University of New York Press, USA.

Vargas Llosa, M. 2023, *The Call of the Tribe*, Farrar, Straus, Giroux, USA.

Veith, G. E. 1994, *Post Modern Times: A Christian Guide to Contemporary Thought and Culture*, Crossway Books, USA.

Vergès, F. 2021, *A Decolonial Feminism*, Pluto Press, London, UK.

Vermeule, A. 2022, *Common Good Constitutionalism*, Polity Press, UK.

Vermeule, A. 2019, *All Human Conflict is Ultimately Theological*, July 26, 2019, Church Life Journal, University of Notre Dame, USA.

Von Boch-Galhau, W. 2020, *Parental Alienation: World-Wide Health Problem*, Journal of Case Reports, Vol. 4:026, October 22, 2020, Wurtzburg, Germany.

Wallison, P. J. 2018, *Judicial Fortitude: The Last Chance to Reign in the Administrative State*, Encounter Books, New York, USA.

Wasserstrom, S. 1999, *Religion after Religion: Gershom Scholem, Mircea Eliade, & Henry Corbin at Eranos*, Princeton University Press, USA.

Weigel, G. 2021, *The Difference Christianity Made*, National Review, Dec. 16, 2021, USA.

Weigel, G. 2022, *Who Invented the Individual?* First Things Journal, Jan. 12, 2022, USA.

Witte, J. 2022, *Blessings of Liberty: Human Rights and Religious Freedom in the Western Legal Tradition*, Cambridge University Press, U.K.

Wollstonecraft, M. 1833, *A Vindication of the Rights of Women*, A. J. Matsell, USA.

Wood, D., Bernasconi, R. (eds.). 1988, *Derrida and Différance*, Northwestern Uni. Press, Evanston, USA.

Yenor, S. 2021, *Lament for the Nations*, June 21, 2021, First Things Journal, USA.

INDEX